Frommer's

PORTABLE
Chicago

4th Edition

W9-CSI-110

by Elizabeth Canning Blackwell

WILEY

Wiley Publishing, Inc.

Published by:

WILEY PUBLISHING, INC.

111 River St.
Hoboken, NJ 07030-5744

ISBN 0-7645-4288-5

Editor: Kendra Falkenstein
Production Editor: Blair J. Pottenger
Photo Editor: Richard Fox
Cartographer: Roberta Stockwell
Production by Wiley Indianapolis Composition Services

Front cover photo: Skyscrapers lining the Chicago River

For information on our other products and services or to obtain technical
support, please contact our Customer Care Department within the U.S. at
800/762-2974, outside the U.S. at 317/572-3993 or fax 317/572-4002.

Wiley also publishes its books in a variety of electronic formats. Some con-
tent that appears in print may not be available in electronic formats.

Manufactured in the United States of America

5   4   3   2   1

Contents

List of Maps

ABOUT THE AUTHOR

Elizabeth Canning Blackwell began life on the East Coast, but 4 years at Northwestern University transformed her into a Midwesterner. She has worked as a writer and editor at *Encyclopedia Britannica,* Northwestern University Medical School, the *Chicago Tribune,* and *North Shore,* a lifestyle magazine for the Chicago suburbs. She also has written for national magazines on everything from planning the perfect wedding to fighting a duel. She lives just outside the city with her husband, daughter, and an extensive collection of long underwear.

AN INVITATION TO THE READER

In researching this book, we discovered many wonderful places—hotels, restaurants, shops, and more. We're sure you'll find others. Please tell us about them, so we can share the information with your fellow travelers in upcoming editions. If you were disappointed with a recommendation, we'd love to know that, too. Please write to:

Frommer's Portable Chicago, 4th Edition

Wiley Publishing, Inc. • 111 River St. • Hoboken, NJ 07030-5744

AN ADDITIONAL NOTE

Please be advised that travel information is subject to change at any time—and this is especially true of prices. We therefore suggest that you write or call ahead for confirmation when making your travel plans. The authors, editors, and publisher cannot be held responsible for the experiences of readers while traveling. Your safety is important to us, however, so we encourage you to stay alert and be aware of your surroundings. Keep a close eye on cameras, purses, and wallets, all favorite targets of thieves and pickpockets.

FROMMER'S STAR RATINGS, ICONS & ABBREVIATIONS

Every hotel, restaurant, and attraction listing in this guide has been ranked for quality, value, service, amenities, and special features using a **star-rating system.** In country, state, and regional guides, we also rate towns and regions to help you narrow down your choices and budget your time accordingly. Hotels and restaurants are rated on a scale of zero (recommended) to three stars (exceptional). Attractions, shopping, nightlife, towns, and regions are rated according to the following scale: zero stars (recommended), one star (highly recommended), two stars (very highly recommended), and three stars (must-see).

In addition to the star-rating system, we also use **seven feature icons** that point you to the great deals, in-the-know advice, and unique experiences that separate travelers from tourists. Throughout the book, look for:

Finds	Special finds—those places only insiders know about
Fun Fact	Fun facts—details that make travelers more informed and their trips more fun
Kids	Best bets for kids—advice for the whole family
Moments	Special moments—those experiences that memories are made of
Overrated	Places or experiences not worth your time or money
Tips	Insider tips—some great ways to save time and money
Value	Great values—where to get the best deals

The following **abbreviations** are used for credit cards:

AE	American Express	DISC	Discover	V	Visa
DC	Diners Club	MC	MasterCard		

FROMMERS.COM

Now that you have the guidebook to a great trip, visit our website at **www.frommers.com** for travel information on more than 3,000 destinations. With features updated regularly, we give you instant access to the most current trip-planning information available. At Frommers.com, you'll also find the best prices on airfares, accommodations, and car rentals—and you can even book travel online through our travel booking partners. At Frommers.com, you'll also find the following:

- Online updates to our most popular guidebooks
- Vacation sweepstakes and contest giveaways
- Newsletter highlighting the hottest travel trends
- Online travel message boards with featured travel discussions

The Best of Chicago

Has Chicago finally gotten over its "Second City" inferiority complex? Sure looks like it. The city is booming, bursting with restaurants, hotels, and shops in every price range. Walk around Chicago these days, and you'll feel an undeniable energy, a sense that the town is on a roll. This isn't the first time Chicago has reinvented itself. From the ashes of the Great Chicago Fire in 1871, Chicagoans not only rebuilt—they reached for the heavens with the first steel-frame skyscrapers.

Today Chicago continues to think big, creating such attractions as an easy-to-navigate Museum Campus; lively Navy Pier; a resurrected North Loop theater district; and a "who's who" of luxury shopping destinations along the city's fabled Magnificent Mile. A busy convention trade has sparked hotel construction, and the city's eclectic mix of restaurants has gained an international reputation, showing that Chicago cuisine goes far beyond deep-dish pizza and bratwurst (although you find plenty of that too).

But the Second City complex still lurks just beneath the surface. Chicago still feels that it has something to prove. Visitors find that Chicagoans like myself will readily brag about our hometown. So without further ado, let me tell you what we locals consider the quintessential Chicago experiences.

1 Frommer's Favorite Chicago Experiences

- **Studying the Skyline:** The birthplace of the modern skyscraper, Chicago is the perfect place to learn about—and appreciate—these dramatic buildings that reach for the sky. See "Sightseeing Tours," beginning on p. 125.
- **Getting Lost at the Art Institute:** This vast art museum offers myriad places for private meditation. Internationally known for its French Impressionist collection, the Art Institute can also transport you to Renaissance Italy, ancient China, or any number of other worlds. See p. 96.

Chicago & Vicinity

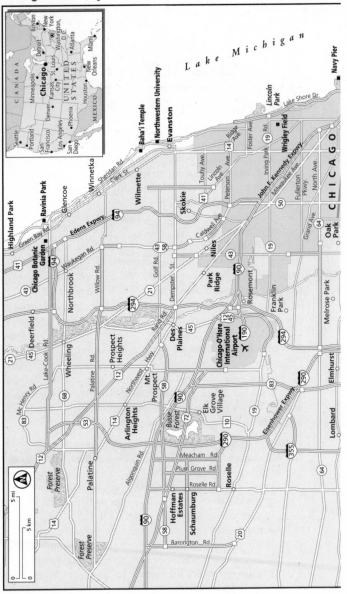

Lake Michigan

Navy Pier

Lincoln Park

Wrigley Field

Baha'i Temple

Northwestern University

Evanston

Winnetka

Glencoe

Highland Park

Ravinia Park

Chicago Botanic Garden

Deerfield

Northbrook

Wheeling

Prospect Heights

Mt. Prospect

Arlington Heights

Palatine

Hoffman Estates

Schaumburg

Roselle

Des Plaines

Park Ridge

Niles

Skokie

Wilmette

Rosemont

Chicago-O'Hare International Airport

Elk Grove Village

Franklin Park

Melrose Park

Elmhurst

Lombard

Oak Park

CHICAGO

Lake Shore Dr.

Foster Ave.

Ridge Ave.

Touhy Ave.

Lincoln Ave.

Peterson Ave.

Irving Park Rd.

Milwaukee Ave.

Fullerton Pkwy.

North Ave.

Grand Ave.

John F. Kennedy Expwy.

Eisenhower Expwy.

Edens Expwy.

Sheridan Rd.

Clark St.

Green Bay Rd.

Waukegan Rd.

Willow Rd.

Golf Rd.

Caldwell Ave.

Dempster St.

Rand Rd.

Northwest Hwy.

Palatine Rd.

Lake-Cook Rd.

Mc Henry Rd.

Algonquin Rd.

Meacham Rd.

Plum Grove Rd.

Roselle Rd.

Barrington Rd.

Busse Forest

Forest Preserve

Forest Preserve

5 mi

5 km

94
41
43
58
21
294
45
68
53
14
12
83
90
72
10
290
355
64
20
58
19
41
14
50
19
190
12
45

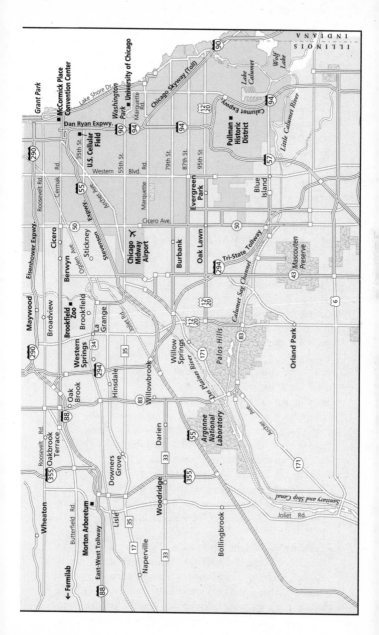

- **Chilling Out on the Lakefront:** It really is cooler by the lake—meteorologically and metaphorically. There are 29 miles of lakefront for biking, 'blading, or simply being, so get out there and contemplate Chicago's very own ocean. See the "Staying Active," section in chapter 6, beginning on p. 129.

- **Getting the Blues:** Here in the world capital of the blues, you've got your pick of places to feel them, from the collegiate atmosphere of Kingston Mines in Lincoln Park to the earthy roadhouse New Checkerboard Lounge on the South Side. See "The Music Scene," beginning on p. 159.

- **Taking in a Show:** The stage lights rarely go dark on one of the country's most bustling theater scenes. See "The Performing Arts," beginning on p. 152.

- **Riding the Rails:** Find out why the Loop is so named by hopping a southbound Brown Line elevated train (or "the El," for short), and watch the city unfold as the train crosses the Chicago River and screeches through downtown canyons. See "Getting Around" (p. 25) and "Sightseeing Tours" (beginning on p. 125).

- **Taking in Some Cool Jazz at the Green Mill:** This atmospheric Uptown jazz club is the place to go to soak up some smooth sounds from some of the hottest up-and-coming performers on the jazz scene today. But don't just go for the tunes—the club, a living museum of 1930s Chicago, is an attraction in itself. See p. 162.

- **Bonding with the Animals at Lincoln Park Zoo:** Occupying a prime spot of Lincoln Park close to the lakefront, the zoo is small enough to explore in an afternoon, and varied enough to make you feel like you've traveled around the world. For families, this is a don't-miss stop. See p. 112.

- **Soaking Up Sun at Wrigley Field:** It's a Chicago tradition to play hooky for an afternoon to sit in the bleachers at this historic baseball park and watch the Cubbies try to hit 'em onto Waveland Avenue. See "In the Grandstand" beginning on p. 131.

- **Exploring the Wright Stuff in Oak Park:** Seeing the earliest examples of Frank Lloyd Wright's Prairie-style homes side by side with rambling Victorian villas is an eye-opening lesson in architectural history. The town of Oak Park—with its funky shops and vibrant community spirit—makes a great side trip. See "Exploring the 'Burbs," beginning on p. 119.

The Best Chicago Websites

- **www.metromix.com** is the *Chicago Tribune*'s entertainment-oriented site.
- **www.ci.chi.il.us/landmarks** is a city website that includes definitions of Chicago architectural styles, tour information, and maps.
- **www.chireader.com** is the site of the *Chicago Reader*, the city's alternative weekly paper.
- **www.chicago.citysearch.com** offers reviews of restaurants, bars, shows, and shops.
- **www.centerstage.net** provides entertainment reviews.

2 Best Hotel Bets

Gone are the days when Chicago hotels catered mainly to a conservative, convention-going crowd. Today, the city has a hotel to suit every taste and budget. For details on these and other Chicago hotels, see chapter 4.

- **Best Historic Hotel: The Drake,** 140 E. Walton Place (© **800/55-DRAKE**), is a master at combining the decorous charm of yesteryear with every modern convenience. See p. 47.
- **Best Rehab of Historic Structure:** The Loop's revered Reliance Building, one of the world's first glass-walled skyscrapers, has regained its dignity, thanks to a thrilling reincarnation as the tony **Hotel Burnham,** 1 W. Washington St. (© **877/294-9712**). See p. 38.
- **Best for Business Travelers:** Virtually every hotel in Chicago qualifies. The **Swissôtel Chicago,** 323 E. Wacker Dr. (© **888/737-9477**), combines extensive business services with stunning city views from all rooms—when you need a mental break from endless paperwork. See p. 41.
- **Best Service:** The attention to detail, regal pampering, and well-connected concierges at both the ultraluxe **Ritz-Carlton,** 160 E. Pearson St. (© **800/621-6906**), and the **Four Seasons,** 120 E. Delaware Place (© **800/332-3442**), make them the hotels of choice for travelers who want to feel like royalty while in town. See p. 46 and p. 44, respectively.

- **Best for a Romantic Getaway:** For a splurge, **The Peninsula,** 108 E. Superior St. (© **866/288-8889**), or the **Park Hyatt,** 800 N. Michigan Ave. (© **800/233-1234**), will pamper you with luxurious rooms and top-notch amenities. See p. 45.

- **Best Trendy Hotel:** The **W Chicago Lakeshore,** 644 N. Lake Shore Dr. (© **877/W-HOTELS**), brings the hip W sensibility to a can't-miss location overlooking Lake Michigan. For a theatrical hotel experience, the **House of Blues Hotel,** 333 N. Dearborn St. (© **877/569-3742**), can't be beat, with its riotous mix of colors and playful attitude. See p. 49 and 53.

- **Best Views:** This isn't an easy call. Consider several hotels for their mix of lake and city views: the **Swissôtel;** the **Four Seasons; The Drake;** the **Ritz-Carlton;** the **Park Hyatt Chicago;** and the **Holiday Inn–Chicago City Centre** (p. 41, 44, 47, 46, 45, and 51, respectively).

- **Best for Families:** With every room a suite, the **Embassy Suites,** 600 N. State St. (© **800/362-2779**), is ideal for families looking for a little more space than the typical hotel room provides. The in-room Nintendo, indoor pool, and location near two popular kid-friendly venues—ESPN Zone and the Hard Rock Cafe—should keep junior happy, too. See p. 52.

- **Best Value:** For the best combination of decent rates and excellent location, try the **Red Roof Inn,** 162 E. Ontario St. (© **800/733-7663**), or the **Hampton Inn & Suites,** 33 W. Illinois St. (© **800/HAMPTON**)—the latter getting bonus points for having a pool. See p. 52 and p. 55, respectively.

3 Best Dining Bets

Yes, we Chicagoans do eat plenty of deep-dish pizza, but we don't stop there. Chicago is home to an ever-expanding galaxy of sophisticated restaurants whose kitchens are energized by culinary stars. For details on these and other terrific restaurants, see chapter 5.

- **Best Spot for a Romantic Dinner:** Few activities are more intimate than dipping lobster tails in fondue by candlelight at **Geja's Cafe,** 340 W. Armitage Ave. (© **773/281-9101**). See p. 84. A strong challenge is being mounted by the **North Pond,** 2610 N. Cannon Dr. (© **773/477-5845**), an Arts and Crafts–styled, Midwestern-flavored restaurant with a postcard-perfect setting in Lincoln Park. Not only does it boast a dramatic vista of the Gold Coast skyline, but the restaurant's out-of-the-way locale also requires diners to begin and end their meal with an idyllic stroll through the park. See p. 85.

- **Best Spot for a Business Lunch:** Stylish **Nine,** 440 W. Randolph St. (✆ **312/575-9900**), offers super-slick environs, prime steaks, fresh seafood, a champagne-and-caviar bar, and—most importantly—tiny TV sets above the men's-room urinals. See p. 59.

- **Best View:** Forty stories above Chicago, **Everest,** 440 S. LaSalle St. (✆ **312/663-8920**), astounds with a spectacular view—and food to match. See p. 58. Closer to earth, diners on the rooftop terrace at Greektown's **Pegasus,** 130 S. Halsted St. (✆ **312/226-3377**), get a panoramic view of the city skyline. See p. 69.

- **Best Value:** At longtime city favorite **Carson's,** 612 N. Wells St. (✆ **312/280-9200**), $20 gets you a full slab of incredible baby back ribs, accompanied by a bowl of Carson's almost-as-famous coleslaw and a choice of potatoes. See p. 79. Lincoln Park residents swarm to **RoseAngelis,** 1314 W. Wrightwood Ave. (✆ **773/296-0081**), where $20 buys a glass of wine, a massive plate of pasta, and a generous slice of possibly the city's best bread pudding. See p. 86.

- **Best for Kids:** A meal at **ESPN Zone,** 43 E. Ohio St. (✆ **312/ 475-0263**). Yes, you'll find a kids' menu here, but the main attraction is the enormous Sports Arena, where kids can work off some excess energy playing the interactive games. See p. 73.

- **Best Pizza:** In the town where deep-dish pies were born, Chicagoans take their out-of-town relatives to either **Gino's East,** 633 N. Wells St. (✆ **312/943-1124**), or **Lou Malnati's,** 439 N. Wells St. (✆ **312/828-9800**), to taste the real thing: mouthwatering slabs of pizza loaded with fresh ingredients atop delectably sweet crusts. See p. 75.

- **Best Fast Food:** A few steps above the standard food court, **foodlife** in Water Tower Place, 835 N. Michigan Ave. (✆ **312/ 335-3663**), offers everything from Asian noodles and vegetarian fare to pizza and burgers. See p. 74.

- **Best Brunch:** The luxury hotels along Michigan Avenue offer all-you-can-eat gourmet spreads, but the locals prefer the funky Southern-inspired combinations at **Soul Kitchen,** 1576 N. Milwaukee Ave. (✆ **773/342-9742**), and the sinfully rich cinnamon rolls at **Ann Sather,** 929 W. Belmont Ave. (✆ **773/ 348-2378**) on p. 87.

2

Planning Your Trip
to Chicago

After choosing a destination, most prospective travelers have two fundamental questions: "What will it cost?" and "How will I get there?" This chapter answers both of these questions and resolves other important issues—such as when to go and where to obtain more information about Chicago before you leave home and once you get there.

1 Visitor Information

The **Chicago Office of Tourism,** Chicago Cultural Center, 78 E. Washington St., Chicago, IL 60602 (© **312/744-2400** or TTY 312/744-2947; www.ci.chi.il.us/tourism), will mail you a packet of materials with information on upcoming events and attractions. The **Illinois Bureau of Tourism** (© **800/2CONNECT** or TTY 800/406-6418; www.enjoyillinois.com) will also send you a packet of information about Chicago and other Illinois destinations.

In addition to the above websites, which offer visitors a good deal of information, see chapter 1 for a list of the best Chicago websites.

2 When to Go

THE CLIMATE

When I tell people from more temperate climates that I live in Chicago, without fail they ask me how I handle the winters. In reality, the winters here are no worse than other northern cities, but it still isn't exactly prime tourist season. The ideal time to visit is summer or fall. Summer offers a nonstop selection of special events and outdoor activities, but you will be contending with the biggest crowds and hot, muggy weather. Autumn days are generally sunny, and the crowds at major tourist attractions grow thinner. Spring here is extremely unpredictable, with dramatic fluctuations of cold and warm weather, and usually lots of rain. If your top priority is indoor cultural sights, winter's not such a bad time to visit: no lines at museums, the cheapest rates at hotels, and the pride that comes in slogging through the slush with the natives.

The key is to be prepared for a wide range of weather with clothing that can take you from a sunny morning to a chilly, drizzly evening. As close to your departure as possible, check the local weather forecast at the websites of the Chicago Office of Tourism (www.ci.chi.il.us/tourism/weather) or the *Chicago Tribune* newspaper (www.chicagotribune.com).

Chicago's Average Temperatures & Precipitation

	Jan	Feb	Mar	Apr	May	June	July	Aug	Sept	Oct	Nov	Dec
High °F	20	34	44	59	70	79	85	82	76	64	48	35
Low °F	14	18	28	39	48	58	63	62	54	42	31	20
High °C	-7	1	7	15	21	26	29	28	24	18	9	2
Low °C	-10	-8	-2	4	9	14	17	17	12	6	-1	-7
Rainfall (in.)	1.60	1.31	2.59	3.66	3.15	4.08	3.63	3.53	3.35	2.28	2.06	2.10

CHICAGO CALENDAR OF EVENTS

The best way to stay on top of the city's current crop of special events is to ask the **Chicago Office of Tourism** (℃ **312/744-2400**; www.ci.chi.il.us/tourism) or the **Illinois Bureau of Tourism** (℃ **800/2CONNECT**; www.enjoyillinois. com) to mail you a copy of *Chicago Calendar of Events,* an excellent quarterly publication that surveys special events, including parades and street festivals, concerts and theatrical productions, and museum exhibitions. Also ask to be sent the latest materials produced by the **Mayor's Office of Special Events** (℃ **312/744-3315**, or call the Special Events Hot Line at ℃ 312/744-3370, TTY 312/744-2964; www.cityofchicago.org/specialevents), which keeps current with citywide and neighborhood festivals.

February

Chicago Auto Show, McCormick Place, 23rd Street and Lake Shore Drive (℃ **630/495-2282**). More than a thousand cars and trucks, domestic and foreign, current and futuristic, are on display. Look for special weekend packages at area hotels that include show tickets. February 6 to 15.

March

St. Patrick's Day Parade. In a city with a strong Irish heritage (and a mayor of Irish descent), this holiday is a big deal. The Chicago River is even dyed green for the occasion. The parade route is along Dearborn Street from Wacker Drive to Van Buren; the best place to view it is around Wacker and Dearborn. Saturday closest to March 17.

April

Opening Day. For the Cubs, call ⓒ **773/404-CUBS;** for the White Sox, call ⓒ **312/674-1000.** Make your plans early to get tickets for this eagerly awaited day. The calendar may say spring, but be warned: Opening Day is usually freezing in Chi-town (in 2003, the first home game was postponed because of snow).

May

Art 2004 Chicago, one of the country's largest international contemporary art fairs, at Navy Pier's Festival Hall, 600 E. Grand Ave. (ⓒ **312/587-3300** or 312/595-PIER). May 7 to 10 (Mother's Day weekend).

June

Chicago Blues Festival, Petrillo Music Shell, at Jackson Drive and Columbus Drive in Grant Park (ⓒ **312/744-3315**). Muddy Waters would scratch his noggin over the sea of suburbanites who flood into Grant Park every summer to quaff Budweisers and accompany local legends Buddy Guy and Lonnie Brooks on air guitar. Still, a thousand-voice chorus of "Sweet Home Chicago" under the stars has a rousing appeal. Blues Fest is free, with dozens of acts performing over 4 days. June 2 through 6.

Printers Row Book Fair, on Dearborn Street from Congress Parkway to Polk Street (ⓒ **312/987-9896**). One of the largest free outdoor book fairs in the country, this weekend-long event celebrates the written word with everything from readings and book signings by big-name authors to panel discussions on penning your first novel. First weekend in June.

Old Town Art Fair, historic Old Town neighborhood, at Lincoln Park West and Wisconsin Street (ⓒ **312/337-1938;** www.oldtown triangle.com). This juried fine arts fair has been drawing crowds for more than 50 years with the work of more than 200 painters, sculptors, and jewelry designers from the Midwest and around the country. It also features an art auction, a garden walk, food and drink, and children's art activities. Second full weekend in June.

Wells Street Art Festival, Wells Street from North Avenue to Division Street (ⓒ **312/951-6106**). Held on the same weekend as the more prestigious Old Town Art Fair, this arts fest is still lots of fun, with 200 arts and crafts vendors, food, music, and carnival rides. Second full weekend in June.

Grant Park Music Festival, Millennium Park Music Pavilion, at Randolph Street and Columbus Drive in Grant Park (ⓒ **312/ 742-4763**). The free outdoor musical concerts in the park begin the last week in June and continue through August.

Chicago Country Music Festival, Petrillo Music Shell, at Jackson Drive and Columbus Drive in Grant Park (© 312/744-3315). Y'all might not think fans of Garth Brooks and Trisha Yearwood would thrive in these northern urban climes. Think again, partner. This free event features big-name entertainers of the country-and-western genre. June 25 and 26, concurrent with the first weekend of the Taste of Chicago (see below).

Taste of Chicago, Grant Park (© 312/744-3315). The city claims that this is the largest free outdoor food fest in the nation. Three-and-a-half million rib and pizza lovers feeding at this colossal alfresco trough say they're right. Over 10 days of feasting in the streets, scores of Chicago restaurants cart their fare to food stands set up throughout the park. Admission is free; you pay for the sampling, of course. June 25 through July 4th.

Gay and Lesbian Pride Parade, Halsted Street, from Belmont Avenue to Broadway, south to Diversey Parkway, and east to Lincoln Park, where a rally and music festival are held (© 773/348-8243). The floats and marching units have to be seen to be believed at this colorful culmination of a month of activities by Chicago's gay and lesbian community. Last Sunday in June.

July

Independence Day Celebration (© 312/744-3315). The holiday is celebrated in Chicago on the third of July, concurrent with the Taste of Chicago. Concerts and fireworks are the highlights of the festivities in Grant Park. Expect huge crowds. July 3.

Sheffield Garden Walk, starting at Sheffield and Webster avenues (© 773/929-WALK). Here's your chance to snoop into the lush backyards of Lincoln Park homeowners. The walk isn't just for garden nuts; the bands, children's activities, and food and drink tents attract lots of swinging singles and young families. Mid-July.

Chicago SummerDance, east side of South Michigan Avenue between Balbo and Harrison streets (© 312/744-6630). From July to early September, the city's Department of Cultural Affairs transforms a patch of Grant Park into a lighted outdoor dance venue. The 3,500-square-foot dance floor provides ample room for throwing down moves while live bands play music from ballroom, jazz, klezmer, and country and western to samba, zydeco, blues, and soul. One-hour lessons are offered from 6 to 7pm. Free admission.

Venetian Night, from Monroe Harbor to the Adler Planetarium (© 312/744-3315). This carnival of illuminated boats on the lake is complete with fireworks and synchronized music by the

Grant Park Symphony Orchestra. Shoreline viewing is fine, but the best way to take it in is from another boat nearby, if you can swing it. July 24.

August

Northalsted Market Days, on Halsted Street between Belmont Avenue and Addison Street (ⓒ 773/868-3010). The largest of the city's street festivals, held in the heart of this gay neighborhood, Northalsted Market Days offers music, lots of food, and the best people-watching of the summer. Early August.

Chicago Air & Water Show, North Avenue Beach (ⓒ 312/ 744-3315). The U.S. Air Force Thunderbirds and Navy Seals usually make an appearance at this hugely popular, perennial aquatic and aerial spectacular. Free admission. August 14 to 15.

Chicago Jazz Festival, Petrillo Music Shell, Jackson Drive and Columbus Drive in Grant Park (ⓒ 312/744-3315). Several national headliners are always on hand at this steamy gathering. The event is free; come early and stay late. August 26 to 29.

September

Mexican Independence Day Parade, along Dearborn Street between Wacker Drive and Van Buren Street (ⓒ 312/744-3315). Saturday in mid-September. Another parade is held the next day on 26th Street in the Little Village neighborhood (ⓒ 773/521-5387).

World Music Festival Chicago, various locations around the city (ⓒ 312/744-6630). The festival brings in top performers from Hungary to Sri Lanka to Zimbabwe, performing traditional, contemporary, and fusion music. Shows are a mix of free and ticketed ($10 or less) events. Late September.

October

Chicago International Film Festival (ⓒ 312/425-9400, or 312/332-FILM for a film schedule). The oldest U.S. festival of its kind screens films from around the world at various theaters over 2 weeks beginning the first Thursday in October.

Chicago Marathon (ⓒ 312/904-9800). A major event on the international long-distance running circuit, this race begins and ends in Grant Park, but can be viewed from any number of vantage points along the race route. Late Sunday in October.

November

Chicago Humanities Festival takes over locations throughout downtown, from libraries to concert halls (ⓒ 312/661-1028;

www.chfestival.org). Over a period of 11 days, the festival presents cultural performances, readings, and symposiums tied to an annual theme. Expect appearances by major authors, scholars, and policymakers, all at a very reasonable cost ($5 per event). Early November.

Christmas Tree Lighting, Daley Center Plaza, in the Loop (© **312/744-3315**). The switch is flipped the day after Thanksgiving, around dusk.

December

A Christmas Carol, Goodman Theatre, 170 N. Dearborn St. (© **312/443-3800**). This seasonal favorite, performed for more than 2 decades, runs from about Thanksgiving to the end of December.

The *Nutcracker* ballet, Joffrey Ballet of Chicago, Auditorium Theatre, 50 E. Congress Pkwy. For tickets, call © **312/559-1212** (Ticketmaster) or 312/739-0120 (Joffrey office). The esteemed company performs its Victorian-American twist on the holiday classic. The production runs 3 weeks from late Thanksgiving to mid-December.

3 Specialized Travel Resources

TRAVELERS WITH DISABILITIES

Most of Chicago's sidewalks, as well as major museums and tourist attractions, are fitted with wheelchair ramps. Many hotels provide special accommodations for visitors in wheelchairs, such as ramps and large bathrooms, as well as telecommunications devices for visitors with hearing impairments; inquire when you make your reservation.

Several of the **Chicago Transit Authority**'s (CTA's) El stations on each line are fitted with elevators. Call the CTA at © **312/ 836-7000** for a list of those that are accessible. All city buses are equipped to accommodate wheelchairs. For other questions about CTA special services, call © **312/432-7025.**

For specific information on facilities for people with disabilities, call or write the **Mayor's Office for People with Disabilities,** 121 N. LaSalle St., Room 1104, Chicago, IL 60602 (© **312/744-6673** for voice; 312/744-4780 for TTY). The office is staffed from 8:30am to 4:30pm Monday through Friday.

Horizons for the Blind, 16A Meadowdale Center, Carpentersville, IL 60110 (© **847/836-1400**), is a social-service agency that can provide information about local hotels equipped with Braille signage and cultural attractions that offer Braille signage and special tours. The **Illinois Relay Center** enables hearing- and speech-impaired TTY callers to call individuals or businesses without TTYs 24 hours a day. Calls are confidential and billed at regular phone rates. Call TTY at ℂ **800/526-0844** or voice 800/526-0857. The city of Chicago operates a 24-hour information service for hearing-impaired callers with TTY equipment; call ℂ **312/744-8599.**

GAY & LESBIAN TRAVELERS

While it's not quite San Francisco, Chicago is a very gay-friendly city. The neighborhood commonly referred to as "Boys Town" (roughly from Belmont Ave. north to Irving Park Ave., and from Halsted St. east to the lakefront) is the center of gay nightlife (and plenty of daytime action, too). Gay and Lesbian Pride Week (ℂ **773/348-8243**), highlighted by a lively parade on the North Side, is a major event on the Chicago calendar each June. You also might want to stop by **Unabridged Books,** 3251 N. Broadway (ℂ **773/883-9119**), an excellent independent bookseller with a large lesbian and gay selection. Here and elsewhere in the Lakeview neighborhood, you can pick up several gay publications, including the newsweekly *Windy City Times* (www.windycitymediagroup.com/index.html), which publishes a useful calendar of events, and *Gay Chicago* (www.gaychicagomag.com), a weekly entertainment magazine. A helpful website, with lists of community and social groups, nightlife options, and an events calendar, is **www.outchicago.org.** **Horizon Community Services** (ℂ **773/929-HELP**), a gay social-service agency with counseling services, support groups, and an antiviolence project, provides referrals daily from 6pm to 10pm; you can also call the main switchboard at ℂ **773/472-6469** during the day.

FAMILY TRAVEL

Chicago is full of sightseeing opportunities and special activities geared toward children. See "Kid Stuff," in chapter 6, for information and ideas for families. Chapter 4 includes a list of the best hotel deals for families, and chapter 5 lists kid-friendly restaurants. For information on finding a babysitter, see "Fast Facts: Chicago," in chapter 3. The guidebook *Frommer's Chicago with Kids* (Wiley Publishing, Inc.) highlights the many family-friendly activities available in the city.

SURFING FOR AIRFARES

The "big three" online travel agencies, **Expedia.com, Travelocity. com,** and **Orbitz.com,** sell most of the air tickets bought on the Internet. Each has different business deals with the airlines and may offer different fares on the same flights, so it's wise to shop around.

Also remember to check **airline websites,** especially those for low-fare carriers such as AirTran, ATA, and Southwest, whose fares are often misreported or simply missing from travel agency websites. Most airlines now offer online-only fares that even their phone agents know nothing about.

If you're willing to give up some control over your flight details, use an **opaque fare service** like **Priceline** (www.priceline.com; www. priceline.co.uk for Europeans) or **Hotwire** (www.hotwire.com). Both offer rock-bottom prices in exchange for travel on a "mystery airline" at a mysterious time of day, often with a mysterious change of planes en route. The mystery airlines are all major, well-known carriers—and the possibility of being sent from Philadelphia to Chicago via Tampa is remote; the airlines' routing computers have gotten a lot better than they used to be. But your chances of getting a 6am or 11pm flight are pretty high. Hotwire tells you flight prices before you buy; Priceline usually has better deals than Hotwire, but you have to play their "name our price" game. If you're new at this, the helpful folks at **BiddingForTravel** (www.biddingfortravel.com) do a good job of demystifying Priceline's prices. Priceline and Hotwire are great for flights within North America and between the U.S. and Europe. But for flights to other parts of the world, consolidators will almost always beat their fares.

SURFING FOR HOTELS

Of the "big three" sites, **Expedia** may be the best choice, thanks to its long list of special deals. **Travelocity** runs a close second. Hotel specialist sites **hotels.com** and **hoteldiscounts.com** are also reliable. An excellent free program, **TravelAxe** (www.travelaxe.net), can help you search multiple hotel sites at once, even ones you may never have heard of.

Priceline and Hotwire are even better for hotels than for airfares; with both, you're allowed to pick the neighborhood and quality level of your hotel before offering up your money. Priceline seems to be much better at getting five-star lodging for three-star prices than at finding anything at the bottom of the scale. ***Note:*** Hotwire overrates its hotels by one star—what Hotwire calls a four-star is a three-star anywhere else.

SURFING FOR RENTAL CARS

For booking rental cars online, the best deals are usually found at rental-car company websites, although all the major online travel agencies also offer rental-car reservations services. Priceline and Hotwire work well for rental cars, too; the only "mystery" is which major rental company you get, and for most travelers the difference between Hertz, Avis, and Budget is negligible.

5 Getting There

BY PLANE

Chicago's **O'Hare International Airport** (© 773/686-2200) is located northwest of the city proper; depending on traffic, the drive to/from downtown can take anywhere from 30 minutes to more than an hour.

O'Hare has information booths in all five terminals; most are located on the baggage level. The multilingual personnel, who are outfitted in red jackets, can assist travelers with everything from arranging ground transportation to getting information about local hotels. The booths also offer a plethora of useful tourism brochures. The booths, labeled "Airport Information," are open daily from 9am to 8pm.

On the opposite end of the city, the Southwest Side, is Chicago's other major airport, **Midway International Airport** (© 773/838-0600). Although it's smaller than O'Hare and fewer airlines have routes here, Midway is closer to the Loop and you may be able to get a cheaper fare flying into here. (Always check fares to both airports if you want to find the best deal.)

All major domestic airlines fly into either O'Hare or Midway; you're more likely to find discount airlines (such as Southwest or ATA) at Midway.

GETTING INTO TOWN FROM THE AIRPORT

Taxis are plentiful at both O'Hare and Midway, but both are quite easily accessible by public transportation as well. A cab ride into the city will cost about $30 to $35 from O'Hare, and $25 to $30 from Midway.

For $1.50, you can take the El (vernacular for the elevated train) straight into downtown. O'Hare is located on the Blue Line; a trip to downtown takes about 40 minutes. Trains leave every 6 to

10 minutes during the day, and every half-hour in the evening and overnight. Getting downtown from Midway is even faster; the ride on the Orange Line takes 20 to 30 minutes. (The Orange Line stops operating each night at about 11:30pm and resumes service by 5am.) Trains leave the station every 6 to 15 minutes.

   Continental Airport Express (© 888/2-THEVAN or 312/454-7800; www.airportexpress.com) services most first-class hotels in Chicago. The cost is $20 one-way ($36 round-trip) to or from O'Hare and $15 one-way ($28 round-trip) to or from Midway. The shuttles operate from 6am to 11:30pm.

BY CAR

Interstate highways from all major points on the compass service Chicago.

BY TRAIN

For tickets, consult your travel agent or call **Amtrak** (© 800/USA-RAIL;** www.amtrak.com). When you arrive in Chicago, the train will pull into **Union Station** at 210 S. Canal St. between Adams and Jackson streets (© **312/655-2385**). Bus nos. 1, 60, 125, 151, and 156 all stop at the station, which is just west across the river from the Loop. The nearest El stop is at Clinton Street and Congress Parkway (on the Blue Line), which is a fair walk away, especially when you're carrying luggage.

6 For International Visitors

ENTRY REQUIREMENTS   Check at any U.S. embassy or consulate for current information and requirements. You can also obtain a visa application and other information online at the **U.S. State Department's** website, at **www.travel.state.gov**.

DRIVER'S LICENSES   Foreign driver's licenses are mostly recognized in the U.S., although you may want to get an international driver's license if your home license is not written in English.

CURRENCY & CURRENCY EXCHANGE   Currency-exchange bureaus are relatively rare in Chicago, so plan accordingly. When arriving in Chicago, you can exchange international currency in **Terminal 5** (the international terminal) at O'Hare Airport. In the city, there are **American Express** offices at 55 W. Monroe St. (© **312/541-5440**) and 605 N. Michigan Ave. (© **312/943-7840**). Most banks will not exchange foreign currency. If you find yourself in need of a foreign-exchange service while in Chicago, the

Chicago consumer Yellow Pages lists names and numbers of foreign-exchange services under the heading "Foreign Exchange Brokers." In the Loop, try **World's Money Exchange, Inc.,** 203 N. LaSalle St. (*©* **312/641-2151**). Otherwise, use your ATM card to get U.S. dollars.

TIPPING   Tips are a very important part of certain workers' income, and gratuities are the standard way of showing appreciation for services provided. In hotels, tip **bellhops** at least $1 per bag and tip the **chamber staff** $2 to $3 per day. Tip the **doorman** or **concierge** only if he or she has provided you with some specific service (for example, calling a cab for you or obtaining difficult-to-get theater tickets). Tip the **valet-parking attendant** $1 every time you get your car. In restaurants, bars, and nightclubs, tip **service staff** 15% to 20% of the check, tip **bartenders** 10% to 15%, and tip **checkroom attendants** $1 per garment. As for other service personnel, tip **cab drivers** 15% of the fare.

CUSTOMS

WHAT YOU CAN BRING IN   For specific information regarding U.S. Customs, contact your nearest U.S. embassy or consulate, or the **U.S. Customs** office (*©* **202/927-1770** or www.customs.ustreas.gov).

WHAT YOU CAN TAKE HOME   **U.K. citizens** should contact HM Customs & Excise at *©* **0845/010-9000** (from outside the U.K., 020/8929-0152), or consult their website at www.hmce.gov.uk. **Canadian** citizens should contact **Canada Customs and Revenue Agency** (*©* **800/461-9999** in Canada, or 204/983-3500; www.ccra-adrc.gc.ca). **Australian citizens** can contact the **Australian Customs Service** at *©* **1300/363-263** or log on to www.customs.gov.au. **Citizens of New Zealand** can contact **New Zealand Customs,** The Customhouse, 17–21 Whitmore St., Box 2218, Wellington (*©* **0800/428-786** or 04/473-6099; www.customs.govt.nz).

3

Getting to Know
the Windy City

The orderly configuration of Chicago's streets and the excellent public transportation system make the city quite accessible—once you identify and locate a few basic landmarks.

This chapter provides an overview of the city's design, as well as some suggestions for how to maneuver within it. The chapter also lists some resources that travelers frequently require, from babysitters to all-night pharmacies

1 Orientation

VISITOR INFORMATION

The **Chicago Office of Tourism** runs a toll-free visitor hot line (© **877/CHICAGO** or 312/744-2400; TTY 312/744-2947; www.cityofchicago.org/specialevents) and operates three visitor information centers staffed with people who can answer questions and stocked with plenty of brochures on area attractions, including materials on everything from museums and city landmarks to lakefront biking maps and even fishing spots. The main visitor center, located in the Loop and convenient to many places that you'll likely be visiting, is on the first floor of the **Chicago Cultural Center,** 78 E. Washington St. (at Michigan Ave.). The center is open Monday through Friday from 10am to 6pm, Saturday from 10am to 5pm, and Sunday from 11am to 5pm; it's closed on holidays.

A second, smaller center is located in the heart of the city's shopping district, in the old pumping station at Michigan and Chicago avenues. Recently renamed the **Chicago Water Works Visitor Center,** its entrance is on the Pearson Street side of the building, across from the Water Tower Place mall. It's open daily from 7:30am to 7pm. This location has the added draw of housing a location of Hot Tix, which offers both half-price day-of-performance and full-price tickets to many theater productions around the city, as well as a gift shop.

A third visitor outpost is located at **Navy Pier** in the Illinois Market Place gift shop; it's open Sunday through Thursday from 10am to 9pm, and Friday and Saturday from 10am to midnight.

The **Illinois Bureau of Tourism** (© **800/2CONNECT** or TTY 800/406-6418; www.enjoyillinois.com) can provide general and specific information 24 hours a day. The agency also has staff at the information desk in the lobby of the **James R. Thompson Center,** 100 W. Randolph St., in the Helmut Jahn–designed building at LaSalle and Randolph streets in the Loop. The desk is open from 8:30am to 4:30pm Monday through Friday.

INFORMATION BY TELEPHONE The **Mayor's Office of Special Events** operates a recorded hot line (© **312/744-3370;** www.ci.chi.il.us/SpecialEvents) listing current special events, festivals, and parades occurring throughout the city. The city of Chicago also maintains a 24-hour information line for those with hearing impairments; call © **312/744-8599.**

PUBLICATIONS Chicago's major daily newspapers are the *Tribune* and the *Sun-Times.* Both have cultural listings, including movies, theaters, and live music, not to mention reviews of the very latest restaurants that are sure to have appeared in the city since this guidebook went to press. The Friday edition of both papers contains a special pullout section with more detailed, up-to-date information on special events happening over the weekend. *Chicago* magazine is an upscale monthly with good restaurant listings.

In a class by itself is the *Chicago Reader,* a free weekly that is an invaluable source of entertainment listings, classifieds, and well-written articles on contemporary issues of interest in Chicago.

Another free weekly, *New City* (© **312/243-8786**), also publishes excellent comprehensive listings of entertainment options. Appealing to a slightly younger audience than the *Reader,* its editorial tone tends toward the edgy and irreverent. Published every Wednesday, it's available in the same neighborhoods and locations as the *Reader.*

CITY LAYOUT

The **Chicago River** forms a Y that divides the city into its three geographic zones: North Side, South Side, and West Side (Lake Michigan is where the East Side would be). The downtown financial district is called **the Loop.** The city's key shopping street is **North Michigan Avenue,** also known as the **Magnificent Mile.** In addition to department stores and vertical malls, this stretch of property

Chicago Neighborhood Map Index

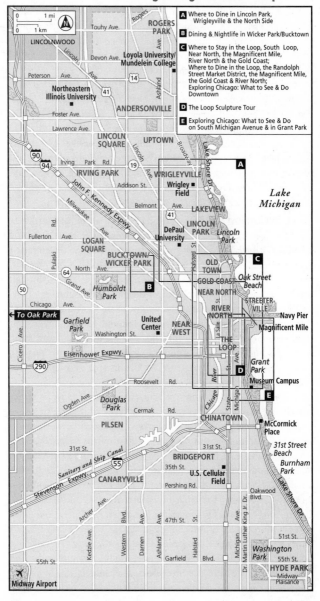

A Where to Dine in Lincoln Park, Wrigleyville & the North Side

B Dining & Nightlife in Wicker Park/Bucktown

C Where to Stay in the Loop, South Loop, Near North, the Magnificent Mile, River North & the Gold Coast; Where to Dine in the Loop, the Randolph Street Market District, the Magnificent Mile, the Gold Coast & River North; Exploring Chicago: What to See & Do Downtown

D The Loop Sculpture Tour

E Exploring Chicago: What to See & Do on South Michigan Avenue & in Grant Park north of the river houses many of the city's most elegant hotels. North and south of this downtown zone, Chicago stretches along 29 miles of Lake Michigan shoreline that is, by and large, free of commercial development, reserved for public use as green space and parkland from one end of town to the other.

Today Chicago proper has about 3 million inhabitants living in an area about two-thirds the size of New York City; another 5 million make the suburbs their home. The towns north of Chicago now stretch in an unbroken mass nearly to the Wisconsin border; the city's western suburbs extend 30 miles to Naperville, one of the fastest-growing towns in the nation over the past 2 decades. The real signature of Chicago, however, is found between the suburbs and the Loop, where a colorful patchwork quilt of residential neighborhoods gives the city a character all its own.

FINDING AN ADDRESS   Having been a part of the Northwest Territory, Chicago is laid out in a **grid system,** with the streets neatly lined up as if on a giant piece of graph paper. Because the city itself isn't rectangular (it's rather elongated), the shape is a bit irregular, but the perpendicular pattern remains. Easing movement through the city are a half-dozen or so major diagonal thoroughfares.

Point zero is located at the downtown intersection of State and Madison streets. **State Street** divides east and west addresses, and **Madison Street** divides north and south addresses. From here, Chicago's highly predictable addressing system begins. Making use of this grid, it is relatively easy to plot the distance in miles between any two points in the city.

Virtually all of Chicago's principal north-south and east-west arteries are spaced by increments of 400 in the addressing system—regardless of the number of smaller streets nestled between them. And each addition or subtraction of 400 numbers to an address is equivalent to a half mile. Thus, starting at point zero on Madison Street and traveling north along State Street for 1 mile, you will come to 800 N. State St., which intersects Chicago Avenue. Continue uptown for another half mile and you arrive at the 1200 block of North State Street at Division Street. And so it goes, right to the city line, with suburban Evanston located at the 7600 block north, 9½ miles from point zero. The same rule applies when you're traveling south, or east to west. The key to understanding the grid is that the side of any square formed by the principal avenues (noted in dark or red ink on most maps) represents a distance of half a mile in any direction. Understanding how Chicago's grid system works is of particular importance to those visitors who want to do a lot of walking in the city's many neighborhoods and who want to plot in advance the distances involved in trekking from one locale to another.

The other convenient aspect of the grid is that every major road uses the same numerical system. In other words, the cross street (Division St.) at 1200 N. Lake Shore Dr. is the same as at 1200 N. Clark St. and 1200 N. LaSalle St.

STREET MAPS   A suitably detailed map of Chicago is published by **Rand McNally,** available at many newsstands and bookstores for less than $5 (the smaller, more manageable laminated versions cost $6.95). Rand McNally operates a thoroughly stocked retail store at 444 N. Michigan Ave. (© **312/321-1751**), just north of the Wrigley Building.

NEIGHBORHOODS IN BRIEF
The Loop & Vicinity
Downtown In the case of Chicago, downtown means the Loop. The Loop refers literally to a core of primarily commercial, governmental, and cultural buildings contained within a corral of elevated train tracks, but greater downtown Chicago overflows these confines and is bounded by the Chicago River to the north and west, by Michigan Avenue to the east, and by Roosevelt Avenue to the south.

The North Side
Near North/Magnificent Mile North Michigan Avenue is known as the Magnificent Mile, from the bridge spanning the Chicago River to its northern tip at Oak Street. Many of the city's best hotels, shops, and restaurants are to be found on and around elegant North Michigan Avenue.

River North Just to the west of the Mag Mile's zone of high life and sophistication is an old warehouse district called River North. Over the past 20 years, the area has experienced a rebirth as one of the city's most vital commercial districts, and today it holds many of the city's hottest restaurants, nightspots, art galleries, and loft dwellings.

The Gold Coast Some of Chicago's most desirable real estate and historic architecture are found along Lake Shore Drive, between Oak Street and North Avenue and along the adjacent side streets. On the neighborhood's southwestern edge, around Division and Rush streets, a string of raucous bars and late-night eateries contrasts sharply with the rest of the area's sedate quality.

Old Town   West of LaSalle Street, principally on North Wells Street between Division Street and North Avenue, is the residential district of Old Town, which boasts some of the city's best-preserved historic homes. Old Town's biggest claim to fame, the legendary Second City comedy club, has served up the lighter side of life to Chicagoans for more than 30 years.

Lincoln Park   Chicago's most popular residential neighborhood is fashionable Lincoln Park. Stretching from North Avenue to Diversey Parkway, it's bordered on the east by the huge park of the same name, which is home to two major museums and one of the nation's oldest zoos (established in 1868). The trapezoid formed by Clark Street, Armitage Avenue, Halsted Street, and Diversey Parkway also contains many of Chicago's most happening bars, restaurants, retail stores, music clubs, and off-Loop theaters—including the nationally acclaimed Steppenwolf Theatre Company.

Lakeview & Wrigleyville   Midway up the city's North Side is a one-time blue-collar, now mainstream middle-class and bohemian quarter called Lakeview. It has become the neighborhood of choice for many gays and lesbians, recent college graduates, and a growing number of residents priced out of Lincoln Park. The main thoroughfare is Belmont Avenue, between Broadway and Sheffield Avenue. Wrigleyville is the name given to the neighborhood in the vicinity of Wrigley Field—home of the Chicago Cubs—at Sheffield Avenue and Addison Street.

The West Side

Near West   On the Near West Side, just across the Chicago River from the Loop, on Halsted Street between Adams and Monroe streets, is Chicago's old Greektown, still the Greek culinary center of the city. Much of the old Italian neighborhood in this vicinity was the victim of urban renewal, but remnants still survive on Taylor Street; the same is true for a few old delis and shops on Maxwell Street, dating from the turn of the 20th century when a large Jewish community lived in the area.

Bucktown/Wicker Park   Centered near the confluence of North, Damen, and Milwaukee avenues, this resurgent area is said to be home to the third-largest concentration of artists in the country. Over the past century, the area has hosted waves of German, Polish, and, most recently, Spanish-speaking immigrants. In recent years, it has morphed into a bastion of hot new restaurants, alternative culture, and loft-dwelling yuppies surfing the gentrification wave that's washing over this still-somewhat-gritty neighborhood.

The South Side

South Loop The generically rechristened South Loop area was Chicago's original "Gold Coast" in the late 19th century, with Prairie Avenue (now a historic district) as its most exclusive address. Stretching from Harrison Street's historic Printers Row south to Cermak Road (where Chinatown begins), and from Lake Shore Drive west to the south branch of the Chicago River, this is one of the fast-growing residential neighborhoods in the city.

Pilsen Originally home to the nation's largest settlement of Bohemian-Americans, Pilsen (which derives its name from a city in Bohemia, the Czech Republic) was for decades the principal entry point in Chicago for immigrants of every ethnic background. Centered at Halsted and 18th streets just southwest of the Loop, Pilsen now contains the second-largest Mexican-American community in the United States.

Hyde Park Hyde Park is like an independent village within the confines of Chicago, right off Lake Michigan and roughly a 30-minute train ride from the Loop. Fifty-seventh Street is the main drag, and the University of Chicago—with all its attendant shops and restaurants—is the neighborhood's principal tenant. The most successful racially integrated community in the city, Hyde Park is an oasis of furious intellectual activity and liberalism.

2 Getting Around

The best way to savor Chicago is by walking its streets. Walking is not always practical, however, particularly when moving between distant neighborhoods and on harsh winter days. In those situations, Chicago's public train and bus systems are efficient modes of transportation.

BY PUBLIC TRANSPORTATION

The **Chicago Transit Authority (CTA)** operates an extensive system of trains and buses throughout the city of Chicago. The sturdy system carries about 1.5 million passengers a day. Subways and elevated trains (known as the El) are generally safe and reliable, although it's advisable to avoid long rides through unfamiliar neighborhoods late at night.

Fares for the bus, subway, and El are $1.50, with an additional 30¢ for a transfer that allows CTA riders to make two transfers on the bus or El within 2 hours of receipt. Children under 7 ride free, and those between the ages of 7 and 11 pay 75¢ (15¢ for transfers).

Adopting a system used by other urban transit agencies, the CTA uses credit-card-size fare cards that automatically deduct the exact fare each time you take a ride. The reusable cards can be purchased with a preset value already stored ($14 for 10 rides, or $17 for 10 rides and 10 transfers), or riders can obtain cards at vending machines located at all CTA train stations and charge them with whatever amount they choose (a minimum of $3 and up to $100). If within 2 hours of your first ride you transfer to a bus or the El, the turnstiles at the El stations and the fare boxes on buses will automatically deduct from your card just the cost of a transfer (30¢). If you make a second transfer within 2 hours, it's free. The same card can be recharged continuously.

Fare cards can be used on buses, but you can't buy a card on the bus. If you get on the bus without a fare card, you'll have to pay $1.50 cash (either in coins or in dollar bills); the bus drivers cannot make change, so make sure that you've got the right amount before hopping on board.

CTA INFORMATION   The CTA operates a useful telephone information service (📞 **836-7000** or TTY 836-4949 from any area code in the city and suburbs) that functions daily from 5am to 1am. When you want to know how to get from where you are to where you want to go, call the CTA. You can also check out the CTA's website at **www.transitchicago.com**. Excellent CTA comprehensive maps, which include both El and bus routes, are usually available at subway or El stations, or by calling the CTA. The CTA also has

Tips Ticket to Ride

Visitors may consider buying a **Visitor Pass,** which works like a fare card and allows individual users unlimited rides on the El and CTA buses over a 24-hour period. The cards cost $5 and are sold at airports, hotels, museums, Hot Tix outlets, transportation hubs, and Chicago Office of Tourism visitor information centers (you can also buy them in advance online at www.transitchicago.com or by calling 📞 888/YOUR-CTA). Also available now are 2-, 3-, and 5-day passes. While the passes save you the trouble of feeding the fare machines yourself, remember that they're economical only if you plan to make at least three distinct trips at least 2 or more hours apart (remember that you get two additional transfers for an additional 30¢ on a regular fare).

Downtown El & Subway Stations

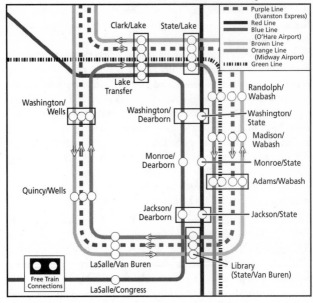

added a toll-free customer service hot line (℅ **888/YOUR-CTA** or TTY 888/CTA-TTY1 Mon–Fri 7am–8pm, with voice mail operating after hours) to field questions and feedback.

BY THE EL & THE SUBWAY The rapid transit system operates five major lines, which the CTA identifies by color: The **Red Line** runs north-south; the **Green Line** runs west-south; the **Blue Line** runs through Wicker Park/Bucktown west-northwest to O'Hare Airport; the **Brown Line** runs in a northern zigzag route; and the **Orange Line** runs southwest, serving Midway airport.

I highly recommend taking at least one El ride while you're here— you'll get a whole different perspective on the city (not to mention fascinating views inside downtown office buildings and North Side homes as you whiz past their windows). While the Red Line is the most efficient for traveling between the Magnificent Mile and points south, your only views along this underground stretch will be of dingy stations. For sightseers, I recommend taking the aboveground Brown Line, which runs around the downtown Loop and then north through residential neighborhoods. You can ride all the way to the end of the line at Kimball (about a 45-min. ride from downtown) or hop off at Belmont to wander the Lakeview neighborhood.

Avoid this scenic ride during rush hour (before about 9am and between 3:30 and 6:30pm), when your only view will be of weary, sweaty commuters.

Study your CTA map carefully (there's one printed on the inside back cover of this guide) before boarding any train. While most trains run every 5 to 20 minutes, decreasing in frequency in the off-peak and overnight hours, some stations close after work hours (as early as 8:30pm) and remain closed on Saturday, Sunday, and holidays. The Orange Line train does not operate from about 11:30pm to 5am, the Brown Line operates only north of Belmont after about 9:30pm, the Blue Line's Cermak branch has ceased operating overnight and on weekends.

The CTA recently posted timetables on the El platforms so that you can determine when the next train should arrive.

BY BUS   The best way to get around Chicago's warren of neighborhoods—the best way to actually see what's around you—is by riding a public bus, especially if you're staying near the lakefront, where the trains don't run. Look for the **blue-and-white signs to locate bus stops,** which are spaced about 1 or 2 blocks apart.

A few buses that are particularly handy for many visitors are the **no. 146 Marine/Michigan,** an express bus from Belmont Avenue on the North Side that cruises down North Lake Shore Drive (and through Lincoln Park during nonpeak times) to North Michigan Avenue, State Street, and the Grant Park museum campus; the **no. 151 Sheridan,** which passes through Lincoln Park en route to inner Lake Shore Drive and then travels along Michigan Avenue as far south as Adams Street, where it turns west into the Loop (and stops at Union Station); and the **no. 156 LaSalle,** which goes through Lincoln Park and then into the Loop's financial district on LaSalle Street.

BY TAXI

Taxis are a pretty affordable way to get around the Loop and to get to the dining, shopping, and entertainment options found beyond downtown, such as on the Near North Side, in Old Town and Lincoln Park, and on the Near West Side. But for longer distances, the fares will add up.

Taxis are easy to hail in the Loop, on the Magnificent Mile and the Gold Coast, in River North, and in Lincoln Park, but if you go much beyond these key areas, you might need to call. Cab companies include **Flash Cab** (✆ **773/561-1444**), **Yellow Cab**

(℃ **312/TAXI-CAB** or 312/829-4222), and **Checker Cab** (℃ **312/ CHECKER** or 312/243-2537).

The meter in Chicago cabs currently starts at $1.90 for the first mile and $1.60 for each additional mile, with a 50¢ surcharge for each additional rider age 12 to 65.

BY CAR

Chicago is laid out so logically that it's relatively easy for visitors to get around the city by car. Although rush-hour traffic jams are just as frustrating as they are in other large U.S. cities, traffic runs fairly smoothly at most times of the day. But Chicagoans have learned to be prepared for unexpected delays; it seems that at least one major highway and several downtown streets are under repair throughout the spring and summer months (some say we have two seasons: winter and construction).

Great diagonal corridors—such as Lincoln Avenue, Clark Street, and Milwaukee Avenue—slice through the grid pattern at key points in the city and shorten many a trip that would otherwise be tedious on the checkerboard surface of the Chicago streets. On scenic **Lake Shore Drive** (also known as the Outer Dr.) you can travel the length of the city (and beyond), never far from the great lake that is Chicago's most awesome natural feature.

DRIVING RULES   One bizarre anomaly in the organization of Chicago's traffic is the occasional absence of signal lights off the principal avenues, notably in the River North and Streeterville neighborhoods. A block east or west of the Magnificent Mile (North Michigan Ave.)—one of the most traveled streets in the city—you will in some cases encounter only stop signs to control the flow of traffic. Once you've become accustomed to the system, it works very smoothly, with everyone—pedestrians and motorists alike—advancing in their proper turn.

Unless otherwise posted, a right turn on red is allowed after stopping and signaling.

PARKING   Parking regulations are vigorously enforced throughout the city. Read signs carefully: The streets around Michigan Avenue have no-parking restrictions during rush hour—and I know from firsthand experience that your car will be towed immediately. Many neighborhoods have adopted resident-only parking that prohibits others from parking on their streets, usually after 6pm each day (even all day in a few areas, such as Old Town). The neighborhood around Wrigley Field is off-limits during Cubs night games, so look for yellow sidewalk signs alerting drivers about the dozen-and-a-half times the Cubs play under lights. You can park in permit zones if you're visiting a friend, who can provide you with a pass to stick on your windshield. Beware of tow zones, and, if visiting in winter, make note of curbside warnings regarding snow plowing.

The very best parking deal in the Loop is the city-run Millennium Park garage, which charges $10 for 12 hours or less (enter on Columbus Dr., 1 block east of Michigan Ave., between Monroe and Randolph sts.). Also relatively affordable are two lots underneath **Grant Park,** with entrances at Michigan Avenue and Van Buren Street (© **312/745-2862**) and Michigan Avenue and Madison Street (© **312/742-7530**). Parking costs $9 for the first hour, $12 for 1 to 2 hours, $15 for 2 to 10 hours, and $18 for 24 hours. You'll find higher prices at most other downtown lots, including **McCormick Place Parking,** 2301 S. Lake Shore Dr. (© 312/747-7194); **Midcontinental Plaza Garage,** 55 E. Monroe St. (© 312/986-6821); and **Navy Pier Parking,** 600 E. Grand Ave. (© 312/595-7437).

CAR RENTAL   Hertz (© 800/654-3131), **Avis** (© 800/831-2847), **National** (© 800/227-7368), and **Budget** (© 800/527-0700) all have offices at O'Hare Airport and at Midway Airport. Each company also has at least one office downtown: Hertz at 401 N. State St., Avis at 214 N. Clark St., National at 203 N. LaSalle St., and Budget at 65 E. Lake St.

BY BOAT

During the summer, boat traffic booms along the Lake Michigan shoreline and the Chicago River. The water taxi service offered by **Shoreline Sightseeing** (© **312/222-9328**) ferries passengers on the lake between Navy Pier and the Shedd Aquarium, and on the Chicago River between Navy Pier and the Sears Tower (Adams St. and the river). The boats run daily from Memorial Day to Labor Day every half-hour from 10am to 6pm and cost $6 for adults, $5 for seniors, and $3 for children.

The "RiverBus" operated by **Wendella Commuter Boats** (© **312/337-1446**) floats daily April through October between a dock below the Wrigley Building (the northwest side of the Michigan Ave. bridge) and North Western Station, a commuter train station across the river from the Loop (near the Sears Tower). The ride, which costs $2 each way (or $3 round-trip) and takes about 8 minutes, is popular with both visitors and commuters. The service operates every 10 minutes from 7am to 7pm.

FAST FACTS: Chicago

American Express Travel-service offices are located in the Loop at 55 W. Monroe St. (📞 **312/541-5440**) and across from the Virgin Megastore, at 605 N. Michigan Ave. (📞 **312/943-7840**).

Area Codes The 312 area code applies to the Loop and the neighborhoods closest to it, including River North, North Michigan Avenue, and the Gold Coast. The code for the rest of the city is 773. Suburban area codes are 847 (north), 708 (west and southwest), and 630 (far west). You must dial "1" plus the area code for all telephone numbers, even if you are making a call within the same area code.

Babysitters Check with the concierge or desk staff at your hotel, who are likely to maintain a list of reliable sitters with whom they have worked in the past. Many of the top hotels work with **American ChildCare Service** (📞 **312/644-7300**), a state-licensed and insured babysitting service that can match you with a sitter. The sitters are required to pass background checks, provide multiple child-care references, and be trained in infant and child CPR. It's best to make a reservation 24 hours in advance; the office is open from 9am to 5pm. Rates are $17 per hour, with a 4-hour minimum.

Business Hours Shops generally keep normal business hours, 10am to 6pm Monday through Saturday. Most stores generally stay open late at least 1 evening a week. And certain businesses, such as bookstores, are almost always open during the evening hours all week. Most shops (other than in the Loop) are now open on Sunday as well, usually from noon to 5pm. Malls are generally open to 7pm and on Sunday as well. Banking hours in Chicago are normally from 9am (8am, in some cases) to 5pm Monday through Friday, with select banks remaining open later on specified afternoons and evenings.

Doctors & Dentists In the event of a medical emergency, your best bet—unless you have friends who can recommend a doctor—is to rely on your hotel physician or go to the nearest hospital emergency room. **Northwestern Memorial Hospital** also has a **Physician Referral Service** (📞 **877/926-4664**). See also "Hospitals" below. The 24-hour **Dental Referral Service** (📞 **630/978-5745**) can refer you to an area dentist.

Emergencies For fire or police emergencies, call ℂ **911.** This is a free call. The nonemergency phone number for the Chicago Police Department is ℂ **311.**

Hospitals The best hospital emergency room in Chicago is, by consensus, at **Northwestern Memorial Hospital,** 251 E. Huron St. (ℂ **312/926-2000**). The emergency department (ℂ **312/926-5188** or 312/944-2358 for TDD access) is located at 251 E. Erie St. near Fairbanks Court. For an ambulance, dial ℂ **911.**

Internet Access Many Chicago **hotels** have business centers with computers available for guests' use. Computers with Internet access are also available to the public at the **Harold Washington Library Center,** 400 S. State St. (ℂ **312/747-4300**) and at the Internet cafe inside the **Apple** computer store, 679 N. Michigan Ave. (ℂ **312/981-4104**).

Liquor Laws Most bars and taverns have a 2am license, allowing them to stay open until 3am on Sunday (Sat night); some have a 4am license and may remain open until 5am on Sunday.

Newspapers & Magazines The *Chicago Tribune* (ℂ **312/222-3232**; www.chicagotribune.com) and the *Chicago Sun-Times* (ℂ **312/321-3000**; www.suntimes.com) are the two major dailies. The *Chicago Reader* (ℂ **312/828-0350**; www.chireader.com) is a free weekly that appears each Thursday, with all the current entertainment and cultural listings. *Chicago Magazine* (www.chicagomag.com) is a monthly that is widely read for its restaurant reviews. *CS* is a free lifestyle monthly that covers nightlife, dining, fashion, shopping, and other cultural pursuits.

Pharmacies **Walgreens,** 757 N. Michigan Ave. (ℂ **312/664-4000**), is open 24 hours. The other big pharmacy chain in town, **Osco Drugs,** has a toll-free number (ℂ **800/654-6726**) that you can call to locate the 24-hour pharmacy nearest you.

Police For emergencies, call ℂ **911.** This is a free call (no coins required). For nonemergencies, call ℂ **311.**

Post Office The main post office is at 433 W. Harrison St. (ℂ **312/983-8182**); free parking is available. You also find convenient branches in the Sears Tower, the Federal Center Plaza at 211 S. Clark St., the James R. Thompson Center at 100 W. Randolph St., and a couple of blocks off the Magnificent Mile at 227 E. Ontario St.

Radio **WBEZ** (91.5 FM) is the local National Public Radio station, which plays jazz in the evenings. **WFMT** (98.7 FM) specializes in fine arts and classical music. **WXRT** (93.1 FM) is a progressive rock station whose DJs mix things up with shots of blues, jazz, and local music. On the AM side of the dial, you'll find talk radio on **WGN** (720) and **WLS** (890). News junkies should tune to **WBBM** (780) for nonstop news, traffic, and weather reports, and sports fans will find company on the talk station **WSCR** (1160).

Safety   Chicago has all the crime problems of any urban center, so use your common sense and stay cautious and alert. At night you might want to stick to well-lighted streets along the Magnificent Mile, River North, Gold Coast, and Lincoln Park (stay out of the park proper after dark, though), which are all high-traffic areas late into the night. Don't walk alone at night, and avoid wandering down dark residential streets, even those that seem perfectly safe. Muggings can—and do—happen anywhere.

After dark, you might want to avoid the Loop's interior, which gets deserted after business hours, as well as neighborhoods such as Hyde Park, Wicker Park (beyond the busy intersection of Milwaukee, Damen, and North aves.), and Pilsen, which border areas with more troublesome reputations. You can also ask your hotel concierge or an agent at the tourist visitor center about the safety of a particular area.

If you're traveling alone, avoid riding the El after the rush-hour crowds thin out. Many of the El stations can be eerily deserted at night, when you'll have to wait around for 15 minutes or longer for the next train. In that case, it's a good idea to spring for a taxi. Buses are a safe option, too, especially nos. 146 and 151, which pick up along North Michigan Avenue and State Street and connect to the North Side via Lincoln Park.

Taxes   The local sales tax is 8.75%. Restaurants in the central part of the city, roughly the 312 area code, are taxed an additional 1%, for a total of 9.75%. The hotel room tax is a steep 14.9%.

Time Zone   All of Illinois, including Chicago, is located in the central time zone.

Weather   For the **National Weather Service**'s current conditions and forecast, dial © **312/976-1212** (for a fee), or check the weather on the Web at www.ci.chi.il.us/Tourism/Weather/.

4

Where to Stay

Downtown Chicago is packed with hotels, thanks to the city's booming convention trade. The competition among luxury hotels is especially intense, with the Ritz-Carlton and Four Seasons winning international awards even as newer properties get in on the action. In recent years, that meant steadily rising prices, with budget lodgings becoming harder to find. But since the September 11, 2001, terrorist attacks and the subsequent stock market woes, both business and tourist traffic has slowed—which means more and more hotels are willing to make a deal.

Most Chicago hotels offer a quintessential urban experience: Rooms come with views of surrounding skyscrapers, and the bustle of city life hits you as soon as you step outside the lobby doors. Although every property listed here caters to business travelers, Chicago attracts lots of tourists as well, and you won't have a problem finding plenty of midrange, family-friendly hotels in the most convenient neighborhoods; this is not a city where luxury hotels have dibs on all the prime real estate.

The rates given in this chapter are per night and do not include taxes, which are quite steep at 14.9%, nor do they take into account corporate or other discounts. Prices are always subject to availability and vary according to the time of week and season.

Because Chicago's hospitality industry caters first and foremost to the business traveler, rates tend to be higher during the week. The city's slow season is from January to March, when outsiders tend to shy away from the cold and the threat of being snowed in at O'Hare.

You never know when some huge convention will gobble up all the desirable rooms in the city (even on the weekends), so you're wise to book a room well in advance at any time of year. To find out if an upcoming convention coincides with your visit, contact the **Chicago Convention & Tourism Bureau** (*C* **312/567-8500;** www.choosechicago.com—click on "Convention Calendar").

RESERVATION SERVICES   You can check on the latest rates and availability, as well as book a room, by calling the **Illinois Reservation Service** (ⓒ **800/491-1800**). The 24-hour service is free. Another reservation service is **Hot Rooms** (ⓒ **800/468-3500** or 773/468-7666; www.hotrooms.com), which offers discounts at selected downtown hotels. The 24-hour service is free, but if you cancel a reservation, you're assessed a $25 fee. For a copy of the annual *Illinois Hotel-Motel Directory,*

BED & BREAKFAST RESERVATIONS   A centralized reservations service called **Bed & Breakfast/Chicago Inc.,** P.O. Box 14088, Chicago, IL 60614 (ⓒ **800/375-7084** or 773/394-2000; fax 773/394-2002; www.chicago-bed-breakfast.com), lists more than 70 accommodations in Chicago. Options range from high-rise and loft apartments to guest rooms carved from a former private club on the 40th floor of a Loop office building.

1 The Loop

Strictly speaking, "downtown" in Chicago means the Loop—the central business district, a 6-by-8-block rectangle enveloped by elevated tracks on all four sides. Within these confines are the city's financial institutions, trading markets, and municipal government buildings, making for a lot of hustle and bustle Monday through Friday. Come Saturday and Sunday, however, the Loop is pretty dead; on Sundays, almost all the stores are closed. If nightlife is a priority, you won't find much here, but you do have some very good dining options.

VERY EXPENSIVE

Fairmont Hotel 𝆑𝆑   The Fairmont is easily one of the city's most luxurious hotels, offering an array of deluxe amenities and services and regularly hosting high-level politicians and high-profile fundraisers. The overall effect is chic but a bit impersonal. The entrance faces anonymous office towers, and you're likely to wander the circular lobby before finding the check-in desk. Still, the rooms are large and decorated in a comfortable, upscale style (ask for one with a lake view, although city-view rooms aren't bad either). The posh bathrooms feature extra-large tubs, separate vanity areas, and swivel TVs. The windows open (a rarity in high-rise hotels), so you can enjoy the breeze drifting off Lake Michigan.

Where to Stay

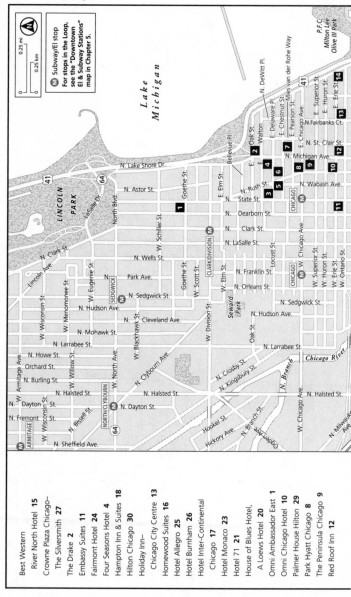

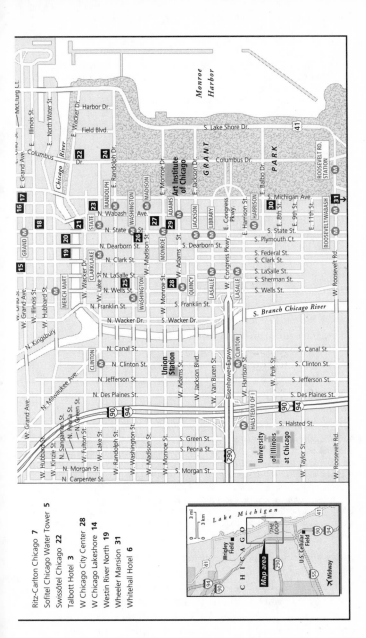

Ritz-Carlton Chicago **7**
Sofitel Chicago Water Tower **5**
Swissôtel Chicago **22**
Talbott Hotel **3**
W Chicago City Center **28**
W Chicago Lakeshore **14**
Westin River North **19**
Wheeler Mansion **31**
Whitehall Hotel **6**

200 N. Columbus Dr. (at Lake St.), Chicago, IL 60601. ℂ **800/526-2008** or 312/
565-8000. Fax 312/856-1032. www.fairmont.com. 692 units. $189–$354 double.
AE, DC, DISC, MC, V. Valet parking $34 with in/out privileges. Subway/El: Red,
Green, Orange, Brown, or Blue line to State/Lake. Small pets accepted. **Amenities:**
Restaurant (American/eclectic); lounge; access to Lakeshore Athletic Club, one of
the top health clubs in the city (with full-court basketball, climbing wall, pool, and
spa); concierge; business center; 24-hr. room service; babysitting; laundry service;
24-hr. dry cleaning. *In room:* A/C, TV w/pay movies, high-speed Internet access,
minibar, hair dryer, iron.

EXPENSIVE

Crowne Plaza Chicago—The Silversmith ᐱᐱ *Finds*   You
might call The Silversmith a hidden gem. The landmark building
was built in 1897 to serve the jewelry and silver trade on Wabash
Avenue. Rooms come in varying configurations, with 12-foot-high
ceilings, 10-foot picture windows, Frank Lloyd Wright–inspired
wrought-iron fixtures, armoires, and homey bedding; bathrooms are
generously sized. Because buildings surround this very urban hotel,
natural light is limited in the rooms; those along the hotel's main
corridor tend to be dark. Rooms at the front on the fifth floor or
higher have a quintessentially Chicago view: hard-working Wabash
Avenue and the El tracks. Yes, the windows are extra-thick to muf-
fle the noise of the rumbling trains, but you'll want to avoid the
lower-level floors if you like things quiet. For the best combination
of natural light and views, request a Wabash Avenue room on the
9th or 10th floor. Word about The Silversmith has been slow getting out (even Loop office workers who pass by it daily don't know
it's there), so rooms don't book up as quickly as other, hotter spots.
That's good news for thrifty travelers looking for deals.

10 S. Wabash Ave. (at Madison St.), Chicago, IL 60603. ℂ **800/2CROWNE** or 312/
372-7696. Fax 312/372-7320. www.ichotelsgroup.com. 143 units. $149–$279 double; from $289 suite; weekend rates available. AE, DC, DISC, MC, V. Valet parking
$28 with in/out privileges. Subway/El: Brown, Green, or Orange line to Madison/
Wabash, or Red Line to Washington/State. **Amenities:** Restaurant (deli); lounge;
tiny fitness room (with access to nearby health club at a charge); concierge;
business center and secretarial services; limited room service; laundry service; dry
cleaning; club-level rooms. *In room:* A/C, TV w/pay movies, dataport, minibar, coffeemaker, hair dryer, iron, safe.

Hotel Burnham ᐱᐱᐱ   If you're looking for a spot with a sense of
history, this is it. A brilliant $30 million restoration in 1999 of the
historic Reliance Building—one of the first skyscrapers ever built
and a highly significant architectural treasure—resulted in this intimate boutique hotel named for Daniel Burnham, whose firm
designed the building in 1895. The prime State Street location is

across from Marshall Field's and 1 block south of the hopping North Loop theater district. The Burnham is a must for architecture buffs: Wherever possible, the restoration retained period elements: terrazzo tile floors, white marble wainscoting, and mahogany door and window frames. Rooms are clubby but glamorous, with plush beds, mahogany writing desks, and chaise lounges. The hotel's 19 suites feature a separate living-room area and CD stereo systems. Don't come to the Burnham if you're looking for extensive amenities—the lobby is tiny, as is the exercise room.

1 W. Washington St. (at State St.), Chicago, IL 60602. ℂ 877/294-9712 or 312/782-1111. Fax 312/782-0899. www.burnhamhotel.com. 122 units. $149–$299 double; $199–$349 suite. AE, DC, DISC, MC, V. Valet parking $29 with in/out privileges. Subway: Red or Blue line to Washington/State. **Amenities:** Restaurant (contemporary American); small fitness room (and access to nearby health club); concierge; business services; 24-hr. room service; laundry service; dry cleaning. *In room:* A/C, TV, fax, dataport, minibar, hair dryer, iron.

Hotel Monaco ✦✦✦   This 14-story boutique hotel may try a little too hard to be "fun": Guests are greeted by derby-hatted doormen, funky house music plays in the lobby, and a goldfish with its own name swims about a fishbowl in your room. But it offers an upbeat alternative to the many cookie-cutter business hotels in the city. The plush, jewel-toned, 1930s-inspired decor makes the sizeable rooms resemble theatrical set pieces. The eclectic furnishings include armoires, mahogany writing desks, and marshmallow-soft beds; suites come with a two-person whirlpool spa and CD player. Rooms on the top three floors have views of the Chicago River and surrounding skyscrapers. The cozy lobby is the spot for free morning coffee and an evening wine reception. Given the hotel's playful spirit, it attracts a younger clientele, with an overall vibe that is laid-back and friendly rather than so-hip-it-hurts (this is Chicago, after all, not New York).

225 N. Wabash Ave. (at Wacker Dr.), Chicago, IL 60601. ℂ 800/397-7661 or 312/960-8500. Fax 312/960-8538. www.monaco-chicago.com. 192 units. $139–$299 double; $279–$429 suite. AE, DC, DISC, MC, V. Valet parking $28 with in/out privileges. Subway: Brown, Green, or Orange line to Randolph/Wabash, or Red Line to Washington/State. Small pets allowed. **Amenities:** Restaurant (American); fitness room (and access to nearby health club); concierge; business center; 24-hr. room service; in-room massage; babysitting; laundry service; dry cleaning. *In room:* A/C, TV w/pay movies, fax, dataport, minibar, coffeemaker, hair dryer, iron.

Hotel 71 ✦✦   The city's newest hotel is actually a complete renovation of a rather drab 1950-era high-rise. Don't let the boring exterior fool you. Hotel 71 is too big to be considered a "boutique hotel" (with more than 400 rooms spread over 30-plus stories), but it is filled with unique touches that reflect the boutique sensibility. The rather-cramped lobby feels like a nightclub, with black curtains covering the walls and atmospheric trance music wafting from the stereo system. The rooms, by contrast, are bright and cheery—and much larger than average. Everything is brand new, from the yellow-checked linens and curtains, to the spotless white bathrooms. Every room has a well-lit work desk and a minibar stocked with gourmet treats from Dean & DeLuca. Rooms on the north side of the hotel (overlooking the Chicago River) have the best views; if you can, snag one of the rooms on the west end of the building, which have views in two directions.

71 E. Wacker Dr. (at Wabash Ave.), Chicago, IL 60601. © **800/621-4005** or 312/346-7100. Fax 312/346-1721. www.hotel71.com. 454 units. $149–$249 double. AE DC, DISC, MC, V. Valet parking $32 with in/out privileges. Subway: Brown, Green, or Orange line to Randolph/Wabash, or Red Line to Washington/State. **Amenities:** Restaurant (contemporary American); fitness room; concierge; business services; 24-hr. room service; laundry service; dry cleaning. *In room:* A/C, TV, high-speed Internet access, minibar, hair dryer, iron, CD player.

Palmer House Hilton *(Overrated* Chicago's oldest hotel, the namesake of legendary State Street merchant prince Potter Palmer, is decidedly from another era—and the massive complex feels somewhat lost in time. The elegance of the grand lobby isn't matched in the rooms (decorated in an anonymous midlevel hotel style) or the clientele (which tends heavily toward conventioneers). And don't expect grand views of surrounding skyscrapers, because most rooms look out into offices across the street. All the rooms are in the process of being renovated, but upgrades at the palatial Palmer House take place, understandably, on a staggered basis; be sure to ask for a refurbished room when making reservations. Bathrooms are on the smallish size (some rooms come with two bathrooms, a plus for families). Kids might appreciate the sheer size of the place, with plenty of room to wander, and the location is good for access to the Museum Campus, but the Palmer House's days as one of Chicago's top hotels are gone.

17 E. Monroe St. (at State St.), Chicago, IL 60603. © **800/HILTONS** or 312/726-7500. Fax 312/917-1797. www.hilton.com. 1,640 units. $129–$350 double; $450–$1,500 suite. AE, DC, DISC, MC, V. Valet parking $31 with in/out privileges; self-parking across the street $21. Subway/El: Red Line to Monroe/State. **Amenities:** 4 restaurants (including the legendary but dated Trader Vic's, a Cajun restaurant, and 2 American bar and grills); 2 lounges; indoor pool; health club; Jacuzzi; sauna; children's programs; concierge; business center; shopping arcade; room service until 2am; babysitting referrals; laundry service; overnight dry cleaning; executive rooms. *In room:* A/C, TV w/pay movies, minibar, coffeemaker, hair dryer, iron.

Swissôtel Chicago 𝒞𝒞   This sleek, modern hotel is all business, and may therefore feel a bit icy to some visitors. Panoramic vistas from every room—of Lake Michigan, Grant Park, the Chicago River, or the nine-hole, par-three FamilyGolf Center next door—are the hotel's best features. The spacious rooms have separate sitting areas and warm contemporary furnishings. Business travelers will appreciate the oversize desks (convertible to dining tables), ergonomic chairs, and—in upgraded executive-level rooms—CD players. Executive suites, with wonderful, 180-degree views, have separate sleeping areas. All executive-level guests also receive complimentary breakfast and hors d'oeuvres and have access to a lounge with Internet connections, library, and personal concierge.

The Swissôtel has a slick, professional aura that's not particularly family-friendly, which makes it especially attractive to business travelers in search of tranquility.

323 E. Wacker Dr., Chicago, IL 60601. © 888/737-9477 or 312/565-0565. Fax 312/565-0540. www.swissotel.com. 632 units. $159–$409 double; $395–$2,500 suite. AE, DC, DISC, MC, V. Valet parking $35 with in/out privileges. Subway/El: Red, Brown, Orange, or Green line to Randolph. **Amenities:** 3 restaurants (steakhouse, American); lounge; penthouse fitness center with indoor pool, spa, Jacuzzi, and sauna; concierge; business center with extensive meeting services; 24-hr. room service; massage; babysitting; laundry service; 24-hr. dry cleaning; executive-level rooms. *In room:* A/C, TV w/pay movies, dataport, minibar, coffeemaker, hair dryer, iron.

W Chicago City Center 𝒞   One of two Chicago properties in the hip W hotel chain (the other is the W Chicago Lakeshore, below), this is an oasis of cool in the button-down Loop. Unfortunately, the rooms tend toward the small and dark (most look out into a central courtyard). The W color scheme—dark purple and gray—doesn't do much to brighten the spaces; don't stay here if you crave lots of natural light. All W properties pride themselves on their "whatever, whenever" service: whatever you want, whenever you want it (the modern version of a 24-hr. on-call concierge). The bar, designed by nightlife wunderkind Rande Gerber (Mr. Cindy Crawford), gives hotel guests a stylish spot to sit and pose amid dance music and cocktail waitresses who look like models.

172 W. Adams St. (at LaSalle St.), Chicago, IL 60603. © 877/W-HOTELS or 312/332-1200. Fax 312/332-5909. www.whotels.com. 390 units. $199–$329 double; from $369 suite. AE, DC, DISC, MC, V. Valet parking $30 with in/out privileges. Subway/El: Brown Line to Quincy. Pets allowed. **Amenities:** Restaurant (European); bar; exercise room; concierge; business services; 24-hr. room service; in-room massage; babysitting; same-day laundry service; dry cleaning. *In room:* A/C, TV w/VCR and pay movies, fax, high-speed Internet access, minibar, coffeemaker, hair dryer, iron, safe, CD player.

MODERATE

Hotel Allegro Chicago ⍟ *Value*   Owned by the same company as the Hotel Monaco and the Hotel Burnham (both listed above), the Allegro is the best choice in the Loop for families in search of a fun vibe. Although its published rates are about the same as those of its sister properties, the Allegro is far larger than the Monaco or the Burnham, and consequently is more likely to offer special rates to fill space (especially on weekends and in the winter). Guests enter a lobby with plush, eclectic, and boldly colorful furnishings: This whimsical first impression segues into the rooms, which vary wildly in size and configuration, so be sure to request the biggest available room when making your reservation. Suites have robes, VCRs, and two-person Jacuzzi tubs. Befitting a place where the concierge wears a stylish leather jacket and the doorman hums along to the tunes playing on speakers out front, the Allegro appeals to younger travelers.

171 W. Randolph St. (at LaSalle St.), Chicago, IL 60601. ℂ 800/643-1500 or 312/236-0123. Fax 312/236-0917. www.allegrochicago.com. 483 units. $149–$299 double; $225–$399 suite. AE, DC, DISC, MC, V. Valet parking $30 with in/out privileges. Subway/El: All lines to Washington. **Amenities:** Restaurant (northern Italian); lounge; exercise room (and access to nearby health club w/indoor pool); concierge; business services; salon; limited room service; same-day laundry service; dry cleaning. *In room:* A/C, TV w/pay movies, high-speed Internet access (upon request), minibar, hair dryer, iron.

2 South Loop

The South Loop is less about glamour and more about old Chicago. Running the length of Grant Park, South Michigan Avenue is ideal for a long city stroll, passing grand museums, imposing architecture, and the park's greenery and statuary.

EXPENSIVE

Hilton Chicago ⍟⍟   When it opened in 1927, this massive brick-and-stone edifice billed itself as the largest hotel in the world. Today, the Hilton still runs like a small city, with numerous restaurants and shops and a steady stream of conventioneers. Its colorful history includes visits by Queen Elizabeth, Emperor Hirohito, and every president since FDR—and riots outside its front door during the 1968 Democratic Convention. The classical-rococo public spaces—including the Versailles-inspired Grand Ballroom and Grand Stair Lobby—are magnificent, but the rest of the hotel is firmly entrenched in the present.

Family-Friendly Hotels

Chicago has plenty of options for families on the go. The **Hampton Inn & Suites** (p. 55) keeps the kids in a good mood with a pool, Nintendo, and proximity to the Hard Rock Cafe and the Rainforest Cafe. Children under 18 stay free. Kiddies also stay free at the **Holiday Inn–Chicago City Centre** (p. 51), which has a large outdoor pool and is near Navy Pier and the beach.

When you want a little extra room to spread out, both **Homewood Suites** (p. 51) and **Embassy Suites** (p. 52) offer affordable ways to travel en masse (and keep your sanity).

Of course, luxury hotels can afford to be friendly to all of their guests. At the **Four Seasons** (p. 44), kids are indulged with little robes, balloon animals, Nintendo, and milk and cookies; the hotel also has a wonderful pool. The concierge at the **Ritz-Carlton** (p. 46) keeps a stash of toys and games for younger guests to borrow, and kids' menu items are available 24 hours; the hotel even provides a special gift pack just for teenage guests. The upscale **Westin River North** (p. 54), the **Omni Chicago Hotel** (p. 48), and the **Omni Ambassador East** (p. 55) also cater to families with baby accessories and programs for older kids, respectively.

Some rooms are on the small side, but all are comfortable and warm, and many of the standard rooms have two bathrooms (great for families). High rooms facing Michigan Avenue offer sweeping views of Grant Park and the lake. The hotel's Tower section has a separate registration area, upgraded amenities (including robes, fax machines, and VCRs), and a lounge, serving complimentary continental breakfast and evening hors d'oeuvres and cocktails (you'll pay about $50 above the standard rate for these rooms).

The Hilton is a great choice for families, thanks to its vast public spaces, proximity to major museums and Grant Park (where kids can run around), and policy of children under 18 staying free in their parents' room.

720 S. Michigan Ave. (at Balbo Dr.), Chicago, IL 60605. ℰ **800/HILTONS** or 312/922-4400. Fax 312/922-5240. www.chicagohilton. 1,544 units. $124–$324 double;

$139–$339 junior suite. AE, DC, DISC, MC, V. Valet parking $32; self-parking $29. Subway/El: Red Line to Harrison/State. **Amenities:** 4 restaurants (Continental, Irish, American); 2 lounges; indoor pool; health club w/indoor track, hot tubs, sauna, and steam room; concierge; business center; 24-hr. room service; massage; babysitting; laundry service; 24-hr. dry cleaning; tower rooms. *In room:* A/C, TV w/pay movies, dataport, minibar, coffeemaker, hair dryer, iron.

Wheeler Mansion *Finds*   This grand Italianate building had fallen on hard times—until Debra and Scott Seger saw its potential as a bed-and-breakfast. Today, completely restored and refurbished, the Wheeler Mansion is one of the city's most charming small hotels. The Segers kept intact whatever was salvageable, including the mosaic tile floor in the vestibule and some of the dark walnut woodwork and fixtures. But they added good-size private bathrooms to each room (some have only shower stalls rather than bathtubs). Antique furniture that the Segers found in Europe fills the house, and guests dine on bone china and sleep on goose-down feather beds. A continental breakfast by the resident chef is served weekdays. On weekends, the buffet features a more elaborate array of dishes.

2020 S. Calumet Ave., Chicago, IL 60616. ⓒ **312/945-2020.** Fax 312/945-2021. www.wheelermansion.com. 11 units. $230–$285 double; $265–$365 suite. Prices include taxes. AE, DC, DISC, MC, V. Free parking. Bus: No. 62 from State Street downtown. **Amenities:** Laundry service; computer rental available. *In room:* A/C, cable TV, fax, dataport, hair dryer, iron.

3 Near North & the Magnificent Mile

Along the Magnificent Mile—a stretch of Michigan Avenue running north of the Chicago River to Oak Street—you'll find most of the city's premium hotels. The location, near some of the city's best shopping and dining, can't be beat.

VERY EXPENSIVE

Four Seasons Hotel *Kids*   Consistently voted one of the top hotels in the world by frequent travelers, the Four Seasons offers an understated luxury that appeals to publicity-shy Hollywood stars and wealthy families. Although the hotel has every conceivable luxury amenity, the overall look is that of an English country manor rather than a glitzy getaway. The real attraction here is the service, not the decor.

The city's tallest hotel, the Four Seasons occupies a rarefied aerie between the 30th and 46th floors above the Mag Mile's most upscale vertical mall. The beautiful rooms have English furnishings, custom-woven carpets and tapestries, and dark-wood armoires.

Each has windows that open to let in the fresh air. Bathrooms boast such indulgences as a lighted makeup mirror, oversize towels and robes, scales, and Bulgari toiletries. Kid-friendly services include little robes, balloon animals, Nintendo, a special room-service menu, and milk and cookies.

120 E. Delaware Place (at Michigan Ave.), Chicago, IL 60611. ℂ **800/332-3442** or 312/280-8800. Fax 312/280-1748. www.fourseasons.com. 343 units. $420–$515 double; $555–$3,500 suite; weekend rates from $305. AE, DC, DISC, MC, V. Valet parking $35 with in/out privileges; self-parking $25. Subway/El: Red Line to Chicago/State. Pets accepted. **Amenities:** 2 restaurants (New American, cafe); lounge; indoor pool; fitness center and spa; concierge; business center; 24-hr. room service; babysitting; laundry service; 24-hr. dry cleaning. *In room:* A/C, TV w/VCR and pay movies, high-speed Internet access, minibar, coffeemaker, hair dryer, iron.

Park Hyatt Chicago ☆☆☆   For those in search of chic modern luxury, the Park Hyatt is the coolest hotel in town (as long as money is no object). The building occupies one of the most desirable spots on North Michigan Avenue and the best rooms are those that face east, overlooking the bustle of the Mag Mile and the lake in the distance.

Luxury might be the watchword here, but the look is anything but stuffy: The lobby feels like a sleek modern art gallery. Rooms feature Eames and Mies van der Rohe reproduction furniture and window banquettes with stunning city views (the windows actually open). The comfortable beds are well appointed with several plush pillows. While most hotels might provide a TV and VCR, this is the kind of place where you get a DVD player and flat-screen TV. The bathrooms are especially wonderful: Slide back the cherrywood wall for views of the city while you soak in the tub.

800 N. Michigan Ave., Chicago, IL 60611. ℂ **800/233-1234** or 312/335-1234. Fax 312/239-4000. www.hyatt.com. 203 units. $375–$425 double; $695–$3,000 suite. AE, DC, DISC, MC, V. Valet parking $36 with in/out privileges. Subway/El: Red Line to Chicago/State. **Amenities:** Restaurant (French/American); lounge; indoor pool; health club with Jacuzzi and spa; concierge; business center with computer technical support; 24-hr. room service; massage; babysitting; laundry service; 24-hr. dry cleaning. *In room:* A/C, TV w/DVD player and pay movies, dataport, minibar, coffeemaker, hair dryer, iron, CD player.

The Peninsula Chicago ☆☆☆   Do believe the hype. The first Midwest location from the luxury Peninsula hotel group promised to wow us, and it does not disappoint. Taking design cues from the chain's flagship Hong Kong hotel, the Peninsula Chicago mixes an Art Deco sensibility with modern, top-of-the-line amenities. Service is practically a religion.

Rooms are average in size (the "junior suites" are fairly small, with living rooms that can comfortably seat only about four people). But the hotel's in-room technology is cutting edge: A small silver "command station" by every bed allows guests to control all the lights, curtains, and room temperature without getting out from under the covers. The marble-filled bathrooms have separate shower stalls and tubs, vanities with plenty of room to sit, and another "command station" by the bathtub. Add in the flat-screen TVs and you have a classic hotel that's very much attuned to the present.

The sultry hotel bar is already one of the city's top spots for romantic assignations (or confidential late-night business negotiations). The bright, airy spa and fitness center fill the top two floors and make a lovely retreat (especially the outdoor deck).

108 E. Superior St. (at Michigan Ave.), Chicago, IL 60611. © 866/288-8889 or 312/337-2888. Fax 312/932-9529. www.peninsula.com. 339 units. $445–$455 double; $500–$4,500 suite. AE, DC, DISC, MC, V. Valet parking $36 with in/out privileges. Subway/El: Red Line to Chicago/State. Pets accepted. **Amenities:** 4 restaurants (seafood, Asian, Continental, and European bakery); bar; indoor pool with outdoor deck; free fitness center; spa; hot tub; sauna; children's amenities; concierge; business center; 24-hr. room service; in-room massage; babysitting; laundry service; same-day dry cleaning. *In room:* A/C, TV w/pay movies (VCRs and DVD players upon request), fax, dataport, minibar, fridge (upon request), hair dryer, safe.

Ritz-Carlton Chicago *★★★ Kids*   Top-notch service and an open, airy setting make this one of Chicago's most welcoming hotels. Perched high atop the Water Tower Place mall, the Ritz-Carlton's lobby is on the 12th floor, with a large bank of windows to admire the city below. Not surprisingly, the quality of the accommodations is of the highest caliber, although the standard rooms aren't very large. Doubles have space for a loveseat and desk but not much more; the bathrooms are elegant but not huge (for extra-large, lavish bathrooms, request a "Premier" room or suite on the 30th floor). Guests staying in any of the hotel's suites (premier or not) are treated to a gratis wardrobe pressing upon arrival, personalized stationery, Bulgari toiletries, and fresh flowers. Lake views cost more but are spectacular (although in all the rooms, you're up high enough that you're not staring into surrounding apartment buildings).

Families will find this luxury crash pad quite welcoming. Every child receives a gift and can borrow toys and games from a stash kept by the concierge. PlayStation and Nintendo are also available, and kids' food is available from room service 24 hours a day.

160 E. Pearson St., Chicago, IL 60611. © 800/621-6906 or 312/266-1000. Fax 312/266-1194. www.fourseasons.com. 430 units. $380–$485 double; $515–$3,500

suite; weekend rates from $305. Valet parking $36 with in/out privileges; self-parking $25 with no in/out privileges. Subway/El: Red Line to Chicago/State. Pets accepted. **Amenities:** 4 restaurants (French, American); 2 lounges; indoor pool; health club with spa, Jacuzzi, and sauna; children's programs; concierge; business center; 24-hr. room service; in-room massage; babysitting; laundry service; same-day dry cleaning; premier suites. *In room:* A/C, TV w/VCR and pay movies, fax, dataport, minibar, hair dryer.

Sofitel Chicago Water Tower ✦✦   The latest addition to Chicago's already-crowded luxury hotel scene, the Sofitel aims to impress by drawing on the city's tradition of great architecture. French architect Jean-Paul Viguier created a building that's impossible to pass without taking a second look: a soaring, triangular white tower that sparkles in the sun. The overall feel of the hotel is European modern; you'll hear French accents from the front-desk staff, and foreign-language magazines are scattered on tables throughout the lobby. The bright, stylish Café des Architects has become a favorite business lunch spot for locals.

The guest rooms feature contemporary decor with natural beechwood walls and chrome hardware for a modern touch. All the rooms enjoy good views of the city (but the privacy-conscious will want to stay on the upper floors, where they won't be on display to surrounding apartment buildings). The standard doubles are fairly compact—but thanks to large picture windows, the spaces don't feel cramped. The luxurious marble bathrooms (with separate tub and shower stall) are quite spacious. The amenities are topnotch.

20 E. Chestnut St. (at Wabash St.), Chicago, IL 60611. ⓒ **800/SOFITEL** or 312/324-4000. Fax 312/324-4026. www.sofitel.com. 415 units. $199–$459 double; $499–$599 suite. AE, DC, DISC, MC, V. Valet parking $35. Subway/El: Red Line to Chicago/State. Small pets accepted. **Amenities:** Restaurant (French cafe); bar; fitness center; concierge; business center; 24-hr. room service; babysitting; laundry service; same-day dry cleaning. *In room:* A/C, TV w/pay movies, high-speed Internet access, minibar, coffeemaker, hair dryer, iron.

EXPENSIVE

The Drake ✦✦✦   If ever the term "grande dame" fit a hotel, it's The Drake, which opened in 1920. Fronting East Lake Shore Drive, this landmark building is Chicago's version of New York's Plaza or Paris's Ritz. Despite a massive renovation in the 1990s, the Drake still feels lost in time compared to places like the glitzy new Peninsula. But for many, that is part of The Drake's charm.

The Drake's public spaces still maintain the regal grandeur of days gone by, but the guest rooms have been modernized with new furniture and linens. Most rooms include a small sitting area with couch and chairs; some have two bathrooms. The lake-view rooms are lovely, and—no surprise—you'll pay more for them. Be forewarned that "city view" rooms on the lower floors look out onto another building, so you'll probably be keeping your drapes shut.

140 E. Walton Place (at Michigan Ave.), Chicago, IL 60611. ✆ **800/55-DRAKE** or 312/787-2200. Fax 312/787-1431. www.hilton.com. 537 units. $255–$295 double; $335–$430 executive floor; from $600 suite; weekend rates start at $289 with continental breakfast. AE, DC, DISC, MC, V. Valet parking $32 with in/out privileges. Subway/El: Red Line to Chicago/State. **Amenities:** 3 restaurants (American, seafood); 2 lounges; fitness center; concierge; business center; shopping arcade (including a Chanel boutique); barbershop; 24-hr. room service; in-room massage; laundry service; 24-hr. dry cleaning; executive-level rooms. *In room:* A/C, TV w/pay movies, dataport, minibar, coffeemaker, hair dryer, iron.

Hotel Inter-Continental Chicago ⭐⭐   The newer hotels might be getting all the attention, but the Hotel Inter-Continental remains a sentimental favorite for many Chicagoans (ranking right up there with The Drake in our affections). A recent renovation removed some of the building's quirky originality, but it has definitely brought the guest rooms up several notches. Built as an athletic club in 1929, the building's original lobby features truly grand details: marble columns, hand-stenciled ceilings, and historic tapestries (for a peek, go in the southern entrance, on the corner of Illinois St.).

Rooms are located in the original club building (the South Tower) and in a 1960s addition (the North Tower). Although all the rooms have new furnishings and fabrics, the North Tower rooms have a more generic, sterile feel; I'd recommend the South Tower for a more distinctive experience—but be prepared for smaller bathrooms.

The Inter-Continental's main claim to fame is the junior Olympic-size pool on the top floor, a beautiful 1920s gem surrounded by elegant mosaics.

505 N. Michigan Ave. (at Grand Ave.), Chicago, IL 60611. ✆ **800/327-0200** or 312/944-4100. Fax 312/944-1320. www.chicago.interconti.com. 807 units. $249–$350 double; $500–$3,000 suite; weekend and promotional rates from $145. AE, DC, DISC, MC, V. Valet parking $27–$34 with in/out privileges. Subway/El: Red Line to Grand/State. **Amenities:** Restaurant (American); 2 lounges; indoor pool; fitness center with sauna; concierge; business center; 24-hr. room service; massage; babysitting; laundry service; same-day dry cleaning; executive rooms. *In room:* A/C, TV w/pay movies, dataport, minibar, coffeemaker, hair dryer, iron.

Omni Chicago Hotel ⭐ *Kids*   The tranquil interior of this business hotel is a welcome retreat from the frenetic shopping activity on Michigan Avenue. No less a Chicago luminary than Oprah Winfrey has given the Omni her stamp of approval, designating it the official crash pad for guests appearing on her show.

All the units are suites with one king-size or two double beds. Each unit has a living room with a sitting area, a dining table, a wet bar, and a refrigerator, all of which are divided from the bedroom by a set of French doors. About a third of the suites have pullout sofas. You can request a corner suite, with lots of light and views looking down Michigan Avenue, for $20 extra.

While the hotel's hushed tones exude a feeling of business rather than pleasure, the Omni Kids Program makes younger guests feel welcome. All children receive a bag of games and ideas for Chicago activities and Nintendo in their rooms, as well as kids' menus.

676 N. Michigan Ave. (at Huron St.), Chicago, IL 60611. © 800/843-6664 or 312/944-6664. Fax 312/266-3015. www.omnihotels.com. 347 units. $259–$329 suite; weekend rates $179–$209. AE, DC, DISC, MC, V. Valet parking $32 with in/out privileges. Subway/El: Red Line to Grand/State. **Amenities:** Restaurant (American/Mediterranean); lounge; lap pool; health club; Jacuzzi; courtesy car available for trips within the downtown area; business services; 24-hr. room service; babysitting; laundry service; 24-hr. dry cleaning; executive-level rooms. *In room:* A/C, TV w/pay movies, fax, dataport, minibar, coffeemaker, hair dryer, iron, safe.

Talbott Hotel ★★ *(Finds)*   The Talbott is not for anyone who needs extensive hotel facilities, but the cozy atmosphere and personal level of service appeal to visitors looking for the feeling of a bed-and-breakfast rather than a sprawling, corporate hotel. Proprietors Basil and Laurie Ann Kromelow take a keen personal interest in the hotel's decor: Most of the gorgeous antiques strewn throughout are purchases from Basil's European shopping trips. The wood-paneled lobby, decorated with leather sofas and velvety armchairs, two working fireplaces, tapestries, and numerous French horns used for fox hunts, is intimate and inviting—all the better in which to enjoy your complimentary continental breakfast.

Although comfortable, the rooms aren't quite as distinctive; they also vary in size, so ask when making reservations. Suites and the hotel's "executive king" rooms entice with Jacuzzi tubs; suites have separate sitting areas with sofa beds and dining tables.

20 E. Delaware Place (between Rush and State sts.), Chicago, IL 60611. © 800/TALBOTT or 312/944-4970. Fax 312/944-7241. www.talbotthotel.com. 149 units. $149–$289 double; $319–$449 suite. AE, DC, DISC, MC, V. Self-parking $21. Subway/El: Red Line to Chicago/State. **Amenities:** Lounge; access to nearby health club; concierge; business services; 24-hr. room service; laundry service; dry cleaning; executive rooms. *In room:* A/C, TV, minibar, hair dryer, iron, safe.

W Chicago Lakeshore ★★   The only hotel in Chicago with a location on the lake, this property prides itself on being a hip boutique hotel—but sophisticated travelers may feel like it's trying way too hard with dance music playing in the lobby and the black-clad staff members doing their best to be eye candy. The compact rooms are decorated in deep red, black, and gray—a scheme that might strike some travelers as gloomy. And although the Asian-inspired bathrooms are stylish, the wooden shades that separate them from the bedroom don't make for much privacy. In W-speak, rooms and suites are designated "wonderful" (meaning standard, with a city view) or "spectacular" (meaning a lake view, for which you'll pay more). Because looking out over the lake means staring at a big expanse of blue, I recommend the "wonderful" rooms with their dramatic city views. Of the few boutique hotels in Chicago, the W Lakeshore has the best location, within easy reach of outdoor activities (the beach, bike paths, and Navy Pier), restaurants, and nightlife—just don't take the place too seriously.

644 N. Lake Shore Dr. (at Ontario St.), Chicago, IL 60611. © **877/W-HOTELS** or 312/943-9200. Fax 312/255-4411. www.whotels.com. 556 units. $229–$429 double; from $369 suite. AE, DC, DISC, MC, V. Valet parking $36 with in/out privileges. Subway/El: Red Line to Grand/State. Pets allowed. **Amenities:** Restaurant (Mediterranean); bar; pool; exercise room; concierge; business services; 24-hr. room service; in-room massage; babysitting; same-day laundry service; dry cleaning. *In room:* A/C, TV w/VCR and pay movies, dataport, minibar, coffeemaker, hair dryer, iron, safe, CD player.

Whitehall Hotel 🏵🏵 Staying here is like visiting a wealthy, sophisticated aunt's town house: elegant but understated, welcoming but not effusive. Before the Four Seasons and Ritz-Carlton entered the picture, the patrician Whitehall reigned as Chicago's most exclusive luxury hotel, with rock stars and Hollywood royalty dropping by when in town. Although those glory days have passed, the independently owned Whitehall still attracts a devoted clientele who relish its subdued ambience and highly personalized service.

Since this is an older property, the hallways are quite narrow and the bathrooms are small. But the rooms are quite spacious and bright, with new furniture. Rooms on the north side of the building come with a wonderful straight-on view of the Hancock Building, with Lake Michigan sparkling in the background. "Pinnacle Level" rooms are the same size as standard rooms, but come with extra amenities, including four-poster beds (with luxury linens), irons and ironing boards, fax machines and umbrellas; Pinnacle guests also receive complimentary breakfast.

Don't miss the hotel's dimly lit, clubby bar, which hasn't changed since the hotel opened in 1928 (ask the staff to point out Katherine Hepburn's favorite seat).

105 E. Delaware Place (west of Michigan Ave.), Chicago, IL 60611. ℭ **800/948-4295** or 312/944-6300. Fax 312/944-8552. www.slh.com/whitehall. 221 units. $179–$279 double; from $500 suite; weekend packages from $199. AE, DC, DISC, MC, V. Valet parking $31 with in/out privileges. Subway/El: Red Line to Chicago/State. **Amenities:** Restaurant (American); lounge; exercise room (and access to nearby health club for an extra charge); concierge; business center (for upper floors); 24-hr. room service; babysitting; laundry service; dry cleaning; club floors. *In room:* A/C, TV w/pay movies, dataport, minibar, hair dryer, safe.

MODERATE

Holiday Inn–Chicago City Centre 𝒜𝒜 (Kids) (Value) Enter the soaring modern atrium, with its vases of blooming fresh flowers, and you won't believe that this place is kin to Holiday Inn's assembly-line roadside staples. Its location is a nice surprise as well: east of the Magnificent Mile and close to the Ohio Street Beach and Navy Pier. Although the rooms are pretty basic, the amenities make this one of the best values in the city.

Fitness devotees will rejoice because the Holiday Inn is located next door to the McClurg Court Sports Complex, where guests may enjoy the extensive facilities free of charge. The hotel also has its own spacious outdoor pool and sun deck. The views are excellent, especially looking north toward the Hancock Building and Monroe Harbor. You might want to splurge on one of the master suites, which boast large living-room areas with wet bars, along with a Jacuzzi-style tub and sauna in the bathroom.

The Holiday Inn is a good bet for the budget-conscious family: Kids under 18 stay free in their parents' room, and those 12 and under eat free in the hotel's restaurants.

300 E. Ohio St. (at Fairbanks Court), Chicago, IL 60611. ℭ **800/HOLIDAY** or 312/787-6100. Fax 312/787-6259. www.chicc.com. 500 units. $128–$270 double; weekend and promotional rates $99–$119. AE, DC, DISC, MC, V. Valet parking $19. Subway/El: Red Line to Grand/State. **Amenities:** 2 restaurants (American, cafe); bar; outdoor and indoor pools; access to nearby health club; whirlpool; sauna; children's programs; concierge; business services; limited room service; babysitting; laundry room; dry cleaning. *In room:* A/C, TV w/pay movies, dataport, coffeemaker, hair dryer, iron.

Homewood Suites 𝒜 (Kids) An excellent choice for families, this hotel offers both fresh, clean rooms and some nice little extras. Because all of the rooms are suites with full kitchens, you can prepare your own meals (a real money saver) and there's plenty of room for everyone to spread out at the end of the day. Distressed-leather sofas, Mediterranean stone tile, wrought-iron chandeliers, and beaded lampshades adorn its sixth-floor lobby. Rooms—one- and two-bedroom suites and a handful of double-double suites, which can connect to king suites—feature velvet sofas that are all sleepers, and the beds have big, thick mattresses. Each comes with a full kitchen, a dining-room table that doubles as a workspace, and decent-size bathrooms. The hotel provides a complimentary hot breakfast buffet as well as beverages and hors d'oeuvres every evening; there is also a free grocery-shopping service and free access to an excellent health club next door.

40 E. Grand Ave. (at Wabash Ave.), Chicago, IL 60611. © 800/CALL-HOME or 312/644-2222. Fax 312/644-7777. www.homewoodsuiteschicago.com. $99–$249 2-room suite. AE, DC, DISC, MC, V. Valet parking $32 with in/out privileges. Subway/El: Red Line to Grand/State. **Amenities:** Fitness room w/small pool and nice views of the city; concierge; business services; babysitting; laundry machines on all floors; dry cleaning. *In room:* A/C, TV w/pay movies, fully equipped kitchen, coffeemaker, hair dryer, iron.

INEXPENSIVE

Red Roof Inn *Value*   This is your best bet for the lowest-priced lodgings in downtown Chicago. The location is the main selling point: right off the Magnificent Mile. The guest rooms are stark and small (much like the off-the-highway Red Roof Inns), but all have new linens and carpeting. Ask for a room facing Ontario Street, where at least you'll get western exposure and some natural light (rooms in other parts of the hotel look right into neighboring office buildings). The bathrooms are tiny but newly renovated (and spotless). You're not going to find much in the way of style or amenities here—but then you don't stay at a place like this to hang out in the lobby.

162 E. Ontario St. (½ block east of Michigan Ave.), Chicago, IL 60611. © 800/733-7663 or 312/787-3580. Fax 312/787-1299. www.redroof.com. 195 units. $86–$102 double. AE, DC, DISC, MC, V. Valet parking $18 with no in/out privileges. Subway/El: Red Line to Grand/State. **Amenities:** Business services; free morning coffee available in the lobby. *In room:* A/C, TV w/pay movies, dataport, hair dryer, iron.

4 River North

The name *River North* designates a vast area parallel to the Magnificent Mile. The zone is bounded by the river to the west and south, and roughly by Clark Street to the east and by Chicago Avenue to the north. The earthy redbrick buildings that characterize the area were once warehouses of various kinds and today hold Chicago's art-gallery district and some very trendy restaurants.

EXPENSIVE

Embassy Suites ★★ *Kids*   Although this hotel does a healthy convention business, its vaguely Floridian ambience—with a gushing waterfall and palm-lined ponds at the bottom of a huge central atrium—makes the place very family-friendly (there's plenty of room for the kids to run around). The accommodations are spacious enough for both parents and kids: All suites have two rooms, consisting of a living room with a sleeper sofa, a round table, and four chairs; and a bedroom with either a king-size bed or two double beds. Guests staying on the VIP floor get nightly turndown service and in-room fax machines and robes. At one end of the atrium, the hotel serves a complimentary cooked-to-order breakfast in the morning and, in the other end, supplies complimentary cocktails and snacks in the evening.

600 N. State St. (at West Ohio St.), Chicago, IL 60610. ℂ **800/362-2779** or 312/943-3800. Fax 312/943-7629. www.embassy-suites.com. 358 units. $199–$259 king suite; $269–$299 double suite. AE, DC, DISC, MC, V. Valet parking $34 with in/out privileges. Subway/El: Red Line to Grand/State. **Amenities:** Restaurant (Greek); coffee bar; indoor pool; exercise room with whirlpool and sauna; concierge; business center; limited room service; babysitting; laundry machines; dry cleaning; VIP rooms. *In room:* A/C, TV w/pay movies and video games, dataport, kitchenette, coffeemaker, hair dryer, iron.

House of Blues Hotel, a Loews Hotel 𝒜𝒜𝒜   The funky vibe here makes this a great choice for teenagers and anyone who wants a hotel to be an experience—not just a place to sleep. Blending Gothic, Moroccan, East Indian, and New Orleans influences, the House of Blues lobby is a riot of crimsons and deep blues (stop by to check it out even if you're not staying here). Banquettes and couches heaped with pillows invite lounging—grab a drink at the Kaz Bar and soak it all in.

You can catch your breath in the lighter, whimsical rooms, which feature some of the most exciting Southern folk art you'll ever come across. The casually dressed, friendly staff invents creative nightly turndowns for guests—such as fragrant mood crystals or a written thought for the day left on your pillow. One of the hotel's biggest selling points is its location in the entertainment-packed Marina Towers complex. Within steps of the hotel you've got the AMF Bowling Center (with billiards), a marina with boat rentals, the riverside Smith & Wollensky steakhouse (an outpost of the New York restaurant), the innovative Bin 36 wine bar and restaurant, and, of course, the House of Blues Music Hall and Restaurant (don't miss the Sunday gospel brunch).

333 N. Dearborn St. (at the river), Chicago, IL 60610. ℂ **877/569-3742** or 312/245-0333. Fax 312/923-2458. www.loewshotels.com. 365 units. $139–$349 double; $500–$1,200 suite; weekend and promotional rates available. AE, DC, DISC, MC, V. Valet parking $28 with in/out privileges. Subway/El: Brown Line to Clark/Lake

or Red Line to Grand/State. Pets accepted. **Amenities:** Lounge; access to the very hip Crunch Health & Fitness Center for $15; concierge; business center; 24-hr. room service; babysitting; laundry service; same-day dry cleaning. *In room:* A/C, TV w/VCR, pay movies and video games, dataport, minibar, coffeemaker (upon request), hair dryer, iron, CD player.

Westin Chicago River North 🏨🏨 *(Kids)*   Geared to upscale business travelers, the Westin Chicago River North has an understated, modern feel that will appeal to those looking for a quiet retreat.

Rooms are handsome, with furniture and artwork that give them a residential feel. New beds were added in 2000. For the best view, get a room facing south, overlooking the river. For those who feel like splurging, a suite on the 19th floor more than satisfies, with three enormous rooms, including a huge bathroom and a large window offering a side view of the river.

Although the Westin River North has the personality of a business hotel, it has made an effort to be family-friendly; especially notable are the many baby and toddler accessories available to guests, from bottle warmers and cribs to night lights and electrical outlet covers. Older kids can while away the hours with in-room Sony PlayStation.

320 N. Dearborn St. (on the river), Chicago, IL 60610. © **800/WESTIN1** or 312/744-1900. Fax 312/527-9761. www.westinchicago.com. 424 units. $199–$498 double; $419–$2,800 suite; weekend rates $199–$249. AE, DC, DISC, MC, V. Valet parking $34 with in/out privileges; self-parking $16. Subway/El: Brown, Orange, or Green line to State/Lake. **Amenities:** Restaurant (contemporary American); lounge; fitness center; concierge; business center; 24-hr. room service; babysitting; laundry service, same-day dry cleaning. *In room:* A/C, TV w/pay movies and video games, fax, dataport, minibar, coffeemaker, hair dryer, iron.

MODERATE

Best Western River North Hotel *(Value)*   This former motor lodge and cold storage structure conceals a very attractive, sharply designed interior that scarcely resembles any Best Western in which you're likely to have spent the night. One of the few hotels located right in the midst of one of the busiest nightlife and restaurant zones in the city, the Best Western lies within easy walking distance of interesting boutiques and Chicago's art-gallery district. Rooms are spacious, and the bathrooms, though no-frills, are spotless. One-room suites have a sitting area, while other suites have a separate bedroom; all suites come with a sleeper sofa. The Best Western's reasonable rates and rooftop pool (with sweeping views) will appeal to families on a budget—and the almost unheard-of free parking can add up to significant savings for anyone planning to stay a week or more.

125 W. Ohio St. (at LaSalle St.), Chicago, IL 60610. ℭ **800/528-1234** or 312/467-0800. Fax 312/467-1665. www.rivernorthhotel.com. 150 units. $105–$149 double; $250 suite. AE, DC, DISC, MC, V. Free parking for guests (1 car per room). Subway/El: Red Line to Grand/State. **Amenities:** Restaurant (American); lounge; indoor pool with sun deck; exercise room; business services; limited room service; laundry service. *In room:* AC, TV w/pay movies and video games, dataport, coffeemaker, hair dryer, iron, safe.

Hampton Inn & Suites Chicago Downtown ⋆ *Kids* *Value*
While the Hampton Inn does attract some business travelers on a budget, it is mainly a family hotel. You can book a room, a two-room suite, or a studio; most don't have much in the way of views, but request one overlooking Illinois Street if you crave natural light. The apartment-style suites feature galley kitchens with fridges, microwaves, dishwashers, and cooking utensils. An American diner is located off the lobby, and a second-floor skywalk connects to Ruth's Chris Steak House next door. Guests with children will appreciate the indoor pool (the suites have VCRs, for when the little ones need to chill out after a busy day). Children under 18 stay free, and there is a complimentary buffet breakfast each morning.

33 W. Illinois St. (at Dearborn St.), Chicago, IL 60610. ℭ **800/HAMPTON** or 312/832-0330. Fax 312/832-0333. www.hamptoninn-suites.com. 230 units. $129–$179 double; $189–$229 suite. AE, DC, DISC, MC, V. Valet parking $32 with in/out privileges; self-parking $14 with no in/out privileges. Subway/El: Red Line to Grand/State. **Amenities:** Restaurant (American diner); indoor pool with sun deck; exercise room with sauna; business services; room service; laundry machines. *In room:* A/C, TV, dataport, coffeemaker, hair dryer, iron, safe.

5 The Gold Coast

The Gold Coast begins approximately at Division Street and extends north to North Avenue, bounded on the west by Clark Street and on the east by the lake. It's a lovely neighborhood for a stroll among the graceful town houses and the several lavish mansions that remain, relics from a glitzier past. The hotels here tend to be upscale, but don't offer amenities as lavish as the top Michigan Avenue hotels.

EXPENSIVE

Omni Ambassador East ⋆⋆ *Kids*   The ring-a-ding glory days of the Ambassador East, when stars including Frank Sinatra, Humphrey Bogart, and Liza Minnelli shacked up here during layovers or touring stops in Chicago, are ancient history. But even though big-name celebs tend to ensconce themselves at the Ritz-Carlton or Four Seasons these days, the Ambassador name still evokes images of high glamour in these parts.

Today, after a face-lift, the Ambassador East has reclaimed its strut and splendor. Rooms here have been spruced up and bathrooms feature the usual higher-end amenities. Executive suites have separate sitting areas; celebrity suites (named for the stars who've crashed in them) come with a separate bedroom, two bathrooms, a small kitchen, and a dining room. Most extravagant is the Presidential Suite, which boasts a canopied terrace and marble fireplace.

The Ambassador East has the same kids' program as the Omni Chicago (p. 48), and both Omnis make an extra effort for guests with disabilities, offering equipment such as TDD telephones and strobe fire alarms for deaf guests.

1301 N. State Pkwy. (1 block north of Division St.), Chicago, IL 60610. ℂ 800/843-6664 or 312/787-7200. Fax 312/787-4760. www.omnihotels.com. 285 units. $160–$200 double; $259–$799 suite. AE, DC, DISC, MC, V. Valet parking $34 with in/out privileges. Subway/El: Red Line to Clark/Division. **Amenities:** Restaurant (contemporary American); small fitness room (and access to nearby health club); concierge; business services; 24-hr. room service; babysitting; 24-hr. laundry service; dry cleaning. *In room:* A/C, TV w/pay movies, dataport, minibar, coffeemaker, hair dryer, iron.

6 Lincoln Park & the North Side

If you prefer the feel of living amid real Chicagoans in a residential neighborhood, several options await you in Lincoln Park and farther north. Although these hotels aren't necessarily more affordable than those downtown, they do provide a different vantage point from which to view Chicago.

EXPENSIVE

Windy City Urban Inn *★★* *Finds*   This grand 1886 home is located on a tranquil side street just blocks from busy Clark Street and Lincoln Avenue—both chock-full of shops, restaurants, and bars. While the inn is charming enough, the true selling point is hosts Andy and Mary Shaw. He's a well-known political reporter, while she has 20 years of experience in the Chicago bed-and-breakfast business. Together, they are excellent resources for anyone who wants to get beyond the usual tourist sites. Plus, their subtle touches give guests a distinctive, Chicago experience: Blues and jazz play during the buffet breakfast, and local food favorites offered to guests include the famous cinnamon buns from Ann Sather's restaurant and beer from Goose Island Brewery.

The more-open-than-typical remodeled Victorian home has five rooms in the main house and three apartment suites in a coach house; all are named after Chicago writers. In good weather, guests are invited to eat breakfast on the back porch or in the garden between the main house and the coach house.

607 W. Deming Place, Chicago, IL 60614. © **877/897-7091** or 773/248-7091. Fax 773/248-7090. www.chicago-inn.com. 8 units. $115–$185 double; $225–$325 suite. Rates include buffet breakfast. AE, DC, DISC, MC, V. Parking $6 in nearby lot with in/out privileges. Subway/El: Red Line to Fullerton. **Amenities:** Laundry machines, kitchenettes, coffeemaker, hair dryer, and iron available for guest use upon request. *In room:* A/C, TV.

MODERATE

City Suites Hotel *Value*   A few doors down from the elevated train stop on Belmont Avenue, this former transient dive has been transformed into a charming small hotel, something along the lines of an urban bed-and-breakfast. Most rooms are suites, with separate sitting rooms and bedrooms, all furnished with first-rate pieces and decorated in a homey and comfortable style. The amenities are excellent for a hotel in this price range, including local limousine service, plush robes, and complimentary continental breakfast. A bonus—or drawback, depending on your point of view—is the hotel's neighborhood setting. Most rooms can be fairly noisy; those facing north overlook Belmont Avenue, where the nightlife continues into the early morning hours, and those facing west look right out over the rumbling El tracks. Blues bars, nightclubs, and restaurants abound hereabouts, making the City Suites a find for the bargain-minded and adventuresome. Suites have fridges and microwaves on request.

933 W. Belmont Ave. (at Sheffield Ave.), Chicago, IL 60657. © **800/248-9108** or 773/404-3400. Fax 773/404-3405. www.cityinns.com. 45 units. $99–$169. Rates include continental breakfast. AE, DC, DISC, MC, V. Parking $17 in nearby lot with in/out privileges. Subway/El: Red Line to Belmont. **Amenities:** Exercise room; business services; concierge; limited room service; laundry service; same-day dry cleaning. *In room:* A/C, TV w/pay movies, dataport, minibar, coffeemaker, hair dryer, iron.

5

Where to Dine

Joke all you want about bratwurst and deep-dish pizza—Chicago has come into its own as a culinary hotspot. Our top local chefs win national cooking awards and show up regularly on the Food Network, while we locals have had a hard time keeping up with all the new restaurant openings. What makes eating out in Chicago fun is the variety: We've got it all, such as stylish see-and-be-seen spots, an amazing array of steakhouses, chef-owned temples to fine dining, and every kind of ethnic cuisine you could possibly crave. Unfortunately, Chicago is no longer the budget-dining destination it once was. (Hipness doesn't come cheap.)

I've divided restaurants into four price categories in this chapter: "Very Expensive" means that entrees cost $20 to $30 (and sometimes more); "Expensive" means that most entrees run from $15 to $25; "Moderate" means that entrees cost between $10 and $20; and, at an "Inexpensive" place, they cost $15 or less.

To find out more about restaurants that have opened since this book went to press, check out the *Chicago Tribune*'s entertainment website at **www.metromix.com**, the website for *Chicago* magazine at **www.chicagomag.com**, or the entertainment/nightlife website **www.chicago.citysearch.com**.

1 The Loop

In keeping with their proximity to the towers of power, many of the restaurants in the Loop and its environs feature expense-account-style prices. Keep in mind that several of the best downtown spots are closed on Sunday.

VERY EXPENSIVE

Everest ★★★ ALSATIAN/FRENCH   Towering high above the Chicago Stock Exchange, Everest is an oasis of four-star fine-dining civility, a place where you can taste the creations of one of Chicago's top chefs while enjoying one of the city's top views. The dining room is nothing dramatic (it looks like a high-end corporate dining room), because diners are meant to focus on the food—and the sparkling lights of surrounding skyscrapers. Chef Jean Joho, who draws inspiration from the earthy cookery of his native Alsace, enjoys mixing what he calls "noble" and "simple" ingredients (caviar or foie gras with potatoes or turnips) for unique flavor combinations. While the menu changes frequently, the salmon soufflé or cream-of-Alsace-cabbage soup with smoked sturgeon and caviar are popular choices as appetizers; signature entrees include roasted Maine lobster in Alsace Gewürztraminer butter and ginger, and poached tenderloin of beef cooked *pot-au-feu* style and served with horseradish cream. Desserts are suitably sumptuous.

440 S. LaSalle St., 40th Floor (at Congress Pkwy.). ✆ 312/663-8920. www.leye. com. Reservations required. Main courses $27–$33; menu degustation $79; 3-course pretheater dinner $44. AE, DC, DISC, MC, V. Tues–Thurs 5:30–9:30pm; Fri–Sat 5:30–10pm. Complimentary valet parking. Subway/El: Brown Line to LaSalle/Van Buren.

EXPENSIVE

Atwood Café ★★ *Finds* AMERICAN If you're tired of the exotic menus of trendy restaurants, Atwood Café will come as a welcome relief. Located in the historic Hotel Burnham, this place combines a gracious, 1900-era feel with a fresh take on American comfort food. The dining room—one of my favorites in the city—mixes elegance and humor with soaring ceilings, lush velvet curtains, and whimsical china and silverware.

Executive chef Heather Terhune plays around with global influences (most notably Asian and Southwestern). Appetizers include smoked salmon piled on sweet-corn cakes in a spicy chipotle chile dressing, chunky clam chowder, and duck quesadillas. Entrees include grilled rack of lamb in a mint-infused port-wine sauce; hoisin-glazed duck breast with snow peas and ginger basmati rice; and fusilli pasta in a roasted-garlic cream sauce with smoked ham, broccoli, and tomatoes. Seasonal fruit is the basis for cobblers, trifles, and pies; for a decadently rich experience, tackle the banana-and-white-chocolate bread pudding.

1 W. Washington St. (at State St.). ✆ 312/368-1900. Reservations accepted. Main courses $16–$24; 3-course prix fixe $39. AE, DC, DISC, MC, V. Mon–Fri 7am–10pm; Sat–Sun 8am–10pm. Formal tea service daily. Subway/El: Red Line to Randolph/ Washington.

Nine ★★★ CONTEMPORARY AMERICAN The sizzle isn't all on the grill at this contemporary Chicago steakhouse–meets–Vegas dining palace. You'll feel like you're making a grand entrance from

Where to Dine in the Loop, the Randolph Street Market District, the Magnificent Mile, the Gold Coast & River North

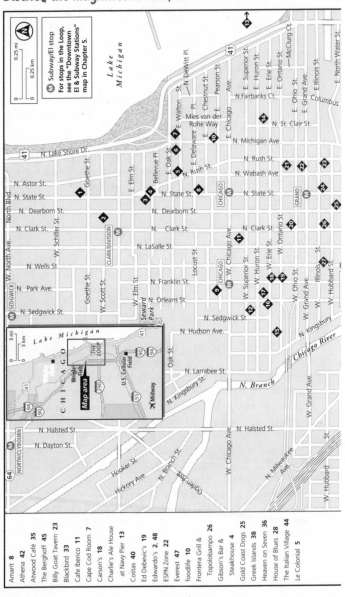

Amarit **8**
Athena **42**
Atwood Café **35**
The Berghoff **45**
Billy Goat Tavern **23**
Blackbird **33**
Cafe Iberico **11**
Cape Cod Room **7**
Carson's **18**
Charlie's Ale House
at Navy Pier **13**
Costas **40**
Ed Debevic's **19**
Edwardo's **2, 48**
ESPN Zone **22**
Everest **47**
foodlife **10**
Frontera Grill &
Topolobampo **26**
Gibson's Bar &
Steakhouse **4**
Gold Coast Dogs **25**
Greek Islands **38**
Heaven on Seven **36**
House of Blues **28**
The Italian Village **44**
Le Colonial **5**

Map legend:

Ⓝ

0   0.25 mi
0   0.25 km

Ⓜ Subway/El stop
For stops in the Loop,
see the "Downtown
El & Subway Stations"
map in Chapter 5.

Lake Michigan

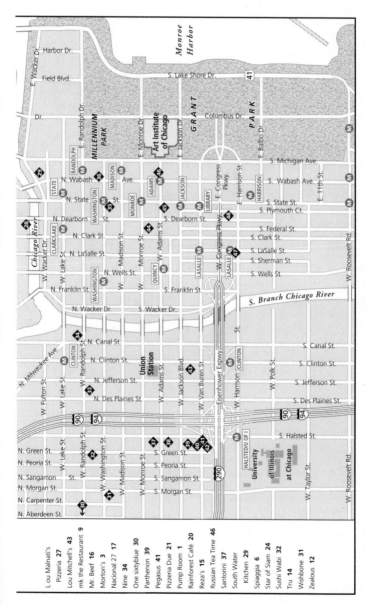

L ou Malnati's
Pizzeria **27**
Lou Mitchell's **43**
mk the Restaurant **9**
Mr. Beef **16**
Morton's **3**
Nacional 27 **17**
Nine **34**
One sixtyblue **30**
Parthenon **39**
Pegasus **41**
Pizzeria Due **21**
Pump Room **1**
Rainforest Café **20**
Reza's **15**
Russian Tea Time **46**
Santorini **37**
South Water
Kitchen **29**
Spiaggia **6**
Star of Siam **24**
Sushi Wabi **32**
Tru **14**
Wishbone **31**
Zealous **12**

the moment you walk in the front door and step down an open staircase into the high-ceilinged, white-and-silver dining room. Nine is all about the beautiful people, so dress the part (that is, leave the khaki shorts at home).

Begin with something from the caviar appetizers or "crustacea" station (clams and oysters, crab, shrimp, and crawfish). The signature starter is the "two cones" appetizer, one overflowing with tuna tartare, another with chunks of lobster and avocado. The prime, dry-aged steaks, particularly the 24-ounce bone-in rib-eye and 22-ounce porterhouse, are the main attraction. Non-red-meat options include a generous veggie chop salad, roast chicken with chipotle marinade, and a daily pasta selection. For dessert, grill your own high-style s'mores on a hibachi grill at your table. The lunch menu adds some burgers, flatbread pizzas, sandwiches, and entree salads.

440 W. Randolph St. ℂ **312/575-9900.** Reservations recommended. Lunch $9–$15; main courses $14–$32. AE, DC, MC, V. Sun–Wed 11:30am–2pm and 5:30–10pm; Thurs 11:30am–2pm and 5:30–11pm; Fri 11:30am–2pm and 5pm–midnight; Sat 5pm–midnight. Subway/El: Blue, Orange, Brown, or Green line to Clark/Lake.

Russian Tea Time ☆☆ *(Finds* RUSSIAN   This is far from being the simple tea cafe that its name implies. The menu offers classic dishes of czarist Russia and the former Soviet republics (for Russian neophytes, all the dishes are well described, sometimes with charming background stories). The atmosphere is old-world and cozy, with lots of woodwork and a friendly staff. Start off a meal with potato pancakes, blini with Russian caviar, or chilled smoked sturgeon; if you can't decide, there are a number of mixed appetizer platters to share. My top entree picks are the beef stroganoff; *kulebiaka* (meat pie with ground beef, cabbage, and onions); and roast pheasant served with a brandy, walnut, and pomegranate sauce and brandied prunes. Nonmeat eaters will also feel very welcome here; both the appetizer and entree listings include vegetarian dishes.

77 E. Adams St. (between Michigan and Wabash aves.). ℂ **312/360-0000.** Reservations recommended. Main courses $15–$27. AE, DC, DISC, MC, V. Sun–Mon 11am–9pm; Tues–Thurs 11am–11pm; Fri–Sat 11am–midnight. Subway/El: Brown, Purple, Green, or Orange line to Adams, or Red Line to Monroe/State or Jackson/State.

MODERATE

The Berghoff ☆ GERMAN/AMERICAN   Having celebrated its centennial in 1998, The Berghoff is a Chicago landmark and its 20-foot ceilings, checked linoleum floor, and sepia photos of old Chicago make you feel like you've stepped back in time. The

Berghoff holds Chicago liquor license no. 1, issued at the close of Prohibition, and it still serves its own brand of beer. This is old-school dining—some of the dark-jacketed waiters seem almost as old as the building.

While the menu rotates seasonally, classic German favorites are always available and promise the most dependable dining experience. The Berghoff serves hundreds of orders of Wiener schnitzel every day, plus bratwurst, sauerbraten, corned beef, and the like. Because some of us have arteries to worry about, the third and fourth generations of family management have added some lighter fare in the form of salads, broiled fish, and vegetarian dishes.

17 W. Adams St. (between State and Dearborn sts.). ✆ 312/427-3170. www. berghoff.com. Reservations recommended. Main courses $7.95–$12 lunch, $11–$17 dinner. AE, MC, V. Mon–Thurs 11am–9pm; Fri 11am–9:30pm; Sat 11:30am–10pm. Subway/El: Red or Blue line to Jackson/State or Monroe/State.

South Water Kitchen 🐟 *Kids* AMERICAN   Loop restaurants cater to office workers and business travelers; there aren't a lot of family-friendly options other than fast food. So while South Water Kitchen isn't breaking any new culinary ground, it deserves a mention as one of the few places in the area that welcomes kids—while featuring food sophisticated enough for discerning moms and dads. Entrees include modern twists on familiar favorites, including a pork chop with sage bread pudding; free-range chicken fricassee with herb dumplings, and a different "blue plate special" every night (at $14, it's an excellent deal for the neighborhood). The restaurant provides not only kids' menus but also games to keep the little ones occupied. Best of all, half the proceeds of all children's meals go to the Chicago Coalition for the Homeless.

In the Hotel Monaco, 225 N. Wabash Ave. (at Wacker Dr.). ✆ 888/306-3507. www. swk.citysearch.com. Reservations accepted. Main courses $8–$17 lunch, $14–$22 dinner. AE, DC, MC, V. Mon–Fri 11:30am–2:30pm and 5–9pm; Sat–Sun 5–9pm. Subway: Red Line to State/Lake.

THE ITALIAN VILLAGE

Along with The Berghoff (see listing above), the Italian Village ranks as a downtown dining landmark. Open since 1927, the building houses three separate Italian restaurants, each with its own menu and unique ambience.

La Cantina Enoteca *Value* ITALIAN/SEAFOOD   La Cantina, the most moderately priced of the three restaurants in the Italian Village, makes the most of its basement location by creating the feel of a wine cellar. Focusing on seafood, La Cantina offers at least five fresh varieties every day. Specialties include a fish soup appetizer, macaroni with scallops and shrimp in a garlic pesto cream sauce, and seafood-filled ravioli. The dinner menu offers a big-time bargain: A la carte dishes (most under $20) include a salad, and for $2 more you also get soup, dessert, and coffee.

71 W. Monroe St. (between Clark and Dearborn sts.). © 312/332-7005. Reservations recommended. Main courses (including soup, salad, dessert, and coffee) $12–$23; salads $9.95–$12; sandwiches $7.50–$7.95. Lunch prices slightly lower. AE, DC, DISC, MC, V. Mon–Thurs 11:30am–11pm; Fri 11:30am–midnight; Sat 5pm–midnight; closed most Sun, except a few in the summer; call to check. Subway/El: Red or Blue line to Monroe.

The Village ⟨ *Finds* SOUTHERN ITALIAN   Upstairs in the Italian Village is The Village, with its charming interpretation of alfresco dining in a small Italian town, complete with a midnight-blue ceiling, twinkling "stars," and banquettes tucked into private, cavelike little rooms. The massive menu includes some time-warp appetizers (oysters Rockefeller, shrimp *de jonghe*) and all the old-time, hearty southern Italian standards. The food is good rather than great, but what sets The Village apart is the bordering-on-corny faux-Italian atmosphere. The service, too, is outstanding, from the Italian maitre d' who flirts with all the ladies, to the ancient waiters who manage somehow to keep up with the nonstop flow.

71 W. Monroe St. (between Clark and Dearborn sts.). © 312/332-7005. Reservations recommended (accepted for parties of 3 or more). Main courses (including salad) $11–$27; salads $5.50–$10; pizza $11–$14; sandwiches $7.95–$15; lunch prices slightly lower. AE, DISC, MC, V. Mon–Thurs 11am–1am; Fri–Sat 11am–2am; Sun noon–midnight. Subway/El: Red or Blue line to Monroe.

Vivere ⟨ REGIONAL ITALIAN   On the main floor of the Italian Village is Vivere, the Italian Village's take on gourmet cooking—and eye-catching design. The bold interior, with rich burgundies, textured walls, spiraling bronze sculptures, and fragmented mosaic floors, makes dinner a theatrical experience. No fettucine Alfredo here; the pasta dishes feature upscale ingredients, from the *pappardelle* with braised duck to the *agnolottini* filled with pheasant. Fresh fish is always on the menu (a recent entree selection was salmon with spiced carrot broth), along with a good selection of meats and game. If you just can't decide, go for the five-course chef's tasting menu ($65).

71 W. Monroe St. (between Clark and Dearborn sts.). © 312/332-4040. Reservations recommended. Main courses $14–$29. AE, DC, DISC, MC, V. Mon–Thurs 11:30am–2:30pm and 5–10pm; Fri 11:30am–2:30pm and 5–11pm; Sat 5–11pm. Subway/El: Red or Blue line to Monroe.

INEXPENSIVE

Heaven on Seven ★★ *Finds* CAJUN/DINER   Hidden on the seventh floor of an office building opposite Marshall Field's, this isn't the kind of place you stumble on by accident, but you'll find it by following the office workers who line up for lunch during the week. Chef/owner Jimmy Bannos's Cajun and Creole specialties come with a cup of soup, and include such Louisiana staples as red beans and rice, a catfish po' boy sandwich, and jambalaya. If you don't have a taste for Tabasco, the enormous coffee shop–style menu covers all the traditional essentials: grilled-cheese sandwiches, omelets, tuna—the works.

Although the Loop original has the most character, Heaven also has locations along the Mag Mile at **600 N. Michigan Ave.** (© **312/280-7774**), adjacent to a cineplex, and in Wrigleyville at

---

Kids Family-Friendly Restaurants

One of the city's first "theme" restaurant's, **Ed Debevic's**, 640 N. Wells St. at Ontario St. (© **312/664-1707**), is a temple to America's hometown lunch-counter culture. The burgers-and-milkshakes menu is kid-friendly, but it's the staff schtick that makes this place memorable. The waitresses play the parts of gum-chewing toughies who make wisecracks, toss out good-natured insults, and even sit right down at your table. It's all a performance—but it works.

One of the best all-around options, and a homegrown place as well, the Southern-style restaurant **Wishbone** (p. 67) has much to recommend it. The food is diverse enough that both adults and kids can find something to their liking, but there's also a menu geared just toward children. Another all-American choice in the Loop is **South Water Kitchen** (p. 63), which offers a kids' menu and coloring books.

At **Gino's East**, the famous Chicago pizzeria, patrons are invited to scrawl all over the graffiti-strewn walls and furniture. Another good pizza spot for older kids, who will find its loft-like space cool, is **Piece** in Wicker Park (p. 92). Sports-minded families should head to **ESPN Zone** (p. 73).

3478 N. Clark St. (© 773/477-7818); unlike the original location, both accept reservations and credit cards and serve dinner daily.

111 N. Wabash Ave. (at Washington St.), 7th floor. © **312/263-6443.** Reservations not accepted. Menu items $3.95–$13. No credit cards. Mon–Fri 8:30am–5pm; Sat 10am–3pm. 1st and 3rd Fri of month 5:30–9pm. Subway/El: Red Line to Washington/State.

2 The Randolph Street Market District

The Market District used to be filled with warehouses and produce trucks that shut down tight after nightfall. But when a few bold restaurant pioneers moved in—and brought their super-hip clientele with them—this short stretch of Randolph Street, west of the Loop, got red hot. There's nothing much to do here besides eat— but if you have a few days in Chicago, try to make it here for at least one meal.

VERY EXPENSIVE

one sixtyblue ✦✦✦ CONTEMPORARY AMERICAN Anchoring the western border of Randolph Street's restaurant row, one sixtyblue has lived down the hype over its not-so-secret silent partner Michael Jordan. Some Chicago foodies consider this the best contemporary American restaurant in town.

The menu changes seasonally; dishes are artfully composed and perfectly satisfying. Chef Martial Noguier brings a French influence to the preparation of the contemporary dishes, but he draws on practically every world cuisine for inspiration. Appetizers run the gamut from ravioli with lobster-tarragon sauce to Thai lobster soup to a modern version of moussaka (made in this case with eggplant purée, braised lamb shoulder, lemon confit, and dried tomatoes). Entrees include thinly sliced loin of lamb with a casserole of fresh vegetables, venison with dried-plum bread pudding, and a rich honey-glazed salmon topped with an emulsion of chestnuts and walnuts. There is also a daily vegetarian entree selection.

1400 W. Randolph St. (at Ogden Ave.). © **312/850-0303.** Reservations recommended. Main courses $21–$30. AE, DC, MC, V. Mon–Thurs 5–10pm; Fri–Sat 5–11pm; Sun 5–9pm.

EXPENSIVE

Blackbird ✦✦✦ CONTEMPORARY AMERICAN Stylishly spare, this restaurant exudes a smart urban chic that could blend into the dining scene of any major city. The narrow room is dense with close-packed tables, and everyone pretends not to be looking around too much. As in many newer restaurants, the noise level can get high, but it's fun for people who like to make the scene.

Chef Paul Kahan's seasonal menu features creative but uncontrived fare, from a charcuterie plate to a modern take on the "soup and sandwich" concept (celery-root bisque garnished with small trout, cucumber, and red-onion sandwiches). An appetizer for more adventurous diners is the sautéed scallop carpaccio accompanied by blood orange, candied ginger, and mint. Familiar comfort foods in new guises make up the entree list: rack of lamb with figs, leeks and honey, and rosemary-infused mashed potatoes; and grilled sturgeon with caramelized carrots and curried cauliflower. Desserts might include lavender crème caramel with pine nuts, tangerines, and caramel sauce; chocolate mousse tower with grapefruit-vanilla salad; and various other enticements.

619 W. Randolph St. ✆ **312/715-0708**. www.blackbirdrestaurant.com. Reservations recommended. Main courses $8–$20 lunch, $16–$29 dinner. AE, DC, DISC, MC, V. Mon–Thurs 11:30am–2pm and 5:30–10:30pm; Fri 11:30am–2pm and 5:30–11:30pm; Sat 5:30–11:30pm.

Sushi Wabi ✿ JAPANESE/SUSHI   Artfully presented sushi and chic crowds are the order of the day here. Sushi highlights include the sea scallop roll with smelt roe, mayonnaise, avocado, and sesame seeds; the dragon roll of shrimp tempura, eel, and avocado; and the spiky, crunchy spider roll of soft-shell crab, smelt roe, mayonnaise, and pepper-vinegar sauce. Simple entrees such as seared tuna, grilled salmon, teriyaki beef, and sesame-crusted chicken breast will satisfy landlubbers who are accommodating their sushi-loving companions. An intriguing side is the Japanese whipped potato salad with ginger, cucumber, carrots, and scallions. The minimal-chic decor is industrial and raw, and the lighting is dark and seductive. Make a reservation or expect quite a wait, even on school nights. Weekend DJ music adds to the clubby feel.

842 W. Randolph St. ✆ **312/563-1224**. www.sushiwabi.com. Reservations recommended. Main courses $9.25–$21. AE, DC, DISC, MC, V. Mon–Fri 11:30am–2pm and 5pm–midnight; Sat 5pm–midnight; Sun 5–11pm.

INEXPENSIVE

Wishbone ✿✿ (Kids) SOUTHERN/CAJUN/BREAKFAST   One of my best friends—a transplanted Chicagoan who now lives in New York—always has one request when she comes back to town: dinner at Wishbone. It's that kind of place, a down-home, casual spot that inspires intense loyalty (even if the food is only good rather than outstanding).

Finds   Ethnic Dining near the Loop

CHINATOWN

Chicago's Chinatown is about 20 blocks south of the Loop. The district is strung along two thoroughfares, Cermak Road and Wentworth Avenue as far south as 24th Place. Hailing a cab from the Loop is the easiest way to get here, but you can also drive and leave your car in the validated lot near the entrance to Chinatown or take the Orange Line of the El to the Cermak stop, a well-lit station on the edge of the Chinatown commercial district.

Chicago dining experts consistently praise affordable **Hong Min,** 221 W. Cermak Rd. (℃ **312/842-5026**), as one of the best Chinese restaurants in the city. The hot and sour soup gets raves, as do the noodle dishes and roast duck. If you can't decide what to get, opt for dim sum.

The spacious, casually elegant **Phoenix,** 2131 S. Archer Ave. (℃ **312/328-0848**), has plenty of room for big tables of family or friends to enjoy the Cantonese (and some Szechwan) cuisine. A good sign: The place attracts lots of Chinatown locals. It's especially popular for dim sum brunch, so come early to avoid the wait.

LITTLE ITALY

Convenient to most downtown locations, a few blocks' stretch of Taylor Street is home to a host of time-honored, traditional, hearty Italian restaurants.

Regulars keep coming back for the straightforward Italian favorites livened up with some adventurous specials at **Francesca's on Taylor,** 1400 W. Taylor St. (℃ **312/829-2828**). I recommend the fish specials above the standard meat dishes. Other standouts include eggplant ravioli in a four-cheese sauce with a touch of tomato sauce and shaved parmigiano, as well as sautéed veal medallions with porcini mushrooms in cream sauce.

Expect to wait well beyond the time of your reservation at **Rosebud on Taylor,** 1500 W. Taylor St. (℃ **312/942-1117**),

Known for Southern food and big-appetite breakfasts, Wishbone's extensive, reasonably priced menu blends hearty, home-style choices with healthful and vegetarian items. Brunch is the 'Bone's claim to fame, when an eclectic crowd of bedheads pack in for the but fear not—your hunger will be satisfied. Rosebud is known for enormous helpings of pasta, most of which lean toward heavy Italian-American favorites: deep-dish lasagna and fettuccine Alfredo that defines the word *rich*. But I highly recommend any of the pastas served with vodka sauce. A newer location is near the Mag Mile at 720 N. Rush St. (© 312/266-6444).

Tuscany, 1014 W. Taylor St. (© 312/829-1990), is one of the most reliable Italian restaurants on Taylor Street. In contrast to the city's more fashionable Italian spots, family-owned Tuscany has the comfortable feel of a neighborhood restaurant. Specialties include anything cooked on the wood-burning grill and Tuscan sausage dishes. A second location is across from Wrigley Field at 3700 N. Clark St. (© 773/404-7700).

GREEKTOWN

A short cab ride across the south branch of the Chicago River will take you to the city's Greektown, a row of moderately priced and inexpensive Greek restaurants clustered on Halsted Street between Van Buren and Washington streets.

To be honest, there's not much here to distinguish one restaurant from the other: They're all standard Greek restaurants with similar looks and similar menus. That said, **Greek Islands,** 200 S. Halsted St. (© 312/782-9855); **Santorini,** 800 W. Adams St., at Halsted Street (© 312/829-8820); **Parthenon,** 314 S. Halsted St. (© 312/726-2407); and **Costas,** 340 S. Halsted St. (© 312/263-0767), are all good bets for gyros, Greek salads, shish kebabs, and the classic moussaka. On warm summer nights, opt for either **Athena,** 212 S. Halsted St. (© 312/655-0000), which has a huge outdoor seating area, or **Pegasus,** 130 S. Halsted St. (© 312/226-3377), with its rooftop patio serving drinks, appetizers, and desserts. Both have incredible views of the Loop's skyline.

plump and tasty salmon cakes, omelets, and red eggs (a lovely mess of tortillas, black beans, cheese, scallions, chile ancho sauce, salsa, and sour cream). However, brunch at Wishbone can be a mob scene, so I suggest lunch or dinner; offerings run from "yardbird" (charbroiled chicken with sweet red-pepper sauce) and blackened catfish to hoppin' John or Jack (vegetarian variations on the black-eyed pea classic). The tart Key lime pie is one of my favorite desserts in the city. The casual ambience is a good bet for families (a children's menu is available).

There's a newer location at 3300 N. Lincoln Ave. (© **773/549-2663**), but the original location has more character.

1001 Washington St. (at Morgan St.). © **312/850-2663.** Reservations accepted for parties of 6 or more (no reservations on Sun). Main courses $3.25–$8.75 breakfast and lunch, $5.75–$14 dinner. AE, DC, DISC, MC, V. Mon 7am–3pm; Tues–Fri 7am–3pm and 5–10pm; Sat–Sun 8am–3pm and 5–11pm.

3 The Magnificent Mile & the Gold Coast

A great many tourists who visit Chicago never stray far from the Magnificent Mile and the adjoining Gold Coast area. From the array of restaurants, shops, and pretty streets in the area, it's not hard to see why. Restaurants here are some of the best in the city—and their prices are right in line with Michigan Avenue's designer boutiques.

VERY EXPENSIVE

Cape Cod Room *Overrated* SEAFOOD   A venerable old restaurant in a venerable old hotel, the Cape Cod Room is the kind of place where waiters debone the Dover sole tableside, while businessmen work out their next deal. There's nothing nouvelle about the Cape Cod Room, which is part of the draw for old-timers; the restaurant, located on the lower level of The Drake hotel, is dimly lit and hasn't changed much since it opened in the 1930s. Although the food is fine, plenty of other restaurants offer similar dishes at much lower prices.

For starters, the hearty Bookbinder red snapper soup is a signature dish; it's flavored to taste with dry sherry brought to the table. Main course offerings include sautéed striped bass served with a potato champagne sauce, New England scrod, red snapper, or Atlantic salmon baked with a potato horseradish crust. You'll also find a small selection of prime meat cuts, steaks, and chops. I wouldn't call the Cape Cod Room a good value, but the people-watching can be priceless.

In The Drake hotel, 140 E. Walton Place (at Michigan Ave.). © **312/787-2200.** Reservations recommended. Main courses $24–$40. AE, DC, DISC, MC, V. Daily noon–11pm. Closed Dec 25. Subway/El: Red Line to Chicago/State.

Gibsons Bar & Steakhouse *🎈🎈* STEAK   Popular with its Gold Coast neighbors, Gibsons is the steakhouse you visit when you want to make the scene. There are sporty cars idling at the valet stand, photos of celebs and near-celebs who've appeared here, and over-dressed denizens mingling and noshing in the bar, which has a life all its own. The dining rooms evoke a more romantic time, from the sleek Art Deco decor to the bow-tied bartenders. The portions are notoriously enormous, so Gibson's is best for groups who are happy to share dishes (I wouldn't recommend it for a romantic dinner *a deux*). The namesake martinis are served in 10-ounce glasses, and the entrees are outlandishly scaled, from the six-piece shrimp cock-tail, so huge you swore you downed a dozen, to the turtle pie that comes with a steak knife (and could easily serve 8 people).

1028 N. Rush St. (at Bellevue Place). ✆ **312/266-8999.** Reservations strongly rec-ommended. Main courses $22–$30. AE, DC, DISC, MC, V. Daily 3pm–midnight (bar open later). Subway/El: Red Line to Clark/Division.

Morton's ✪✪✪ STEAK Morton's is a well-known chain with a couple dozen locations nationwide; but it's Chicago born and bred, and many people still consider it the king of the Chicago-style steakhouses. Named for its founding father, renowned Chicago restaurateur Arnie Morton, Morton's holds its own against an onslaught of steakhouse competition with gargantuan portions of prime, wet-aged steaks, football-size baking potatoes, and trees of broccoli rolled out on a presentation cart. The restaurant is some-what hidden in an undistinguished high-rise, and the decor hasn't changed in years. Neither has the menu: starters include lobster bisque, Caesar salad, shrimp, or jumbo lump crabmeat cocktail, but meat is the main event. House specialties include the double filet mignon with sauce béarnaise, and classic cuts of porterhouse, New York strip, and rib-eye.

1050 N. State St. ✆ **312/266-4820.** www.mortons.com. Reservations recom-mended. Main courses $20–$33. AE, DC, DISC, MC, V. Mon–Sat 5:30–11pm; Sun 5–10pm. Subway/El: Red Line to State/Chicago.

Pump Room *(Overrated* AMERICAN/FRENCH Come here for the nostalgia, not the food. Back when celebrities journeyed by train between Hollywood and New York and stopped in Chicago to court the press, they always had a meal at the Pump Room. Diners at Booth One inevitably showed up in the morning papers. Today, it's the kind of place that's thought of fondly as a local institution, but a recent turnover of chefs has made the cuisine inconsistent.

Like the interior, the menu has had a few makeovers over the years; today, the focus is on classic American dishes with a sophisti-cated twist. Appetizers run the range from simple escargot in garlic butter to foie gras served with hibiscus nectar or sea scallops with mushrooms and caviar. For entrees, try the three preparations of lamb served together (seared rack, oven roasted, and braised shank), or veal chop stuffed with prosciutto and asiago cheese. A more exotic choice is the roasted Muscovy duck breast with seaweed salad and mango sauce.

In the Omni Ambassador East Hotel, 1301 N. State Pkwy. (at Goethe St.). ℂ 312/ 266-0360. Reservations required. Jackets required. Main courses $23–$36. AE, DC, DISC, MC, V. Mon–Thurs 7am–2:30pm and 6–10pm; Fri–Sat 7am–2:30pm and 5pm–midnight; Sun 11am–2:30pm and 5–10pm. Subway/El: Red Line to Clark/ Division.

Spiaggia ⭐⭐⭐ ITALIAN   *Spiaggia* means "beach" in Italian, and the restaurant's name is a tribute to its spectacular view of Lake Michigan and the Oak Street Beach. But this is no casual beach cafe. Spiaggia is widely acknowledged as the best fine-dining Italian restaurant in the city. The dining room is bright, airy, and sophisticated, an atmosphere far removed from your neighborhood trattoria (wear your jackets, gentlemen).

You can order a la carte or from two different degustation menus. The menu changes often and emphasizes seasonal ingredients. This ain't your Mama's pasta: Recent offerings have included pheasant-stuffed ravioli, pumpkin risotto, and gnocchi with wild mushrooms. Entree examples include classic *zuppa di pesce* and products of the restaurant's wood-burning oven, including monkfish; salmon; duck breast with Ligurian black olives, tomatoes, fennel, and baby artichokes; and grilled squab over lentils with foie gras. The classic Spiaggia dessert is the *baba all'arancia,* a cake soaked in orange liqueur and served with orange cream; the chilled mascarpone-cheese torte with rich chocolate gelato and espresso sauce is another high point.

Adjacent to the restaurant in a narrow, window-lined space is the informal, lower-priced **Café Spiaggia** (ℂ **312/280-2764**), which has the same hours but also (unlike the main restaurant) serves Sunday brunch.

980 N. Michigan Ave. (at Oak St.). ℂ **312/280-2750.** www.levyrestaurants.com. Reservations required on weekends. Main courses $17–$25 lunch; $29–$38 dinner; menu degustation $95–$135; fixed-price 3-course lunch $35. AE, DC, DISC, MC, V. Tues–Thurs 5:30–9:30pm; Fri–Sat 11:30am–2pm and 5:30–10:30pm; Sun 5:30–9pm. Subway/El: Red Line to Chicago/State.

Tru ⭐⭐⭐ PROGRESSIVE FRENCH   The sense of humor of chefs Rick Tramonto and Gale Gand shines through this menu (which recently included Insane Black Truffle Soup and Nut 'n

Honey Foie Gras), making Tru an approachable fine-dining experience. The menu is divided into a series of prix-fixe options; if your wallet and stomach permits, shell out the big bucks for the 7-course Grand Collection or 8-course Tramonto's Collection. Appetizers include a visually sensational caviar staircase (caviars and fixin's climbing a glass spiral staircase), black-truffle risotto with rabbit confit and chanterelles, or venison carpaccio with sweet-potato compote and cherry sauce. For entrees, Surf, Turf, and Turf combines roasted lobster with sweetbreads and foie gras; also, a grilled beef tenderloin is paired with gratin of artichoke and marrow sauce. The latest additions to the menu are dishes that are prepared and served tableside, such as roasted duck with duck consommé and duck foie gras ravioli. Gand's desserts perfectly echo Tramonto's savory menus.

676 N. St. Clair St. (at Huron St.). ℂ 312/202-0001. www.trurestaurant.com. Reservations required. Dinner 3-course prix-fixe menu $75; 7- or 8-course menu $75–$125. AE, DC, DISC, MC, V. Mon–Thurs 5:30–10pm; Fri–Sat 5:30–11pm. Subway/El: Red Line to Chicago/State.

MODERATE

ESPN Zone *(Kids* AMERICAN   Sports fans, welcome to nirvana. This massive 35,000-square-foot sports-themed dining and entertainment complex features three components: the Studio Grill, designed with replicas of studio sets from the cable networks' shows (including *SportsCenter*); the Screening Room, a sports pub featuring a 16-foot screen and an armada of TV monitors and radio sets carrying live broadcasts of games; and the Sports Arena, a gaming area with interactive and competitive attractions. The food here is better-than-average tavern fare, including quite a few salads and upscale items such as a salmon filet baked on cedar and served with steamed rice and grilled vegetables. There's also a special kids' menu.

43 E. Ohio St. (at Wabash Ave.). ℂ 312/644-3776. Main courses $7.25–$20. Sun–Thurs 11:30am–11:30pm; Fri–Sat 11:30am–midnight. Subway/El: Red Line to Grand.

Le Colonial *(★★* *Finds* VIETNAMESE/FRENCH   Le Colonial has one of the loveliest dining rooms in the city—and the second-floor lounge is a sultry, seductive cocktail destination. The restaurant evokes 1920s Saigon, with bamboo shutters, rattan chairs, potted palms and banana trees, fringed lampshades and ceiling fans, and evocative period photography. While the ambience certainly merits a visit, the flavorful cuisine is a draw on its own. Start with the hearty oxtail soup or the light and refreshing beef-and-watercress salad. Entrees include grilled lime-glazed sea scallops with garlic noodle salad; sautéed jumbo shrimp in curried coconut sauce; and roasted chicken with lemon grass–and-lime dipping sauce. Refresh with the orange-mint iced tea, and finish with banana tapioca pudding or gooey Le Colonial macaroon—or an after-dinner drink upstairs.

937 N. Rush St. (just south of Oak St.). © 312/255-0088. Reservations recommended. Main courses $14–$19. AE, DC, MC, V. Mon–Fri noon–2:30pm and 5–11pm; Sat noon–2:30pm and 5pm–midnight; Sun 5–10pm. Subway/El: Red Line to Chicago/State.

INEXPENSIVE

Billy Goat Tavern ☆ *Value* BURGERS/BREAKFAST "Cheezeborger, Cheezeborger—No Coke . . . Pepsi." Viewers of the original *Saturday Night Live* will certainly remember the classic John Belushi routine, a moment in the life of a crabby Greek short-order cook. The comic got his material from the Billy Goat Tavern, located under North Michigan Avenue near the bridge that crosses to the Loop (you'll find it by walking down the steps across the street from the Chicago Tribune building). The tavern is a classic dive: dark, seedy, and no-frills. But unlike the *Saturday Night Live* skit, the guys behind the counter are friendly. The Billy Goat is a hangout for the newspaper workers and writers who occupy the nearby Tribune Tower and Sun-Times Building, so you might overhear the latest media buzz. After work, this is a good place to watch a game, chitchat at the bar, and down a few beers.

430 N. Michigan Ave. © 312/222-1525. Reservations not accepted. Menu items $4–$8. No credit cards. Mon–Fri 7am–2am; Sat 10am–2am; Sun 11am–2am. Subway/El: Red Line to Chicago/State.

foodlife ☆☆ *Finds* ECLECTIC Taking the standard food court up a few notches, foodlife consists of a dozen or so kiosks offering both ordinary and exotic specialties on the mezzanine of Water Tower Place mall. Seats are spread out cafe-style in a very pleasant environment under realistic boughs of artificial trees festooned with strings of lights. A hostess will seat you, give you an electronic card, and then it's up to you to stroll around and get whatever food strikes your fancy (each purchase is recorded on your card, then you pay on the way out).

The beauty of a food court, of course, is that it offers something for everybody. At foodlife, diners can choose from burgers and pizza, south-of-the-border dishes, an assortment of Asian fare, and veggie-oriented, low-fat offerings. A lunch or a snack is basically

Only in Chicago

PIZZA

We have three pizza styles in Chicago: Chicago style, also known as deep-dish, which is thick-crusted and often demands a knife and fork; stuffed, which is similar to a pie, with a crust on both top and bottom; and thin crust. Many pizzerias serve both thick and thin, and some make all three kinds.

Three of Chicago's best gourmet deep-dish restaurants are **Pizzeria Uno**, **Pizzeria Due**, and **Gino's East**. In River North, **Lou Malnati's Pizzeria,** at 439 N. Wells St. (© 312/828-9800), bakes both deep-dish and thin-crust pizza and even has a low-fat cheese option. **Edwardo's** is a local pizza chain that serves all three varieties, but with a wheat crust and all-natural ingredients (spinach pizza is the specialty here); locations are in the Gold Coast, at 1212 N. Dearborn St. at Division Street (© 312/337-4490); in the South Loop, at 521 S. Dearborn St. (© 312/939-3366); and in Lincoln Park, at 2662 N. Halsted St. (© 773/871-3400). Not far from Lincoln Park Zoo is **Ranalli's Pizzeria, Libations & Collectibles,** 1925 N. Lincoln Ave. (© 312/642-4700), with its terrific open-air patio and extensive selection of beers.

HOT DOGS

The classic Chicago hot dog includes a frankfurter by Vienna Beef (a local food processor and hallowed institution), heaps of chopped onions and green relish, a slather of yellow mustard, pickle spears, fresh tomato wedges, a dash of celery salt, and, for good measure, two or three "sport" peppers, those thumb-shaped holy terrors that turn your mouth into its own bonfire.

Chicago is home to many standout hot-dog spots such as **Gold Coast Dogs**, 418 N. State St., at Hubbard Street (© 312/527-1222), two blocks off North Michigan Avenue. **Fluky's**, in The Shops at North Bridge mall at 520 N. Michigan Ave. (© 312/245-0702), is part of a local chain that has been serving great hot dogs since the Depression (Dan Aykroyd and Jay Leno are fans). **Portillo's**, at 100 W. Ontario St. (© 312/587-8930), is another local chain that specializes in hot dogs but also serves excellent pastas and salads.

inexpensive, but the payment method makes it easy to build up a big tab while holding a personal taste-testing session at each kiosk.

In Water Tower Place, 835 N. Michigan Ave. © **312/335-3663.** Reservations not accepted. Most items $5–$10. AE, DC, DISC, MC, V. Juice, espresso, and corner bakery Sun–Thurs 7:30am–9pm; Fri–Sat 7:30am–10pm. All other kiosks Sun–Thurs 11am–9pm; Fri–Sat 11am–10pm. Subway/El: Red Line to Chicago/State.

4 River North

River North, the area north of the Loop and west of Michigan Avenue, is home to the city's most concentrated cluster of art galleries and to a something-for-everyone array of restaurants—from fast food to theme and chain restaurants, to some of our trendiest dining destinations.

VERY EXPENSIVE

mk ☆☆☆ CONTEMPORARY AMERICAN Considered by foodies to be one of the top American restaurants in the city, mk doesn't flaunt its pedigree. The loftlike dining room is as understated as the lowercase initials that give the restaurant its name. Chef Michael Kornick specializes in creative combinations, such as sautéed whitefish and Maine lobster with sweet corn, mushrooms, and a light cream sauce; a nouvelle surf and turf of grilled filet mignon and lobster with truffle aioli, red-wine sauce, and potato purée; and a New York sirloin steak with veal porterhouse. The presentations are tasteful rather than dazzling; Kornick wants you to concentrate on the food, and that's just what the chic, mixed-age crowd does. Pastry chef Mindy Segal is mk's not-so-secret weapon: her sweet seasonal masterpieces, from intriguing homemade ice creams to playful adaptations of classic fruit desserts, shouldn't be missed.

868 N. Franklin St. (1 block north of Chicago Ave.). © **312/482-9179.** www. mkchicago.com. Reservations recommended. Main courses $19–$34; menu degustation $55. AE, DC, MC, V. Mon–Thurs 11:30am–2pm and 5:30–10pm; Fri 11:30am–2pm and 5:30–11pm; Sat 5:30–11pm; Sun 5:30–10pm. Subway/El: Brown Line to Chicago/Franklin.

Zealous ☆☆☆ CONTEMPORARY AMERICAN One of the most stylish contemporary restaurants in town, Zealous also has one of the most eclectic menus. Chef Michael Taus's cooking combines American ingredients with the subtle complexity of Chinese, Vietnamese, Korean, and Indian cuisines. Diners order from the a la carte menu or from one of three degustation menus; there is always a vegetarian menu, and Taus welcomes vegan diners as well. Recent entrees have ranged from Asian-inspired (sesame-crusted Chilean sea bass with red coconut curry sauce) to heartland hearty (roasted pork rack stuffed with dried peaches and served with carrot pierogi). The lunch menu features mostly pastas, along with some upscale sandwiches (all quite reasonably priced for a restaurant of this quality). The dining room is bright and airy (thanks to a central skylight); the purple chairs, green banquettes, and silver accents make the space feel trendy but not intimidating. The 6,000-bottle wine collection and glass-enclosed wine cellar show that Zealous takes its libations just as seriously as it takes its food (450 label selections appear on the wine list).

419 W. Superior St. ⓒ **312/475-9112.** www.zealousrestaurant.com. Reservations recommended. Main courses $12–$19 lunch, $15–$32 dinner; menu degustation $75–$105. AE, DISC, MC, V. Tues–Fri 11:30am–2:30pm and 5:30–11pm; Sat 5:30–11pm. Subway/El: Brown Line to Chicago.

EXPENSIVE

Frontera Grill & Topolobampo ⭐⭐⭐ MEXICAN Forget all your notions of burritos and chalupas. Owners Rick and Deann Groen Bayless are widely credited with bringing authentic Mexican regional cuisine to a wider audience. The building actually houses two restaurants: the casual Frontera Grill and the fine-dining Topolobampo.

At Frontera, the signature appetizer is the *sopes surtidos,* corn tortilla "boats" with a sampler of fillings (chicken in red mole, black beans with homemade chorizo, and so on). The ever-changing entree list features fresh, organic ingredients: pork loin in a green mole sauce; smoked chicken breast smothered in a sauce of chiles, pumpkin seeds, and roasted garlic; or a classic *sopa de pan* ("bread soup" spiced up with almonds, raisins, grilled green onions, and zucchini). The Baylesses up the ante at the adjacent Topolobampo, where both the ingredients and presentation are more upscale.

It can be tough to snag a table at Frontera during prime dining hours, so do what the locals do: Put your name on the list and order a few margaritas in the lively, large bar area.

445 N. Clark St. (between Illinois and Hubbard sts.). ⓒ **312/661-1434.** Reservations accepted at Frontera Grill only for parties of 5–10; accepted at Topolobampo for parties of 1–8. Main courses Frontera Grill $15–$21; Topolobampo $20–$29 (chef's 5-course tasting menu $70). AE, DC, DISC, MC, V. Frontera Grill Tues 11:30am–2:30pm and 5:30–10pm; Wed–Thurs 11:30am–2:30pm and 5–10pm; Fri 11:30am–2:30pm and 5–11pm; Sat 10:30am–2:30pm and 5–11pm. Topolobampo Tues 11:45am–2pm and 5:30–9:30pm; Wed–Thurs 11:30am–2pm and 5:30–9:30pm; Fri 11:30am–2pm and 5:30–10:30pm; Sat 5:30–10:30pm. Subway/El: Red Line to Grand.

Dining Alfresco

Cocooned for 6 months of the year, with furnaces and electric blankets blazing, Chicagoans revel in the warm months of late spring, summer, and early autumn. Dining alfresco is an ideal way to experience the sights, sounds, smells, and social fabric of this multifaceted city.

LOOP & VICINITY

Athena This Greektown mainstay offers a stunning three-level outdoor seating area. It's paved with brick and landscaped with 30-foot trees, flower gardens, and even a waterfall. Best of all: an incredible view of the downtown skyline with the Sears Tower right in the middle. 212 S. Halsted St.; ✆ 312/655-0000.

Charlie's Ale House at Navy Pier One of several outdoor dining options along Navy Pier, this outpost of the Lincoln Park restaurant wins for lip-smacking pub fare and a great location on the southern promenade overlooking the lakefront and Loop skyline. 700 E. Grand Ave.; ✆ 312/595-1440.

MAGNIFICENT MILE & GOLD COAST

Le Colonial This lovely French-Vietnamese restaurant, located in a vintage Gold Coast town house and evocative of 1920s Saigon, has a sidewalk cafe. But you'd do better to reserve a table on the tiny second-floor porch, overlooking the street and close to Le Colonial's atmospheric cocktail

Nacional 27 *☆☆* *Finds* CONTEMPORARY LATIN   Part sleek supper club, part sultry nightclub, Nacional 27 showcases the cuisine of 27 Latin American nations, including Venezuela, Argentina, Costa Rica, and Brazil. Rich walnut and bamboo woods and gauzy curtains lend a tropical air to the grand dining room, which has cozy booth seating and tables arranged around a central dance floor. Steaks and seafood, along with exotic fruits and vegetables, are the stars of the menu (and all seem to call for one of the innovative Latin cocktails on the drink menu). House specialties include chimichurri churrasco steak, a pounded sirloin with black-bean salsa, roasted peppers, and *papas fritas* (fried potatoes); and Chilean sea bass *en zarzuela en cazuela* (poached in shellfish and spicy lounge. For a full review, see p. 73. 937 N. Rush St.; © **312/ 255-0088.**

LINCOLN PARK

North Pond Set on the banks of one of Lincoln Park's beautiful lagoons, the excellent North Pond serves American cuisine in a romantic and sylvan setting. One caveat: Alcohol is not permitted on the outdoor patio. See also p. 85. 2610 N. Cannon Dr.; © **773/477-5845.**

O'Brien's Restaurant Wells Street in Old Town is lined with several alfresco options, but the best belongs to O'Brien's, the unofficial nucleus of neighborhood life. The outdoor patio has teakwood furniture, a gazebo bar, and a mural of the owners' country club on a brick wall. Order the dressed-up chips, a house specialty. 1528 N. Wells St. (2 blocks south of North Ave.); © **312/787-3131.**

WICKER PARK/BUCKTOWN

Meritage Café and Wine Bar Meritage wins my vote for most romantic outdoor nighttime seating. The food (American cuisine with Pacific Northwest influences) is top-notch, but it's the outdoor patio, twinkling with overhead lights, that makes for a magical experience. Best of all, the patio is covered and heated in the winter, so you can enjoy the illusion of outdoor dining even in February. 2118 N. Damen Ave.; © **773/235-6434.**

tomato broth and served over annatto rice). The food can tend toward the spicy, so ask before you order if you've got sensitive taste buds. Nacional 27 heats up on Friday and Saturday nights after 10pm, when a DJ starts spinning fiery Latin tunes and couples take to the dance floor.

325 W. Huron St. (between Franklin and Orleans sts.). © **312/664-2727.** Reservations recommended. Main courses $14–$25. AE, DC, DISC, MC, V. Dining room Mon–Thurs 5:30–9:30pm; Fri–Sat 5:30–11pm. Bar Mon–Thurs 5–10pm; Fri–Sat 5pm–2am. Subway/El: Brown Line to Chicago.

MODERATE

Carson's ⍟ AMERICAN/BARBECUE   A true Chicago institution, Carson's calls itself "The Place for Ribs," and, boy, is it ever.

The barbecue sauce is sweet and tangy, and the ribs are meaty. Included in the $20 price for a full slab of baby backs are coleslaw and one of four types of potatoes (the most decadent are au gratin), plus right-out-of-the-oven rolls.

For dinner there's often a wait, but don't despair: In the bar area, you'll find a heaping mound of some of the best chopped liver around and plenty of cocktail rye to go with it. When you're seated at your table, tie on your plastic bib—and indulge. In case you don't eat ribs, Carson's also barbecues chicken, pork chops, and (in a nod to health-consciousness) even salmon. But let's be honest: You don't come to a place like this for the seafood. The waitstaff will be shocked if no one in your group orders the famous ribs.

612 N. Wells St. (at Ontario St.). ℂ **312/280-9200.** Reservations not accepted. Main courses $8.95–$30. AE, DC, DISC, MC, V. Mon–Thurs 11am–11pm; Fri 11am–12:30am; Sat noon–12:30am; Sun noon–11pm. Subway/El: Red Line to Grand.

Reza's ⭐⭐ *Value* MIDDLE EASTERN   Reza's doesn't look like the typical Middle Eastern restaurant; housed in a former microbrewery, it has high ceilings and expansive, loftlike dining rooms. But the Persian-inspired menu will soon make you forget all about pints of ale. Specialties include a deliciously rich chicken in pomegranate sauce and a variety of kebabs (make sure you ask for the dill rice). Can't decide what to order? Go for an appetizer combo, a generous sampler of Middle Eastern dishes.

432 W. Ontario St (at Orleans St.). ℂ **312/664-4500.** Main courses $9.95–$17. AE, DC, DISC, MC, V. Daily 11am–midnight. Subway/El: Red Line to Grand.

INEXPENSIVE
Cafe Iberico ⭐⭐ SPANISH/TAPAS   This no-frills tapas spot won't win any points for style, but the consistently good food and festive atmosphere makes it a long-time local favorite for singles in their 20s and 30s. Crowds begin pouring in at the end of the workday, so you'll probably have to wait for a table. Not to worry: Order a pitcher of fruit-filled sangria at the bar along with everyone else. Put a dent in your appetite with a plate of *queso de cabra* (baked goat cheese with fresh tomato-basil sauce), and when your waiter returns with the first dish, put in a second order for a round of both hot and cold tapas. (The waiters may take some effort to flag down.) Then continue to order as your hunger demands. A few standout dishes are the vegetarian Spanish omelet, spicy potatoes with tomato sauce, chicken brochette with caramelized onions and rice, and grilled octopus with potatoes and olive oil.

739 N. LaSalle St. (between Chicago Ave. and Superior St.). © 312/573-1510. Reservations accepted during the week for parties of 6 or more. Tapas $3.50–$4.95; main courses $7.95–$13. DC, DISC, MC, V. Mon–Thurs 11am–11pm; Fri 11am–1:30am; Sat noon–1:30am; Sun noon–11pm. Subway/El: Red Line to Chicago/State or Brown Line to Chicago.

Mr. Beef ✪ *Finds* AMERICAN   Mr. Beef doesn't have much atmosphere or seating room, but it's a much-loved Chicago institution. Its claim to fame is the classic Italian beef sandwich, the Chicago version of a Philly cheese steak. The Mr. Beef variety is made of sliced beef dipped in jus, piled high on a chewy bun, and topped with sweet or hot peppers. Heavy, filling, and *very* Chicago, Mr. Beef really hops during lunchtime, when dusty construction workers and suit-wearing businessmen crowd in for their meaty fix.

666 N. Orleans St. (at Erie St.). © 312/337-8500. Sandwiches $5.95–$8.50. No credit cards. Mon–Fri 7am–4:45pm; Sat 10am–2pm. Subway/El: Red Line to Grand.

5 Lincoln Park

Singles and upwardly mobile young families inhabit Lincoln Park, the neighborhood roughly defined by North Avenue on the south, Diversey Parkway on the north, the park on the east, and Clybourn Avenue on the west. No surprise, then, that the neighborhood has spawned a dense concentration of some of the city's best restaurants.

VERY EXPENSIVE

Ambria ✪✪ FRENCH   Across the street from the Lincoln Park Zoo and housed in the impressive former Belden-Stratford Hotel, Ambria has enjoyed an enviable 20-year run as one of Chicago's finest restaurants. The dimly lit, wood-paneled interior is intimate, almost clublike, and eminently civilized.

The menu, masterfully orchestrated by Chef Gabino Sotelino, changes frequently but always features beautifully prepared French-influenced dishes. Appetizers might include lobster medallions in a caviar beurre blanc, or a pastry stuffed with escargot and seasonal vegetables. Main courses run the gamut from roasted rack of lamb with stuffed baby eggplant, couscous, and artichoke chips to roasted medallions of New Zealand venison with wild-rice pancakes, caramelized rhubarb, and root vegetables. You can order a la carte or from a selection of fixed-price menus (including a five-course shellfish degustation and the "Ambria Classic Menu" of tried-and-true favorites). The wine list is extensive; take advantage of the top-notch sommelier if you need guidance.

Where to Dine in Lincoln Park, Wrigleyville & the North Side

Ambria **13**
Ann Sather **6**
Arun's **1**
Bamee Noodle Shop **7**
Byron's Hot Dog Haus **2**
Charlie's Ale House **12**
Charlie Trotter's **15**
Edwardo's **10**
Geja's Cafe **16**
Goose Island Brewing
 Company **18**
Nookies **4, 14, 19**
North Pond **11**
O'Brien's Restaurant **21**
Orange **5**
Penny's Noodle Shop **8**
Ranalli's Pizzeria, Libations
 & Collectibles **17**
RoseAngelis **9**
Thai Classic **3**
Twin Anchors **20**

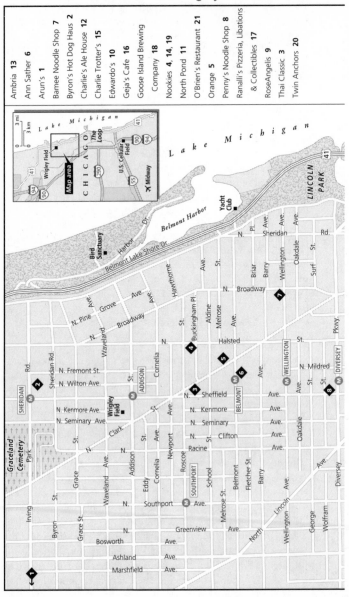

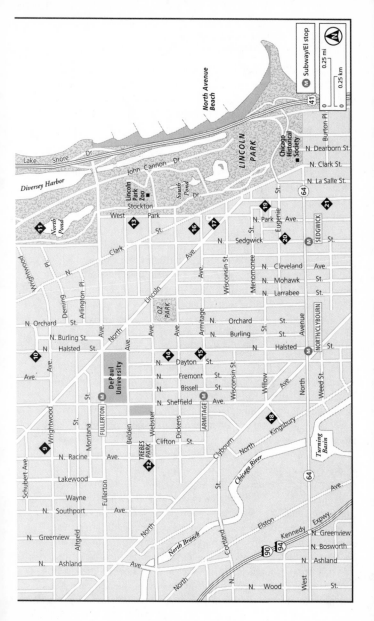

North Avenue Beach

Lake Shore Dr.

Diversey Harbor

North Pond

LINCOLN PARK

John Cannon Dr.

Lincoln Park Zoo
Stockton

South Pond Dr.

West Park St.

Chicago Historical Society

N. Dearborn St.
N. Clark St.
N. La Salle St.

Clark Ave.

N. Park Ave.

N. Sedgwick St.

N. Cleveland Ave.
N. Mohawk St.
N. Larrabee St.

Wisconsin St.

Menomonee St.

Eugenie St.

SEDGWICK

Wrightwood Pl.

N. Deming Pl.

Arlington Pl.

Lincoln Ave.

OZ PARK

Armitage

N. Orchard St.
N. Burling St.
N. Halsted St.

North Ave.

N. Orchard St.
N. Burling St.
N. Halsted St.

NORTH/CLYBOURN

Weed St.

N. Wrightwood Ave.

DePaul University

FULLERTON

N. Dayton St.
N. Fremont St.
N. Bissell St.
N. Sheffield Ave.

Wisconsin St.

Willow St.

ARMITAGE

North Ave.

Kingsbury St.

Turning Basin

N. Racine Ave.

TREBES PARK

Belden

Webster

Dickens

Clifton St.

Clybourn St.

Chicago River

Lakewood

Wayne

N. Southport Ave.

Fullerton Ave.

Montana

Schubert Ave.

North Branch

North Ave.

North Branch

Cortland St.

Elston Ave.

Kennedy Expwy.

N. Greenview

N. Bosworth

N. Ashland

N. Greenview

N. Ashland

N. Wood St.

West St.

N.

M Subway/El stop

0   0.25 mi
0   0.25 km

83

2300 N. Lincoln Park West (at Belden Ave.). ✆ 773/472-0076. Reservations recommended. Main courses $24–$36; fixed-price meals $60–$75. AE, DC, DISC, MC,
V. Mon–Fri 6–10pm; Sat 5–10:30pm. Bus: No. 151.

Charlie Trotter's ✫✫✫ NOUVELLE   Foodies flock to the
namesake restaurant of chef Charlie Trotter, Chicago's first celebrity
chef. Yes, he's done TV shows and authored a series of cookbooks
(with almost impossible-to-follow recipes), but Trotter's focus is this
restaurant, a shrine to creative fine dining.

There is no a la carte menu, so this is not the place to come if
you're a picky eater. Decide at the outset if you would like the vegetable ($90) or grand ($110) degustation menu. Trotter delights in
presenting diners with unfamiliar ingredients and presentations, and
prides himself on using only organic or free-range products (so you
can feel good about indulging). The very long entree descriptions signal Trotter's attention to detail; sample dishes from a recent menu
include ragout of leek confit, braised carrots, salsify, and cauliflower
with Perigord black-truffle emulsion; and black buck venison with
Japanese *kumai* (jasmine rice cake and red-wine Kalamata olive
emulsion). Be prepared to linger; dinner here can take up to 3 hours.
The dining room may be formal, but the staff are not intimidating.

816 W. Armitage Ave. (at Halsted St.). ✆ 773/248-6228. www.charlietrotters.com.
Reservations required. Jackets required, ties requested. Fixed-price menus $90 and
$110. AE, DC, DISC, MC, V. Tues–Sat 6–10pm. Subway/El: Brown Line to Armitage.

Geja's Cafe ✫ FONDUE   A dark, subterranean hideaway, Geja's
(pronounced gay-*haz*) regularly shows up on lists of the most
romantic restaurants in Chicago (cozy couples should request a
booth off the main dining room). If there are at least two in your
party (all main courses are served for two or more), choose the con-
noisseur fondue dinner, the best Geja's has to offer. The meal begins
with a Gruyère cheese fondue appetizer with apple wedges and
chunks of dark bread. Next, a huge platter arrives, brimming with
squares of beef tenderloin, lobster tails, and jumbo shrimp—all
raw—and a caldron of boiling oil to cook them in. These delicacies
are accompanied by a variety of raw vegetables, and eight different
dipping sauces. When the flaming chocolate fondue arrives for
dessert, with fresh fruit and pound cake for dipping and marshmal-
lows for roasting, you'll want to beg for mercy. One word of caution:
You have to work for your fondue—keeping track of how long each
piece of meat has been cooking—so Geja's is not the best choice if
you just want to sit back and be pampered.

340 W. Armitage Ave. (between Lincoln Ave. and Clark St.). © 773/281-9101. Reservations accepted every day except late Fri–Sat. Main courses $20–$37. AE, DC, DISC, MC, V. Mon–Thurs 5–10:30pm; Fri 5pm–midnight; Sat 5pm–12:30am; Sun 4:30–10pm. Subway/El: Brown Line to Armitage. Bus: No. 22.

North Pond *★★★ (Finds* AMERICAN   Tucked away in Lincoln Park, North Pond is a hidden treasure. There are no roads leading here—you must follow a path to reach the restaurant, which was formerly a warming hut for ice skaters. The building's Arts and Crafts–inspired interior blends perfectly with the park outside, and a recently added glass-enclosed addition lets you dine "outside" all year long.

In keeping with the natural setting, chef Bruce Sherman emphasizes organic, locally grown ingredients and favors simple preparations—although the overall result is definitely upscale (at these prices, it better be). Examples of seasonal menu items include herbed Parmesan gnocchi with braised rabbit, fava beans, asparagus, Wisconsin ramps, and lovage (a celerylike green); poached farm-fresh egg with wilted baby spinach and lemon-caviar butter sauce; and grilled sea scallops with orange-Parmesan grain salad, glazed organic baby carrots, and spiced lobster sauce. To enjoy the restaurant's setting with a slightly lower price tag, try the fixed-price Sunday brunch ($28).

2610 N. Cannon Dr. (south of Diversey Pkwy.). © 773/477-5845. www.northpond restaurant.com. Reservations recommended. Main courses $24–$30. AE, DC, MC, V. Tues–Sat 5:30–10pm; Sun 11am–2pm and 5:30–10pm. Bus: No. 151.

INEXPENSIVE

Goose Island Brewing Company AMERICAN PUB   Some of the best beer in Chicago is manufactured at this comfy, award-winning microbrewery in the Clybourn corridor (an impressive cast of professional beer critics agrees). In the course of a year, Goose Island produces about 100 varieties of lagers, ales, stouts, pilsners, and porters that change with the seasons.

For many years, the food here didn't live up to the beer. But fans of the foamy are now dining at the Goose with almost the same gusto they devote to their guzzling. Cut-above bar food includes burgers (including a killer, dragon-breath-inducing Stilton burger with roasted garlic), sandwiches (pulled pork, catfish po' boy, chicken Caesar), and some serious salads. Goose Island is also known for its addictive homemade potato chips, fresh-brewed root beer, and orange cream soda. The zero-attitude, come-as-you-are ambience is very refreshing for a lazy afternoon pit stop or a casual lunch or dinner. A second location at 3535 N. Clark St. in Wrigleyville (© 773/832-9040) has an enclosed beer garden.

1800 N. Clybourn Ave. (at Sheffield Ave.). © 312/915-0071. www.gooseisland. com. Reservations recommended on weekends. Sandwiches $7.50–$9.95; main courses $11–$17. AE, DC, DISC, MC, V. Mon–Fri 11:30am–1am; Sat 11am–2am; Sun 11am–midnight; main dining room closes at 10pm daily. Subway/El: Red Line to North/Clybourn.

RoseAngelis ★★ *Value* NORTHERN ITALIAN   What is it about RoseAngelis that keeps me coming back, when there's not exactly a shortage of Italian restaurants in this city? The secret is simple: This is neighborhood dining at its best, a place with reliably good food and very reasonable prices. Tucked in a residential side street in Lincoln Park, the restaurant fills the ground floor of a former private home, with a charming series of cozy rooms and a garden patio. The menu emphasizes pasta (my favorites are the rich lasagna and the ravioli al Luigi, filled with ricotta and served with a sun-dried-tomato cream sauce). The garlicky chicken Vesuvio is excellent, but it's not offered on Friday and Saturday nights because of preparation time. While RoseAngelis is not a vegetarian restaurant per se, there's no red meat on the menu, and many of the pastas are served with vegetables rather than meat. Finish up with the deliciously decadent bread pudding with warm caramel sauce, one of my favorite desserts in the city (and big enough to share). I suggest stopping by on a weeknight because you'll be fighting lots of locals on weekend nights (when you'll wait 2 hr. for a table).

1314 W. Wrightwood Ave. (at Lakewood Ave.). © 773/296-0081. Reservations accepted for parties of 8 or more. Main courses $9.95–$15. DISC, MC, V. Tues–Thurs 5–10pm; Fri–Sat 5–11pm; Sun 4:30–9pm. Subway/El: Red Line to Fullerton.

Twin Anchors ★ BARBECUE   A landmark in Old Town since the end of Prohibition, Twin Anchors manages to maintain the flavor of old Chicago. It's a friendly, family-owned pub with Frank Sinatra on the jukebox and on the walls (he apparently hung out here on swings through town in the 1960s). It's a totally unpretentious place with a long mahogany bar up front and a modest dining room in back with red Formica-topped tables crowded close. Of course, you don't need anything fancy when the ribs—the fall-off-the-bone variety—come this good. All of this means that you should prepare for a long wait on weekends. Ribs and other entrees come with coleslaw and dark rye bread, plus your choice of baked potato, tasty fries, and the even-better crisp onion rings.

1655 N. Sedgwick St. (1 block north of North Ave.). © 312/266-1616. Reservations no accepted. Main courses $9.95–$20; sandwiches $3.50–$7.50. AE, DC, DISC, MC, V. Mon–Thurs 5–11:30pm; Fri 5pm–12:30am; Sat noon–12:30am; Sun noon–10:30pm. Subway/El: Brown Line to Sedgwick.

6 Wrigleyville & the North Side

The area surrounding Wrigley Field has a long history as a working-class neighborhood. But Wrigleyville quickly gentrified as developers built new town houses and apartments. And with that affluence has come several popular restaurants spanning a range of culinary offerings and prices.

VERY EXPENSIVE

Arun's ☆☆☆ THAI   It has been called the best Thai restaurant in the city—possibly the country. Here, chef/owner Arun Sampanthavivat prepares a refined version of traditional Thai cuisine, authentic and flavorful but not palate-scorching. The only downside is its out-of-the-way location—you can get here by public transportation, but I recommend a taxi at night when the bus schedules are less reliable.

The 12-course chef's menu is your only option here, and different tables receive different dishes on a given night. This sequential banquet begins with degustation-style appetizers, followed by four family-style entrees and two desserts. You might see courses of various delicate dumplings accented with edible, carved dough flowers; an alchemist's Thai salad of bitter greens and peanuts with green papaya, tomatoes, chiles, and sticky rice; and a medley of clever curries, including a surprisingly delightful sea bass and cabbage sour curry. When classic dishes appear, such as pad thai, they're always above the norm. Hope your dessert selections include the sticky rice with papaya (don't tell them if you're celebrating an occasion or they may serve you chocolate cake). The menu is paired with an award-winning wine list, and the restaurant provides a smoke-free environment.

4156 N. Kedzie Ave. (at Irving Park Rd.). © 773/539-1909. Reservations required with credit card. 12-course chef's menu $85. AE, DC, DISC, MC, V. Sun and Tues–Thurs 5–9pm; Fri–Sat 5–10pm. Subway/El and bus: Blue Line to Irving Park, and then transfer to eastbound no. 80 bus; or Brown Line to Irving Park, and then transfer to westbound no. 80 bus.

INEXPENSIVE

Ann Sather ☆☆ SWEDISH/AMERICAN/BREAKFAST   A sign hanging by Ann Sather's door bears the following inscription: "Once one of many neighborhood Swedish restaurants, Ann Sather's is the only one that remains." It's a real Chicago institution, where you can enjoy Swedish meatballs with buttered noodles and brown gravy, or the Swedish sampler of duck breast with lingonberry glaze, meatball, potato-sausage dumpling, sauerkraut, and brown beans. All meals are full dinners, including appetizer, main course, vegetable, potato, and dessert. Sticky cinnamon rolls are a highlight of Sather's popular (and very affordable) weekend brunch menu (it can get frenzied, but you'll be fine if you get here before 11am). The people-watching is priceless here: a cross section of gay and straight, young and old, from club kids to elderly couples.

929 W. Belmont Ave. (between Clark St. and Sheffield Ave.). © 773/348-2378. Reservations accepted for parties of 6 or more. Main courses $7–$12. AE, DC, MC, V. Sun–Thurs 7am–10pm; Fri–Sat 7am–11pm. Free parking with validation. Subway/El: Red Line to Belmont.

Penny's Noodle Shop 🔍 *Value* ASIAN/THAI Predating many of Chicago's pan-Asian noodle shops, Penny's has kept its loyal following even as others have joined the fray. Penny Chiamopoulous, a Thai native, has assembled a concise menu of delectable dishes, all of them fresh and made to order—and all at prices that will make you do a double-take. The two dining rooms are clean and spare; single diners can usually find a seat along the bar that wraps around the grill. The Thai spring roll, filled with seasoned tofu, cucumber, bean sprouts, and strips of cooked egg, makes a refreshing starter. Of course, noodles unite everything on the menu, so your main decision is choosing among the options (crispy wide rice, rice vermicelli, Japanese udon, and so on) served in a soup or spread out on a plate.

The original Penny's, tucked under the El tracks at 3400 N. Sheffield Ave. near Wrigley Field (© 773/281-8222), is small and often has long waits; you stand a better chance of scoring a table at the Diversey Avenue location or the one in Wicker Park, at 1542 N. Damen Ave. (© 773/394-0100). All locations are BYOB.

950 W. Diversey Ave. (at Sheffield St.). © 773/281-8448. Reservations not accepted. Main courses $4.50–$7.95. MC, V. Sun and Tues–Thurs 11am–10pm; Fri–Sat 11am–10:30pm. Subway/El: Brown Line to Diversey.

7 Wicker Park/Bucktown

The booming Wicker Park/Bucktown area followed closely in the race to gentrification on the heels of Lincoln Park and Wrigleyville. Get yourself to the nexus of activity at the intersection of North, Damen, and Milwaukee avenues, and you won't have to walk more than a couple of blocks in any direction to find a hot spot.

Dining & Nightlife in Wicker Park/Bucktown

DINING ◆

Bongo Room **11**
Le Bouchon **2**
Mas **14**
Mirai Sushi **12**
Piece **7**
Spring **6**

NIGHTLIFE ●

Big Wig **15**
The Borderline **3**
Davenport's Piano Bar & Cabaret **10**
Double Door **9**
Get Me High Lounge **4**
The Map Room **1**
Phyllis' Musical Inn **13**
Red Dog **5**
Sinibar **8**

EXPENSIVE

Mas *ĠĠ* LATIN AMERICAN   Urban, cozy, and dark, "nuevo Latino" Mas is almost always packed with faithful regulars who come for the Latin cocktails and modern takes on traditional Central and South American cuisine. The "primero" list includes spicy lime-marinated tuna tacos with papaya, rosemary, and Dijon salsa; and a succulent ceviche of the day (such as yellowtail snapper with smoked poblano chile or blue marlin with rum and vanilla). Entrees worth the wait include chile-cured pork tenderloin over smoky white beans; the achiote-roasted mako shark with crawfish-lentil salsa and avocado salad; and traditional Brazilian *xinzim* (shrimp and chicken stew with coconut broth and black beans). Out-of-the-ordinary desserts include lightly fried pound cake with fresh plum compote, roasted hazelnuts, and caramel-praline ice cream.

With long waits on weekends (there are no reservations) and plenty of loud conversation, Mas may not be to everyone's taste. They do offer the same menu at its second location, **Otro Mas,** at 3651 N. Southport Ave., ℭ **773/348-3200.**

1670 W. Division St. ℭ 773/276-8700. www.masrestaurant.com. Reservations not accepted. Main courses $17–$27. AE, DC, MC, V. Mon–Thurs 5:30–10:30pm; Fri–Sat 5:30–11:30pm; Sun 11am–2pm and 5:30–10pm. Subway/El: Blue Line to Damen.

Mirai Sushi *ĠĠ* SUSHI/JAPANESE   Blending a serious devotion to sushi and sake with a decidedly youthful, funky-chic ambience, Mirai is one hot destination for cold raw fish (it serves other Japanese fare as well). The futuristic second-floor sake lounge is the hippest place in town to slurp down sushi, chilled sakes, and "red ones," the house cocktail of vodka with passion fruit, lime, and cranberry juices. The bright, smoke-free main-floor dining room offers a comparatively traditional environment.

Fish is flown in daily for the sushi bar, where several chefs are hard at work master-crafting a lovely list of offerings—from the beginner sushi standards such as California roll and *ebi* (boiled shrimp) to escalating classifications of tuna, three additional shrimp varieties, five types of salmon, a half-dozen varieties of fresh oysters, and a tantalizing list of four caviars (in addition to the four roes offered). The informative sake menu of about a dozen selections opens up a new world to diners accustomed to the generic carafe of heated sake.

2020 W. Division St. ℭ 773/862-8500. Reservations recommended. Main courses $13–$21. AE, DC, DISC, MC, V. Sun–Wed 5–10pm; Thurs–Sat 5–11pm. Upstairs lounge open until 2am. Subway/El: Blue Line to Division.

Spring ⭐⭐⭐ CONTEMPORARY AMERICAN   This former Russian bathhouse has been transformed into an oasis of Zen calm and soothing, neutral colors. Chef Shawn McClain is Chicago's newest culinary celebrity, and his restaurant has been attracting national attention. Spring is not a scene; diners step down into a dining room hidden from the street, sink into the banquettes that zigzag across the center of the room, and concentrate on the food. Unlike other chefs who feel pressured to keep outdoing themselves, McClain sticks to a focused menu, with a heavy emphasis on seafood and pan-Asian preparations. Appetizers include an aromatic lemon grass–red curry broth with rice noodles, and sea scallop–and-potato ravioli with sautéed mushrooms and truffle essence. Most of the entrees are seafood-based: New Zealand snapper with lemon couscous and fennel salad, or the braised baby monkfish and escargots with roasted eggplant in smoked tomato bouillon, for example. Desserts also go the Asian route, focusing on seasonal fruits, although the coconut mochi brûlée with warm pineapple puts a whole new twist on rice pudding.

2039 W. North Ave. (at Milwaukee Ave.). © **773/395-7100.** Reservations recommended. Main courses $16–$25. AE, DC, DISC, MC, V. Tues–Thurs 5:30–10pm; Fri–Sat 5:30–11pm; Sun 5:30–9pm. Subway: Blue Line to Damen.

MODERATE

Le Bouchon ⭐⭐ *Finds* FRENCH/BISTRO   Opened in 1994, Jean-Claude Poilevey's trend-setting Le Bouchon was a well-received precursor of the bistro boom. This tiny storefront restaurant quickly caught on for the intimate yet boisterous atmosphere and authentic bistro fare at reasonable prices.

Whatever the season, the food here is fairly heavy, although specials are lighter in warmer months. Poilevey could pack this place every night just with regulars addicted to the house specialty of roast duck for two bathed in Grand Marnier–orange marmalade sauce. The fare covers bistro basics, with starters including steamed mussels in white wine and herbs, country pâté, onion tart, codfish *brandade* (a pounded mixture of cod, olive oil, garlic, milk, and cream), and *salade Lyonnaise* (greens with bacon lardons, croutons, and poached egg). The authenticity continues in the entree department, with steak frites, sautéed rabbit in white wine, veal kidneys in mustard sauce, and garlicky frogs legs on the bill of fare. The sounds of prominent music and voices from closely packed tables create an atmosphere that some perceive as cozy and romantic, and others as claustrophobic and noisy.

1958 N. Damen Ave. (at Armitage Ave.). ℂ **773/862-6600**. www.lebouchonof
chicago.com. Reservations recommended. Main courses $13–$15. AE, DC, DISC,
MC, V. Mon–Thurs 5:30–11pm; Fri–Sat 5pm–midnight. Subway/El and bus: Blue
Line to Damen and transfer to bus no. 50.

INEXPENSIVE

Northside Café AMERICAN/BURGERS   Among the best
cheap eats in the city, Northside cooks up great burgers, sandwiches,
and salads, all for less than $10. This is strictly neighborhood din-
ing, without attitude and little in the way of decor; the back dining
room looks like a rec room circa 1973, complete with a fireplace,
pinball machines, and a pool table. In nice weather, Northside
opens up its large front patio for dining, and a skylit cover keeps it
in use during the winter. You're always sure to find entertaining people-watching, as Northside attracts all sorts. During the week, it's
more of a neighborhood hangout, while on weekends, a touristy
crowd from Lincoln Park and the suburbs piles in. A limited late-
night menu is available from 10pm to 1am.

1635 N. Damen Ave. (at North and Milwaukee aves.). ℂ **773/384-3555**. Reservations not accepted. Menu items $5.95–$11. AE, DC, DISC, MC, V. Sun–Fri
11:30am–2am; Sat 11am–3am. Subway/El: Blue Line to Damen.

Piece ℱ (Kids) AMERICAN/PIZZA   A casual, welcoming hangout, Piece makes a great family lunch stop during the day; at night,
it becomes a convivial scene full of young singles sipping one of the
restaurant's seasonal microbrew beers. The large, airy dining
room—a former garage that's been outfitted with dark wood tables
and ceiling beams—is flooded with light from the expansive skylights overhead; even when it's crowded (as it gets on weekend
evenings), the soaring space above keeps the place from feeling
claustrophobic.

Piece offers a selection of salads and sandwiches on satisfyingly
crusty bread, but thin-crust pizza in the style of New Haven, Con-
necticut (hometown of one of the owners), is the house specialty.
You pick from three styles: plain (tomato sauce, Parmesan cheese,
and garlic), red (tomato sauce and mozzarella), or white (olive oil,
garlic, and mozzarella), then add on your favorite toppings. Sausage
and/or spinach work well with the plain or red, but the adventurous
shouldn't miss the house specialty: clam and bacon on white pizza.

1927 W. North Ave. (at Milwaukee Ave.). ℂ **773/772-4422**. Reservations not
accepted. Main courses $6.95–$15. AE, DISC, MC, V. Mon–Thurs 11:30am–11pm;
Fri–Sat 11:30am–12:30am; Sun 11am–11pm. Subway: Blue Line to Damen.

Exploring Chicago

Chicago may still be stereotyped as the home of sausage-loving, overweight guys who babble on endlessly about "da Bears" or "da Cubs," but in reality the city offers some of the most sophisticated cultural and entertainment options in the country. You'll have trouble fitting in all of Chicago's museums, which offer everything from action (the virtual-reality visit to the Milky Way galaxy at the Adler Planetarium) to quiet contemplation (the Impressionist masterpieces at the Art Institute of Chicago). Gape at Sue, the biggest T-rex fossil ever discovered, at the Field Museum of Natural History, or be entranced by the colorful world of the Butterfly Haven at the Peggy Notebaert Nature Museum. Stroll through picture-postcard Lincoln Park Zoo on the Near North Side, and then enjoy the view from the top of the Ferris wheel on historic Navy Pier.

Extensive public transportation makes it simple to reach almost every tourist destination, but some of your best memories of Chicago may come from simply strolling the sidewalks. Chicago's neighborhoods each have their own distinct style and look, and you'll have a more memorable experience if you don't limit yourself solely to the prime tourist spots. And if you *really* want to talk about da Bears or da Cubs, chances are you'll find someone more than happy to join in.

1 In & Around the Loop: The Art Institute, the Sears Tower & Grant Park

The heart of the Loop is Chicago's business center, where you'll find some of the city's most famous early skyscrapers (not to mention the Sears Tower). If you're looking to soak in a real big-city experience, wander the area on a bustling weekday (just make sure you don't get knocked down by a commuter rushing to catch the train). The Loop is also home to one of the city's top museums, the Art Institute of Chicago.

Exploring Chicago: What to See & Do Downtown

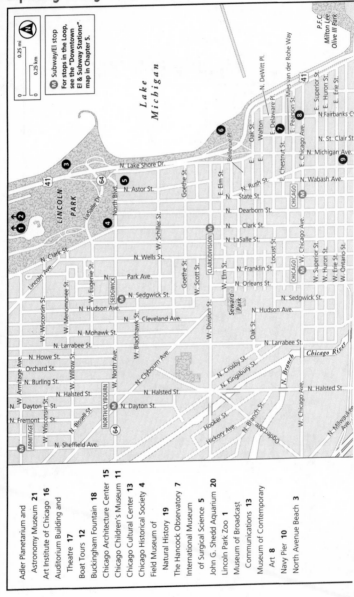

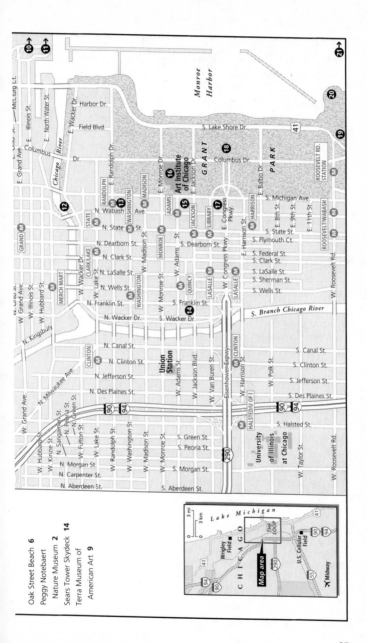

Oak Street Beach **6**
Peggy Notebaert
Nature Museum **2**
Sears Tower Skydeck **14**
Terra Museum of
American Art **9**

W. Grand Ave.
W. Hubbard St.
W. Illinois St.
W. Hubbard St.

N. Kingsbury

N. Milwaukee Ave.
W. Kinzie St.
N. Sangamon St.
N. Peoria St.
N. Green St.
W. Fulton St.

N. Morgan St.
N. Carpenter St.
N. Aberdeen St.

W. Grand Ave.
W. Lake St.
W. Randolph St.
W. Washington St.
W. Madison St.
W. Monroe St.

S. Green St.
S. Peoria St.

S. Morgan St.
S. Aberdeen St.

90 94

290

University
of Illinois
at Chicago

S. Halsted St.
W. Taylor St.
W. Roosevelt Rd.

S. Canal St.
S. Clinton St.
S. Jefferson St.
S. Des Plaines St.

90 94

W. Polk St.

S. Branch Chicago River

W. Harrison St.

W. Van Buren St.
W. Jackson Blvd.
W. Adams St.

Union
Station

N. Canal St.
N. Clinton St.
N. Jefferson St.
N. Des Plaines St.

CLINTON

Eisenhower-Expwy

HALSTED/U of I

CLINTON

N. Wacker Dr.
S. Wacker Dr.

MERCH MART

W. Wacker Dr.

CLARK/LAKE

WASHINGTON

QUINCY

LASALLE

LASALLE

N. Franklin St.
W. Franklin St.

N. Wells St.
N. LaSalle St.
N. Clark St.
N. Dearborn St.

S. Wells St.
S. Sherman St.
S. LaSalle St.
S. Clark St.
S. Federal St.
S. Plymouth Ct.
S. State St.

W. Congress Pkwy
E. Congress Pkwy

QUINCY

MONROE

W. Monroe St.
W. Adams St.

N. State St.
N. State

N. Wabash Ave.

STATE

GRAND

RANDOLPH

WASHINGTON

MADISON

MONROE

ADAMS

JACKSON

LIBRARY

HARRISON

ROOSEVELT/WABASH

ROOSEVELT RD.
STATION

W. Roosevelt Rd.

E. 8th St.
E. 9th St.
E. 11th St.

S. Michigan Ave.

E. Harrison St.

E. Balbo Dr.

E. Jackson Dr.
E. Congress Pkwy

E. Adams St.

E. Monroe Dr.

E. Randolph Dr.

E. Wacker Dr.

12
13
14
15
16
17
18
19
20
21

Art Institute
of Chicago

Columbus Dr.

S. Lake Shore Dr.

41

GRANT
PARK

Monroe
Harbor

Harbor Dr.
Field Blvd.

Columbus
Dr.

Chicago
River

E. Grand Ave.
E. Illinois St.
E. North Water St.
McClurg Ct.

10
11

Lake Michigan

0   3 mi
0   3 km

CHICAGO

Wrigley
Field

THE
LOOP

Map area

U.S. Cellular
Field

Midway

41

90

94

290

94

90

55

95

THE TOP ATTRACTIONS IN THE LOOP

Art Institute of Chicago ✮✮✮ *(Kids)*   You can't (and shouldn't)
miss the Art Institute: Choose a medium and a century and the Art
Institute has the works in its collection to captivate you: Japanese
ukiyo-e prints, ancient Egyptian bronzes and Greek vases, 19th-cen-
tury British photography, masterpieces by most of the greatest
names in 20th-century sculpture, or modern American textiles. For
a good general overview of the museum's collection, take the free
"Highlights of the Art Institute" tour, offered at 2pm on Saturdays,
Sundays, and Tuesdays.

If you've got limited time, you'll want to head straight to the
museum's renowned collection of **Impressionist art** ✮✮✮ (including one of the world's largest collections of Monet paintings); this is
one of the most popular areas of the museum, so arriving early pays
off. Among the treasures, you'll find Seurat's pointillist masterpiece
Sunday Afternoon on the Island of La Grande Jatte. Your second must-
see areas are the galleries of **European and American contemporary
art** ✮✮, ranging from paintings, sculptures, and mixed-media works
from Pablo Picasso, Henri Matisse, and Salvador Dalí through
Willem de Kooning, Jackson Pollock, and Andy Warhol. Visitors are
sometimes surprised when they discover many of the icons that
hang here. (Grant Wood's *American Gothic* and Edward Hopper's
Nighthawks are two that bring double takes from many visitors.)

The Art Institute goes the extra mile to entertain kids. The **Kraft
Education Center** on the lower level features interactive exhibits for
children and has a list of "gallery games" to make visiting the
museum more fun. When I was a kid, I was entranced by the
Thorne Miniature Rooms ✮, filled with tiny reproductions of furnished interiors from European and American history (heaven for a
dollhouse fanatic).

The museum also has a cafeteria and an elegant full-service
restaurant, a picturesque courtyard cafe (open June–Sept), and a
large shop. Allow 3 hours.

111 S. Michigan Ave. (at Adams St.). ✆ **312/443-3600.** www.artic.edu. Suggested
admission $10 adults; $6 seniors, children, and students with ID. Additional cost for
special exhibitions. Free admission Tues. Mon, Wed–Fri, and holidays 10:30am–
4:30pm; Tues 10:30am–8pm; Sat–Sun 10am–5pm. Closed Thanksgiving and Dec
25. Bus: No. 3, 4, 60, 145, 147, or 151. Subway/El: Green, Brown, Purple, or Orange
line to Adams, or Red Line to Monroe/State or Jackson/State.

Sears Tower Skydeck *(Overrated)*   First Sears sold the building and
moved to cheaper suburban offices in 1992. Then the skyscraper got

(Tips) Insider Tips for Touring the Art Institute

Many people don't realize the museum is open on Mondays; so keep this secret to yourself, and visit when the galleries are relatively subdued. Wednesdays are a close second. Tuesdays tend to draw the masses because the Art Institute is free that day and open late (until 8pm). Try to arrive when the doors open in the morning or else during the lunchtime lull. Another tip: If the Michigan Avenue entrance is crowded, head around to the entrance on the Columbus Drive side, which is usually less congested and is more convenient to the Grant Park underground parking garage. There's a small gift shop near the Columbus Drive entrance, too, if the main shop is too bustling.

an ego blow when the Petronas Towers in Kuala Lumpur, Malaysia, went up and laid claim to the title of world's tallest buildings. (The Sears Tower has since put up a 22-ft. antenna in an attempt to win back the title.) Tallest-building posturing aside, this is still a great place to orient yourself to the city, but I wouldn't put it on the top of must-see sights for anyone with limited time (and limited patience for crowds).

The view from the 103rd-floor Skydeck is everything you'd expect it to be—once you get there. Unfortunately, you're often stuck in a very long, very noisy line, so by the time you make it to the top, your patience could be as thin as the atmosphere up there. (Come in the late afternoon to avoid most of the crowds.) On a clear day, visibility extends up to 50 miles, and you can catch glimpses of four surrounding states. Despite the fact that it's called a "skydeck," you can't actually walk outside. Recent upgrades include multimedia exhibits on Chicago history and *Knee High Chicago,* an exhibit for kids. The 70-second high-speed elevator trip will feel like a thrill ride for some, but it's a nightmare for anyone with even mild claustrophobia. Allow 1 to 2 hours, depending on the length of the line.

233 S. Wacker Dr. (enter on Jackson Blvd.). © 312/875-9696. www.sears-tower. com. Admission $9.50 adults, $7.75 seniors, $6.75 children 3–12, free for children under 3 and military with active-duty ID. May–Sept daily 10am–10pm; Oct–April daily 10am–8pm. Bus: No. 1, 7, 126, 146, 151, or 156. Subway/El: Brown, Purple, or Orange line to Quincy, or Red or Blue line to Jackson; then walk a few blocks west.

THE LOOP SCULPTURE TOUR

Downtown Chicago is a veritable "museum without walls." Examples of public art—in the form of traditional monuments, murals, and monumental contemporary sculpture—are located widely throughout the city, but their concentration within the Loop and nearby Grant Park is worth noting. The best known of these works are by 20th-century artists, including Picasso, Chagall, Miró, Calder, Moore, and Oldenburg.

With the help of a very comprehensive booklet, *Loop Sculpture Guide* ($3.95 at the gift shop in the Chicago Cultural Center, 78 E. Washington St.), you can steer yourself through Grant Park and much of the Loop to view some 100 examples of Chicago's monumental public art. It provides locations and descriptions of 37 major works, including photographs, plus about 60 other nearby sites.

You also can conduct a self-guided tour of the city's public sculpture by following our "The Loop Sculpture Tour" map (p. 99).

The single-most-famous sculpture is **Pablo Picasso's** *Untitled,* located in Daley Plaza and constructed out of Cor-Ten steel, the same gracefully rusting material used on the exterior of the Daley Center behind it. Viewed from various perspectives, its enigmatic shape alternately suggests that of a woman, bird, or dog. Its installation in 1967 was met with hoots and heckles, but today "The Picasso" enjoys semiofficial status as the logo of modern Chicago.

GRANT PARK

Modeled after the gardens at Versailles, Grant Park is Chicago's front yard, composed of giant lawns segmented by *allées* of trees, plantings, and paths, and pieced together by major roadways and a network of railroad tracks. Covering the greens are a variety of public recreational and cultural facilities. Incredibly, the entire expanse was

Oprah in Person

Oprah Winfrey tapes her phenomenally successful talk show at Harpo Studios, 1058 W. Washington Blvd., just west of the Loop. If you'd like to be in her studio audience, you'll have to plan ahead: Reservations are taken by phone only (📞 312/591-9222), at least one month in advance.

The Loop Sculpture Tour

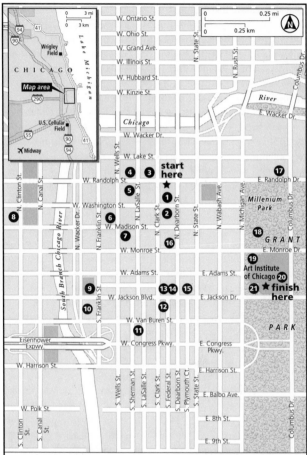

1 *Untitled ("The Picasso")*, Pablo Picasso (1967)
2 *Chicago*, Joan Miro (1981)
3 *Monument with Standing Beast*, Jean Dubuffet (1984)
4 *Freeform*, Richard Hunt (1993)
5 *Flight of Daedalus and Icarus*, 120 N. LaSalle St., Roger Brown (1990)
6 *Dawn Shadows*, Louise Nevelson (1983)
7 *Loomings and Knights and Squires*, Frank Stella
8 *Batcolumn*, Claes Oldenburg (1977)
9 *The Universe*, Alexander Calder (1974)
10 *Gem of the Lakes*, Raymond Kaskey (1990)
11 *San Marco II*, Ludovico de Luigi (1986)
12 *The Town-Ho's Story*, Frank Stella (1993)
13 *Ruins III*, Nita K. Sutherland (1978)
14 *Flamingo*, Alexander Calder (1974)
15 *Lines in Four Directions*, Sol Lewitt (1985)
16 *The Four Seasons*, Marc Chagall (1974)
17 *Untitled Sounding Sculpture*, Harry Bertoia (1975)
18 *Alexander Hamilton*, Bela Lyon Pratt (1918)
19 *Large Interior Form*, Henry Moore (1983)
20 *Celebration of the 200th Anniversary of the Founding of the Republic*, Isamu Noguchi (1976)
21 *The Fountain of the Great Lakes*, Lorado Taft (1913)

created from sandbars, landfill, and Chicago Fire debris; the original shoreline extended all the way to Michigan Avenue.

The immense **Buckingham Fountain,** accessible along Congress Parkway, is the baroque centerpiece of the park, composed of pink Georgia marble and patterned after—but twice the size of—the Latona Fountain at Versailles, with adjoining esplanades beautified by rose gardens in season. From April through October, the fountain spurts columns of water up to 150 feet in the air every hour on the hour; beginning at 4pm, a whirl of colored lights and dramatic music amps up the drama (the fountain shuts down at 11pm). Concession areas and bathrooms are available on the plaza.

The northwest corner of Grant Park (bordered by Michigan Ave. and Randolph St.) is the site of **Millennium Park,** one of the city's grandest recent public-works projects. Who cares that the park cost hundreds of millions more than it was supposed to, or the fact that it's finally opening a whole 4 years after the actual millennium? It's a winning combination of beautiful landscaping, elegant architecture (the classically inspired Peristyle), and public entertainment spaces (an ice rink, the music and dance theater). The park's centerpiece is the dramatic, Frank Gehry–designed **Music Pavilion,** featuring massive curved ribbons of steel. The Grant Park Symphony Orchestra and Chorus stages a popular series of free outdoor classical music concerts here most Wednesday through Sunday evenings in the summer. For a schedule of concert times and dates, contact the **Grant Park Music Festival** (© 312/742-7638).

Through the summer, Grant Park is taken over by a variety of music and food festivals. Annual events that draw big crowds include a blues music festival (in June) and a jazz festival (Labor Day). The **Taste of Chicago** (© 312/744-3315), purportedly the largest food festival in the world (the city estimates its annual attendance at around 3½ million), takes place every summer for 10 days around the July 4th holiday. Local restaurants serve up more ribs, pizza, hot dogs, and beer than you'd ever want to see, let alone eat. (See chapter 2 for a comprehensive listing of summer events in Grant Park.)

To get to Grant Park, take bus no. 3, 4, 6, 60, 146, or 151. If you want to take the subway or the El, get off at any stop in the Loop along State or Wabash, and walk east.

MORE ATTRACTIONS IN THE LOOP
ALONG SOUTH MICHIGAN AVENUE
The following attractions are listed from north to south.

Exploring Chicago: What to See & Do on South Michigan Avenue & in Grant Park

Adler Planetarium and Astronomy Museum **7**
Art Institute of Chicago **3**
Buckingham Fountain **4**
Chicago Cultural Center **1**
Field Museum of Natural History **6**
John G. Shedd Aquarium **5**
Millennium Park/ Music Pavilion **2**
National Vietnam Veterans Art Museum **8**

Chicago River
E. Wacker Dr.
N. Michigan Ave.
N. Wabash Ave.
Columbus Dr.
Field Blvd.
Harbor Dr.
STATE
State St.
RANDOLPH   E. Lake St.
1   E. Randolph Dr.
MILLENNIUM PARK
Richard J. Daley Bicentennial Plaza
E. Washington St.
WASHINGTON
WASHINGTON
2
E. Madison St.
MONROE
ADAMS   E. Monroe Dr.
E. Adams St.
JACKSON
3 Art Institute of Chicago
E. Jackson Dr.
Monroe Harbor
E. Van Buren St.   GRANT
Congress Pkwy.
4
E. Harrison St.
HARRISON
41
E. Balbo Ave.
E. 8th St.   PARK
Lake Shore Dr.
E. 9th St.
Columbus Dr.
E. 11th St.
ROOSEVELT
Roosevelt Dr.
Lake Michigan
S. Michigan Ave.
E. 13th St.   Roosevelt
Museum Campus **5**
Solidarity Dr.   **7**
6
Wm. McFetridge Dr.
E. 14th St.
S. State St.
S. Wabash Ave.
S. Indiana Ave.
Soldier Field
Burnham Harbor
S. Lake Shore Dr.
M Subway/El stop
E. 16th St.   E. Waldron Dr.
8
0   0.25 mi
0   0.25 km
N

0   3 mi
0   3 km
94   41
90   Wrigley Field
CHICAGO
Lake Michigan
Map area
290
U.S. Cellular Field
55   90   41
Midway   94

Chicago Cultural Center ★ *Finds*   Built in 1897 as the city's public library, and transformed into a showplace for visual and performing arts in 1991, the Chicago Cultural Center is an overlooked civic treasure. Its basic beaux arts exterior conceals a sumptuous interior of rare marble, fine hardwood, stained glass, polished brass, and mosaics of Favrile glass, colored stone, and mother-of-pearl inlaid in white marble. The crowning centerpiece is Preston Bradley Hall's majestic Tiffany dome, said to be the largest of its kind in the world.

The building also houses one of the Chicago Office of Tourism's visitor centers, which makes it an ideal place to kick-start your visit. If you stop in to pick up tourist information and take a quick look around, your visit won't take longer than half an hour. But the Cultural Center also hosts an array of art exhibitions, concerts, films, lectures, and other special events (many free), which might convince you to extend your time here.

Guided architectural tours of the Cultural Center are offered Wednesday, Friday, and Saturday at 1:15pm. For information, call © **312/744-8032.**

Allow a half-hour.

78 E. Washington St. © **312/744-6630,** or 312/FINE-ART for weekly events. Fax 312/744-2089. www.ci.chi.il.us/tour/culturalcenter. Free admission. Mon–Wed 10am–7pm; Thurs 10am–9pm; Fri 10am–6pm; Sat 10am–5pm; Sun 11am–5pm. Closed holidays. Bus: No. 3, 4, 20, 56, 60, 127, 131, 145, 146, 147, 151, or 157. Subway/El: Brown, Green, Orange, or Purple line to Randolph, or Red Line to Washington/State.

Chicago Architecture Center   Chicago's architecture is one of the city's main claims to fame, and a quick swing through this center will help you understand why. Run by the well-regarded Chicago Architecture Foundation, it's conveniently located across the street from the Art Institute. Still trying to figure out the difference between Prairie School and postmodern? Stop in here for a quick lesson. Exhibits include a scale model of downtown Chicago, profiles

---

Moments   **Photo Op**

For a great photo op, walk on Randolph Street toward the lake in the morning. That's when the sun, rising in the east over the lake, hits the cliff of buildings along South Michigan Avenue—giving you the perfect backdrop for an only-in-Chicago picture.

of the people and buildings that shaped the city's look, and a searchable database with pictures and information on many of Chicago's best-known skyscrapers. "Architecture ambassadors" are on hand to provide information on tours run by the foundation (see "Sightseeing Tours," p. 125). There's also an excellent gift shop filled with architecture-focused books, decorative accessories, and gifts. Allow a half-hour, more if you want to browse in the store.

224 S. Michigan Ave. (℡) **312/922-3432**. www.architecture.org. Free admission. Daily 9:30am–5pm. Bus: No. 3, 4, 60, 145, 147, or 151. Subway/El: Brown, Green, Purple, or Orange line to Adams, or Red Line to Jackson.

Auditorium Building and Theatre ✶✶   A truly grand theater with historic landmark status, the Auditorium is worth a visit to experience late-19th-century Chicago opulence. Designed and built in 1889 by Louis Sullivan and Dankmar Adler, the Auditorium was a wonder of the world: the heaviest (110,000 tons) and most massive modern edifice on earth. It was also the first large-scale building to be electrically lighted, and its theater was the first in the country to install air-conditioning.

The 4,000-seat theater, which today is the scene for Broadway touring musicals, is a marvel of visionary design and engineering. Originally the home of the Chicago Opera Company, Sullivan and Adler's masterpiece is defined by powerful arches lit by thousands of bulbs and features Sullivan's trademark ornamentation—in this case, elaborate golden stenciling and gold plaster medallions. It's equally renowned for otherworldly acoustics and unobstructed sight lines.

Don't miss the lobby fronting Michigan Avenue, with its faux ornamental marble columns, molded ceilings, mosaic floors, and Mexican onyx walls. Another inside tip: Take the elevator to the 10th-floor and have a look at what was once the city's first top-floor dining room. Its palatial, barrel-vaulted ceiling, and marvelous views of Grant Park and the lake will make you want to brush up on your Dewey Decimal System.

The best way to see everything is to take a 1-hour guided tour, offered on Mondays between 10am and 4pm (call (℡) **312/431-2354** to make reservations). Tours cost $6 for adults, $3 for seniors and students.

Allow a half-hour, 1 hour if you take the guided tour.

50 E. Congress Pkwy. (℡) **312/922-2110**. www.auditoriumtheatre.org. For ticket reservations or box-office information, call Ticketmaster at (℡) 312/902-1500. Bus: No. 145, 147, or 151. Subway/El: Brown, Green, Orange, or Purple line to Library/ Van Buren, or Red Line to Jackson.

(Value) Museum Free Days

Plan your time in Chicago carefully and you can save yourself admission fees to some of the city's major museums.
However, keep in mind that you will still have to pay for
special exhibitions and films on free days.

Monday: Adler Planetarium (Sept–Feb only), Field Museum
of Natural History (Sept–Feb only), Museum of Science and
Industry (Sept–Feb only), Shedd Aquarium (Sept–Feb,
Oceanarium admission extra)

Tuesday: Adler Planetarium (Sept–Feb only), Art Institute
of Chicago, Field Museum of Natural History (Sept–Feb
only), International Museum of Surgical Science, Museum
of Contemporary Art, Museum of Science and Industry
(Sept–Feb only), Terra Museum of American Art, Shedd
Aquarium (Sept–Feb, Oceanarium admission extra)

Thursday: DuSable Museum of African-American History,
Chicago Children's Museum (5–8pm only), Terra Museum
of American Art

Friday: Spertus Museum

Always Free: Chicago Cultural Center, Garfield Park Con-
servatory, David and Alfred Smart Museum of Art, Jane
Addams Hull-House Museum, Lincoln Park Conservatory,
Lincoln Park Zoo, Martin D'Arcy Gallery of Art, Mexican
Fine Arts Center Museum, Museum of Contemporary Pho-
tography, Newberry Library

2 The Earth, the Sky & the Sea: The Big Three in the Grant Park Museum Campus

With terraced gardens and broad walkways, the Museum Campus
at the southern end of Grant Park makes it easy for pedestrians to
visit three of the city's most beloved institutions: our natural history
museum, aquarium, and planetarium. The campus is about a 15- to
20-minute walk from the Loop, and is easily reached by bus or subway (a trolley runs from the Roosevelt Rd. El stop). To get to the
Museum Campus from the Loop, head east across Grant Park on
East Balbo Drive from South Michigan Avenue, and then trek south

along the lakeshore path to the museums. Or, you can make your approach on the path that begins at 11th Street from South Michigan Avenue. Follow 11th to the walkway that spans the Metra tracks. Cross Columbus Drive and then pick up the path that will take you under Lake Shore Drive and into the Museum Campus. The CTA no. 146 bus will take you from downtown to all three of these attractions. Call ℃ **836-7000** (from any city or suburban area code) for the stop locations and schedule.

Adler Planetarium and Astronomy Museum ✮✮   The don't miss experience here is the **StarRider Theater** ✮✮, which takes you on an interactive virtual-reality trip through the Milky Way and into deep space, featuring a computer-generated 3D-graphics projection system and controls in the armrest of each person's seat. Six high-resolution video projectors form a seamless image on the domed ceiling—you'll feel like you're literally floating in space. If you're looking for more entertainment, the **Sky Theater** shows movies with an astronomical bent (*Skywatchers of Africa* looks at the way different African cultures have interpreted the sky, and *Images of the Infinite* highlights discoveries from the Hubble Telescope). The planetarium's exhibit galleries feature a variety of displays and interactive activities designed to foster understanding of our solar system and more. The best current exhibit is ***Bringing the Heavens to Earth*** ✮, which traces the ways different cultures have tried to make sense of astronomical phenomena.

Allow 2 hours, more if you want to see more than one show.

Value **Museums for Less**

If you're planning on visiting lots of Chicago museums, you should invest in a CityPass, a prepaid ticket that gets you into the biggest attractions (The Art Institute, Field Museum of Natural History, Shedd Aquarium, Adler Planetarium, Museum of Science and Industry, and Hancock Observatory). The cost at press time was $49 for adults and $38 for children, which is about 50% cheaper than paying all the museums' individual admission fees. You can buy a CityPass at any of the museums listed above, or purchase one online before you get to town (www.citypass.net). Also, see the "Museum Free Days" box, above, for schedules of when some of these museums are free.

1300 S. Lake Shore Dr. ℂ **312/922-STAR.** Fax 312/922-2257. www.adler planetarium.org. Admission (including 1 show) $13 adults, $12 seniors, $11 children 4–17, free for children under 4. Free admission Mon and Tues Sept–Feb only. Mon–Fri 9:30am–4:30pm, Sat–Sun 9am–4:30pm; from June 1–Sept 1 Sat–Wed until 6pm and Thurs–Fri until 9pm; 1st Fri of every month until 10 pm. StarRider Theater and Sky Shows at numerous times throughout the day; call ℂ 312/922-STAR for current times. Bus: No. 12, 127, or 146.

Field Museum of Natural History 𝒌𝒌𝒌 *Kids*   Is it any wonder that Steven Spielberg thought the Field Museum of Natural History suitable home turf for the intrepid archaeologist and adventurer hero of his *Indiana Jones* movies? Spread over the museum's 9 acres of floor space are scores of permanent and temporary exhibitions—some interactive, but most requiring the old-fashioned skills of observation and imagination.

You'll start out in the grand Stanley Field Hall, which you enter from either the north or south end. Standing proudly at the north side is the largest, most complete *Tyrannosaurus rex* fossil ever unearthed. Named **Sue** 𝒌𝒌𝒌 for the paleontologist who found the dinosaur in 1990 in South Dakota, the specimen was acquired by the museum for a cool $8.4 million following a high-stakes bidding war. The real skull is so heavy that a lighter copy had to be mounted on the skeleton; the actual one is displayed nearby.

Families should head downstairs for two of the most popular kid-friendly exhibits. The pieces on display in *Inside Ancient Egypt* 𝒌𝒌 were brought to the museum in the early 1900s. Visitors can explore aspects of the day-to-day world of ancient Egypt, viewing 23 actual mummies and realistic burial scenes, a living marsh environment and canal works, the ancient royal barge, a religious shrine, and a reproduction of a typical marketplace of the period. Many of the exhibits allow hands-on interaction, and there are special activities for kids, such as making parchment from living papyrus plants.

Next to the Egypt exhibit, you'll find *Underground Adventure* 𝒌𝒌, a "total immersion environment" populated by giant robotic earwigs, centipedes, wolf spiders, and other subterranean critters. The Disneyesque exhibit is a big hit with kids, but—annoyingly—requires an extra admission charge ($5 on top of regular admission for adults, $2 for kids).

You might be tempted to skip the "peoples of the world" exhibits, but, trust me—some are not only mind-opening, but they're also great fun. *Traveling the Pacific* 𝒌 is hidden up on the second floor, but it's definitely worth a stop. Hundreds of artifacts from the museum's oceanic collection re-create scenes of island life in the

South Pacific (there's even a full-scale model of a Maori meeting house). *Africa* 𝕂, an assemblage of African artifacts and provocative, interactive multimedia presentations, takes viewers to Senegal, to a Cameroon palace, to the savanna and its wildlife, and on a "virtual" journey aboard a slave ship to the Americas.

The museum hosts special traveling exhibits (recent blockbusters included shows on Cleopatra and the jewels of Russia), as well as numerous lectures, book signings, multiethnic musical and dance performances, storytelling events, and family activity days throughout the year. The Corner Bakery cafe, located just off the main hall, is a cut above the usual museum victuals (to avoid the lunchtime lines, pick up one of the premade salads or sandwiches and head for the cash register). Families also flock to the McDonald's on the lower level. Allow 3 hours.

Roosevelt Rd. and Lake Shore Dr. ℂ **312/922-9410** or 312/341-9299 TDD (for hearing-impaired callers). www.fmnh.org. Admission $10 adults; $7 seniors, children 3–11, and students with ID; free for teachers, armed-forces personnel in uniform, and children 2 and under. Free admission mid-Sept to Feb. Daily 9am–5pm. Open Thurs to 8pm June 17–Aug 26. Closed Dec 25 and Jan 1. Bus: No. 6, 10, 12, 130, or 146.

John G. Shedd Aquarium 𝕂𝕂𝕂   The Shedd is a city treasure and well deserving of its title as world's largest indoor aquarium. A mix of standard aquarium tanks and elaborate new habitats, this marble octagon building is filled with thousands of denizens of river, lake, and sea. The only problem with the Shedd is its steep admission price. You can keep your costs down by buying the "Aquarium Only" admission, but then you'll be missing some of the most stunning exhibits.

The first thing you'll see as you enter is the **Caribbean Coral Reef** 𝕂. This 90,000-gallon circular tank occupies the beaux arts–style central rotunda, entertaining spectators who press up against the glass to ogle divers feeding nurse sharks, barracudas, stingrays, and a hawksbill sea turtle.

The exhibits surrounding the Caribbean coral reef re-create different marine habitats around the world. The best is *Amazon Rising: Seasons of the River* 𝕂, a recreation of the Amazon basin that showcases far more than fish (although you'll get to see some sharp-toothed piranhas as well).

You'll pay extra to see the other Shedd highlights, but they're quite impressive, so I'd suggest shelling out for at least one. The *Oceanarium* 𝕂𝕂𝕂, with a wall of windows revealing the lake outside, re-creates a Pacific Northwest coastal environment and creates a stunning optical illusion of one uninterrupted expanse of sea. On a fixed performance schedule in a large pool flanked by an amphitheater, a crew of friendly trainers puts dolphins through their paces of leaping dives, breaches, and tail walking. Check out the Oceanarium schedule as soon as you get to the Shedd; seating space fills up quickly for the shows, so you'll want to get there early. If you're visiting during a summer weekend, you may also want to buy your Oceanarium ticket in advance to made sure you can catch a show that day. The newest signature exhibit is **Wild Reef—Sharks at Shedd** 𝕽𝕽, a series of 26 interconnected habitats that house a Philippine coral reef patrolled by sharks and other predators. The floor-to-ceiling windows bring those toothy swimmers up close and personal (they even swim over your head at certain spots).

Allow 2 to 3 hours.

1200 S. Lake Shore Dr. ℭ **312/939-2438**. www.sheddaquarium.org. All-Access Pass (to all exhibits) $21 adults, $15 seniors and children 3–11; admission to aquarium and either *Oceanarium* or *Wild Reef,* $17 adults, $13 seniors and children 3–11; aquarium only $8 adults, $6 children and seniors. Free admission to aquarium Mon and Tues Oct–Feb. Summer Fri–Wed 9am–6pm, Thurs 9am–10pm; fall–spring Mon–Fri 9am–5pm, Sat–Sun 9am–6pm. Bus: No. 6, 10, 12, 130, or 146.

3 North of the Loop: The Magnificent Mile & Beyond

North of the Chicago River are a number of attractions you should not overlook. Most of these sites are either on the Magnificent Mile (North Michigan Ave.) and its surrounding blocks or not too far from there, on the Near North Side.

The Hancock Observatory 𝕽𝕽   While not as famous as the Sears Tower, for many locals the Hancock remains the archetypal Chicago skyscraper, with its bold, tapered shape and exterior steel cross-bracing design. The Hancock Observatory delivers an excellent panorama of the city and an intimate view over nearby Lake Michigan and the various shoreline residential areas. The view from the top of Chicago's third-tallest building is enough to satisfy, but some high-tech additions to the experience include "talking telescopes" with sound effects and narration in four languages, history walls illustrating the growth of the city, and the Skywalk open-air viewing deck—a "screened porch" that allows visitors to feel the rush of the wind at 1,000 feet. The view up the North Side is particularly dramatic, stretching from the nearby Oak Street and North Avenue beaches, along the green strip of Lincoln Park, to the line of high-rises you can trace up the shoreline until they suddenly halt just below the boundary of the northern suburbs. A high-speed elevator carries passengers to the observatory in 40 seconds, and the entrance and observatory are accessible for people with disabilities. Allow 1 hour.

"Big John," as it's referred to by some locals, also has a sleek restaurant, the Signature Room at the 95th, with an adjoining lounge. For about the same cost as the observatory, you can take in the views from the latter with a libation in hand.

94th floor of the John Hancock Center, 875 N. Michigan Ave. (enter on Delaware St.). ℂ 888/875-VIEW or 312/751-3681. Fax 312/751-3675. www.hancock-observatory. com. Admission $9.75 adults, $7.75 seniors, $6 children 5–12, free for children under 4 and military personnel in uniform or with active-duty cards. Daily 9am–11pm. Bus: No. 125, 145, 146, 147, or 151. Subway/El: Red Line to Chicago/State.

Museum of Contemporary Art ⭐⭐   Sitting on a front-row piece of property between the lake and the historic Water Tower, this gloomy, imposing building (designed by Berlin's Josef Paul Kleihues) looks like something out of Communist Russia, but the interior spaces are more vibrant, with a sun-drenched two-story central corridor, elliptical staircases, and three floors of exhibition space. The MCA has tried to raise its national profile to the level of New York's Museum of Modern Art by hosting major touring retrospectives of working artists such as Cindy Sherman and Chuck Close.

You can see the MCA's highlights in about an hour, although art lovers will want more time to wander (especially if a high-profile exhibit is in town). Your first stop should be the handsome barrel-vaulted galleries on the top floor, dedicated to pieces from the permanent collection. For visitors who'd like a little guidance for making sense of the rather challenging works found here, there is an audio tour for rent as well as a free tour (1 and 6pm Tues; 1pm Wed–Fri; 11am, noon, 1, and 2pm Sat–Sun). In addition to a range of special activities and educational programming, including films, performances, and a lecture series in a 300-seat theater, the museum features Puck's at the MCA, a cafe operated by Wolfgang Puck of Spago restaurant fame, with seating that overlooks a 1-acre terraced sculpture garden. There's also a store, Culturecounter, with one-of-a-kind gift items, that's worth a stop even if you don't make it into the museum. Allow 1 to 2 hours.

220 E. Chicago Ave. (1 block east of Michigan Ave.). ℂ 312/280-2660. Fax 312/ 397-4095. www.mcachicago.org. Admission $10 adults, $6 seniors and students with ID, free for children under 12. Free admission on Tues. Tues 10am–8pm; Wed–Sun 10am–5pm. Bus: No. 3, 10, 11, 66, 125, 145, 146, or 151. Subway/El: Red Line to Chicago/State.

Navy Pier ⋆ *Kids*   Built during World War I, this 3,000-foot-long pier was used by the Navy during World War II as a training center for pilots. But any military aura is long gone, now that the place has been transformed into a bustling tourist mecca. A combination of carnival, food court, and boat dock, the pier makes a fun place to stroll (if you don't mind crowds), but you'll have to walk all the way to the end to get the best views back to the city.

Midway down the pier are the Crystal Gardens, with 70 full-size palm trees, dancing fountains, and other flora in a glass-enclosed atrium; a white-canopied open-air Skyline Stage that hosts concerts, dance performances, and film screenings; a carousel; and a 15-story Ferris wheel that's a replica of the original that debuted at Chicago's 1893 World's Fair. The 50 acres of pier and lakefront property also are home to the **Chicago Children's Museum** (p. 124), a **3D IMAX theater** (𝄐 312/595-5629), a small ice-skating rink, and the **Chicago Shakespeare Theatre** (p. 156). The shops tend to be bland and touristy (except for independently owned Barbara's Bookstore [p. 146]). Summer is one long party at the pier, with fireworks on Wednesday and Saturday evenings.

If the commercialism of the place becomes too much for you, take the half-mile stroll to the end of the pier, east of the ballroom, where you can find a little respite and enjoy the wind, the waves, and the city view, which is the real delight of a place like this. Or unwind in **Olive Park,** a small sylvan haven with a sliver of beach that lies just to the north of Navy Pier.

You'll find, moored along the south dock, more than half a dozen different sailing vessels, including a couple of dinner cruise ships, the pristine white-masted tall ship *Windy,* and the 70-foot speedboats *Seadog I, II,* and *III.* In the summer months, water taxis speed between Navy Pier and other Chicago sights. For more specifics on sightseeing and dinner cruises, see "Lake & River Cruises" on p. 126.

Allow 1 hour.

600 E. Grand Ave. (at Lake Michigan). 𝄐 **800/595-PIER** (outside 312 area code), or 312/595-PIER. www.navypier.com. Free admission. Summer Sun–Thurs 10am–10pm, Fri–Sat 10am–midnight; fall–spring Mon–Sat 10am–10pm, Sun 10am–7pm. Bus: No. 29, 56, 65, 66, 120, or 121. Parking: Rates start at $9.50 for the 1st hr. and go up to $17.50 for up to 8 hr. However, the lots fill quickly. Valet parking is $7 with a restaurant validation. There are also surface lots west of the pier, and free trolley buses make stops on Grand Ave. and Illinois St. from State St. Subway/El: Red Line to Grand/State; transfer to city bus or board a free pier trolley bus.

Terra Museum of American Art 🍀 *(finds)*   The core of the Terra's holdings was originally the private collection of Daniel Terra, a wealthy industrialist and rainmaker for Ronald Reagan who founded his eponymous museum in north-suburban Evanston in 1980. Moved to the present location in 1987, its excellent collection has grown to include some 700 pieces of American art from the late 18th century to the present. The museum is particularly known for its outstanding American Impressionism collection. And, from time to time, the Terra can bowl you over with a truly stellar traveling exhibition, so it's worth checking out the museum's website before you come to town. Allow 1 hour.

664 N. Michigan Ave. (near Erie St.). © **312/664-3939.** Fax 312/664-2052. www. terramuseum.org. Admission $5 adults; $3.50 seniors, students, educators; free for children under 12 and veterans with valid ID. Free admission on Tues, Thurs, and 1st Sun of each month. Tues 10am–8pm; Wed–Sat 10am–6pm; Sun noon–5pm. Bus: No. 3, 11, 125, 145, 146, 147, or 151. Subway/El: Red Line to Grand/State or Chicago/State.

4 Lincoln Park Attractions

Lincoln Park is the city's largest park, and certainly one of the longest. Straight and narrow, Lincoln Park begins at North Avenue and follows the shoreline of Lake Michigan northward for several miles. Within its elongated 1,200 acres are a world-class zoo, a half-dozen bathing beaches, two excellent museums, and the usual meadows, formal gardens, sporting fields, and tennis courts typical of urban parks. To get to the park, take bus no. 22, 145, 146, 147, 151, or 156.

Chicago Historical Society 🍀   At the southwestern tip of Lincoln Park stands one of Chicago's oldest cultural institutions (founded in 1856). Inside the Historical Society's lovely redbrick and glass-walled building, you'll find well-designed displays of significant objects, artifacts, and artwork—but the overall effect is instructive rather than interactive (this isn't the place to bring young children).

Casual visitors can get a good overview of the highlights in about an hour; history buffs will need more time. The must-see permanent exhibit is *A House Divided: America in the Age of Lincoln* 🍀🍀, which explores the institution of slavery in America and the devastation of the Civil War (items on display include the bed that Lincoln died in and an original copy of the 13th amendment abolishing slavery, signed by Honest Abe himself). Another highlight is the

CHS's **costume collection** 🔎, which includes clothing worn by George Washington, John Adams, and, of more current vintage, one of Michael Jordan's uniforms, along with numerous gowns by contemporary fashion designers (pieces from the collection are displayed on a rotating basis). Another worthy stop is *We the People,* a permanent exhibit that explores how "ordinary people" founded the United States.

The museum's website is worth checking out before your visit, especially the impressive online "exhibit" on the Great Chicago Fire. Allow 1 to 2 hours.

1601 N. Clark St. (at North Ave.). ⓒ **312/642-4600.** www.chicagohistory.org. Admission $5 adults, $3 seniors and students, $1 children 6–12, free for children under 6. Free admission on Mon. Mon–Sat 9:30am–4:30pm; Sun 12–5pm. Research center Tues–Sat 10am–4:30pm. Bus: No. 11, 22, 36, 72, 151, or 156.

Lincoln Park Zoo 🔎🔎🔎 *Value* This is one of Chicago's don't-miss attractions (especially if the weather is decent), and because it's free, it's worth at least a quick stop during a stroll through Lincoln Park. But you'll probably want to wander for a while. The term "zoological gardens" truly fits here: Landmark Georgian Revival brick buildings and modern structures sit among gently rolling pathways, verdant lawns, and a kaleidoscopic profusion of flower gardens.

The zoo has taken on an ambitious modernization campaign, which is good news for animal lovers. While many zoo residents used to wander listlessly in stark concrete pens, exhibits have been renovated and expanded to reflect natural habitats. For years, the zoo's star attraction has been the **Great Ape House** 🔎🔎🔎, which will reopen in the summer of 2004 after a complete renovation. Lincoln Park Zoo has had remarkable success breeding gorillas and chimpanzees, and watching these ape families interact can be mesmerizing (and touching). The new **Regenstein African Journey** 🔎🔎 is home to elephants, giraffes, rhinos, and other large mammals; large glass-enclosed tanks allow visitors to go face-to-face with swimming pygmy hippos and (not for the faint of heart) a rocky ledge filled with Madagascar hissing cockroaches.

The **Small Mammal–Reptile House** is a state-of-the-art facility, housing 200 species and featuring a glass-enclosed walk-through ecosystem simulating river, savanna, and forest habitats. The popular **Sea Lion Pool,** situated in the center of the zoo and home to harbor seals, gray seals, and California sea lions, features an underwater viewing area spanning 70 feet and an updated amphitheater.

Allow 2 to 3 hours. For the adjoining children's zoo, see "Kid Stuff," on p. 124.

2200 N. Cannon Dr. (at Fullerton Pkwy.). ℭ **312/742-2000.** www.lpzoo.com. Free admission. Year-round Mon–Fri 10am–5pm, grounds open at 9am; fall–spring Sat–Sun 10am–6:30pm. Bus: No. 151 or 156. Free trolley service from area CTA stations and parking garages on Sat–Sun and holidays 11am–7pm.

Peggy Notebaert Nature Museum 𝒦 *Kids*   Built into the rise of an ancient sand dune—once the shoreline of Lake Michigan—Chicago's newest museum bills itself as "an environmental museum for the 21st century." Throughout, the focus is on interactivity, making this a good stop for active kids.

Inside, large windows create a dialogue between the outdoor environment and the indoor exhibits designed to illuminate it. Don't miss the **Butterfly Haven** 𝒦𝒦, a greenhouse habitat where about 25 Midwestern species of butterflies and moths carry on their complex life cycles (wander through as a riot of color flutters all around you). Another top exhibit is **City Science** 𝒦, a 3,000-square-foot, two-story "house" with functional rooms where visitors can view the pipes and ducts that connect our homes with power sources miles away. **Water Lab** is a model river system demonstrating the uses and abuses that a waterway undergoes as it meanders from rural to urban environments. It's probably safe to say that the **Children's Gallery** is the only place in town where kids can clamber in and out of a model ground-squirrel town or explore a beaver lodge from the inside.

Allow 1 hour.

Fullerton Ave. and Cannon Dr. ℭ **773/871-2668.** www.chias.org. Admission $7 adults, $5 seniors and students, $4 children ages 3–12, free for children under 3. Mon–Fri 9am–4:30pm; Sat–Sun 10am–5pm. Closed Thanksgiving, Dec 25, and Jan 1. Bus: No. 151 or 156.

5 Exploring Hyde Park: The Museum of Science and Industry & More

Birthplace of atomic fission, home to the University of Chicago, and site of the popular Museum of Science and Industry, Hyde Park is worth a trip south of the Loop. You should allow at least half a day to explore the campus and neighborhood, one of Chicago's most successfully integrated; set aside a full day if you want to explore museums as well.

GETTING THERE   From the Loop, the ride to Hyde Park on the **no. 6 Jeffrey Express bus** takes about 30 minutes. The bus originates on Wacker Drive, travels south along State Street, and ultimately follows Lake Shore Drive to Hyde Park. The bus runs from early morning to late evening 7 days a week, with departures about every 5 minutes on weekdays and every 10 minutes on weekends and holidays. The southbound express bus adds a surcharge of 25¢ to the normal fare of $1.50 (there's no surcharge if you use a CTA transit card). The **no. 1 local bus** originates at Union Station on Jackson Boulevard and Canal Street and takes about an hour.

For a faster trip, take the **Metra Electric train** on the South Chicago line, which goes from downtown to Hyde Park in about 15 minutes. Trains run every hour (more frequently during rush hr.) Monday through Saturday from 5:15am to 12:50am, and every 30 to 90 minutes on Sunday and holidays from 5am to 12:55am. Downtown stations are at Randolph Street and Michigan Avenue, Van Buren Street and Michigan Avenue, and Roosevelt Road and Michigan Avenue (near the Museum Campus in Grant Park). Printed schedules are available at the stations. The fare is approximately $2 each way.

For CTA bus and Metra train information, call © **836-7000** (from any city or suburban area code).

For taxis, dial © **312/TAXI-CAB** (© 312/829-4222) for **Yellow Cab** or © **312/CHECKER** (© 312/243-2537) for **Checker.** The one-way fare from downtown is around $15.

THE TOP ATTRACTIONS
The Museum of Science and Industry ☆☆☆ *(Kids)*   The massive Museum of Science and Industry is the granddaddy of interactive museums, with some 2,000 exhibits. You should plan on spending at least a couple of hours here, and a comprehensive visit can take all day, especially if you catch an Omnimax movie while you're here. Although it's quite a distance from the rest of Chicago's tourist attractions, it's easy enough to get here without a car; your best options are the no. 6 Jeffrey Express bus or the Metra Electric train from downtown (the no. 10 bus runs from downtown to the museum's front entrance during the summer).

While the museum is constantly adding new exhibits to cover the latest scientific breakthroughs, you shouldn't miss certain tried-and-true exhibits that have been here for years and epitomize the museum for Chicagoans. The **U-505** ☆☆☆, a German submarine that was captured in 1944 and brought to the museum 10 years later, brings home the claustrophobic reality of underwater naval life. The full-scale **Coal Mine** ☆☆, which dates back to 1934, now incorporates modern mining techniques into the exhibit—but the best part is the simulated trip down into a dark, mysterious mine.

Get to these exhibits quickly after the museum opens because they attract amusement-park-length lines during the day.

Kids who love planes, trains, and automobiles shouldn't miss *All Aboard the Silver Streak,* a refurbished Burlington Pioneer Zephyr train with on-board interactive exhibits; the massive model train exhibit that makes up *The Great Train Story;* or *Take Flight,* an aviation exhibit featuring a full-size 727 airplane that revs up its engines and replays the voice recordings from a San Francisco–Chicago flight periodically throughout the day. Well-designed educational exhibits include *AIDS: The War Within* (which was the 1st permanent museum exhibit on the immune system and HIV) and *Reusable City,* which teaches children ecological tips with implements that they might find in their own backyard.

And, not to be sexist, but girls (myself included) love **Colleen Moore's Fairy Castle** ⟨⟩, a lavishly decorated miniature palace filled with priceless treasures (yes, those are real diamonds and pearls in the chandeliers).

A major newer addition to the museum is the **Henry Crown Space Center** ⟨⟩⟨⟩, where the story of space exploration is documented in copious detail, highlighted by a simulated space-shuttle experience through sight and sound at the center's five-story Omnimax Theater. The theater offers double features on the weekends; call for show times.

Allow 3 hours.

57th St. and Lake Shore Dr. ⓒ **800/468-6674** outside the Chicago area, 773/684-1414, or TTY 773/684-3323. www.msichicago.org. Admission to museum only, $9 adults, $7.50 seniors, $5 children 3–11, free for children under 3. Free admission Mon and Tues Sept 15–Nov 25 and Jan–Feb. Combination museum and Omnimax Theater $15 adults, $12.50 seniors, $10 children 3–11, free for children under 3 on an adult's lap. Omnimax Theater only, evening shows $10 adults, $8 seniors, $6 children, free for children under 3 on an adult's lap. Mon–Sat 9:30am–4pm; Sun 11am–4pm. Closed Christmas. Bus: No. 6, 10, 55, 151, or 156.

Oriental Institute Museum ⟨⟩⟨⟩ *(Finds)*   The Oriental Institute houses one of the world's major collections of Near Eastern art. Your first stop should be the **Egyptian Gallery** ⟨⟩⟨⟩, which showcases the finest objects among the 35,000 artifacts from the Nile Valley held by the museum. At the center stands a monumental 17-foot solid-quartzite statue of King Tutankhamen. The surrounding exhibits have a wonderfully accessible approach that emphasizes themes, not chronology. Among them are: mummification (there are 14 mummies on display—five people and nine animals, including hawks, an ibis, a shrew, and a baby crocodile), kingship, society, and writing (including a deed for the sale of a house, a copy of the *Book of the Dead,* and a schoolboy's homework).

The Oriental Institute also houses the nation's premier archaeological collection of artifacts from civilizations that once flourished in what is now Iran on display in the **Persian Gallery** 🔎. Other galleries are filled with artifacts from Sumer, ancient Palestine, Israel, Anatolia, Nubia, and Mesopotamia (including a re-creation of a royal courtyard of Assyrian King Sargon II).

The excellent gift shop, called the Suq, stocks many one-of-a-kind items, including reproductions of pieces in the museum's collection. Allow 2 hours.

1155 E. 58th St. (at University Ave.). ✆ **773/702-9514.** www.oi.uchicago.edu. Free admission; suggested donation $5 adults, $2 children. Tues and Thurs–Sat 10am–4pm; Wed 10am–8:30pm; Sun noon–4pm. Bus: No. 6.

Robie House 🔎🔎   One of Frank Lloyd Wright's finest works, the Robie House is considered among the masterpieces of 20th-century American architecture. The open layout, linear geometry of form, and craftsmanship are typical of Wright's Prairie School design. Completed in 1909 for inventor Frederick Robie, a bicycle and motorcycle manufacturer, the home is also notable for its exquisite leaded- and stained-glass doors and windows. Docents from Oak Park's Frank Lloyd Wright Home and Studio Foundation lead tours here, even though the house is undergoing a massive, 10-year restoration (the house will be open throughout the process, but your photos may include plenty of scaffolding). A Wright specialty bookshop is located in the building's former three-car garage—which was highly unusual for the time in which it was built. Allow 2 hours.

5757 S. Woodlawn Ave. (at 58th St.). ✆ **773/834-1847.** Admission $9 adults, $7 seniors and children 7–18. Mon–Fri tours at 11am, 1pm, and 3pm; Sat–Sun every half-hr. 11am–3:30pm. Bookshop open daily 10am–5pm. Bus: No. 6.

EXPLORING THE UNIVERSITY OF CHICAGO

Walking around the Gothic spires of the University of Chicago campus is bound to conjure up images of the cloistered academic life. Allow at least an hour to stroll through the grassy quads and dramatic stone buildings. If you're visiting on a weekday, your first stop should be the university's **Visitors Information Desk** (✆ **773/702-9739**), located on the first floor of Ida Noyes Hall, 1212 E. 59th St., where you can pick up campus maps and get information on university events. The center is open Monday through Friday from 10am to 7pm. The university also offers free architecture tours on Saturdays (paid tours can be arranged for other days); call the **Office** of Special Events ((C) 773/702-9636). If you stop by on a weekend when the Visitors Information Desk is closed, you can get the scoop on campus events at the **Reynolds Clubhouse** student center ((C) 773/702-8787).

Start your tour of the campus at the **Henry Moore statue, *Nuclear Energy,*** on South Ellis Avenue between 56th and 57th streets. It's next to the Regenstein Library, which marks the site of the old Stagg Field, where, on December 2, 1942, the world's first sustained nuclear reaction was achieved in a basement laboratory below the field. Then turn left at 57th Street until you reach the grand stone Hull Gate; walk straight to reach the main quad, or turn left through the column-lined arcade to reach **Hutchinson Court** (designed by John Olmsted, son of revered landscape designer Frederick Law Olmsted). The Reynolds Clubhouse, the university's main student center, is located here; you can take a break at the C-Shop cafe or settle down at a table at Hutchinson Commons, a dining room/hangout spot right next to the cafe which will bring to mind the grand dining halls of Oxford or Cambridge.

Other worthy spots on campus include the charming, intimate **Bond Chapel,** located behind Swift Hall on the main quad, and the blocks-long **Midway Plaisance,** a wide stretch of green that was the site of carnival sideshow attractions during the World's Columbian Exposition in 1893 (the term "midway" has been used ever since to refer to carnivals in general).

The **Seminary Co-op Bookstore,** 5757 S. University Ave. ((C) 773/752-4381; www.semcoop.com), is a treasure trove of academic and scholarly books. Its selection of more than 100,000 titles has won it an international reputation as "the best bookstore west of Blackwell's in Oxford." It's open Monday through Friday from 8:30am to 9pm, Saturday from 10am to 6pm, and Sunday from noon to 6pm.

6 More Museums

Chicago has a slew of smaller museums devoted to all manner of subjects. Many of their collections preserve the stories and heritage of a particular immigrant group that has become inseparable from the history of the city as a whole.

Historic Pullman   Railway magnate George Pullman may have been a fabulously wealthy industrialist, but he fancied himself more enlightened than his 19th-century peers. So when it came time to build a new headquarters for his Pullman Palace Car Company, he dreamed of something far more than the standard factory surrounded by tenements. Instead, he built a model community for his workers. As one of the first "factory towns," Pullman caused an international sensation and was seen as a model for other companies to follow. The happy workers that Pullman envisioned, however, did go on strike in 1894, frustrated by the company's control of every aspect of their lives.

Today, the Pullman district makes a fascinating stop for anyone with a historical or architectural bent. While many of the homes are private residences, a number of public buildings still stand (including the lavish Hotel Florence, the imposing Clock Tower, and the two-story colonnaded Market Hall). You can walk through on your own during opening hours (stop by the Visitor Center for a map), or take a guided a tour at 12:30 or 1:30pm on the first Sunday of the month from May through October ($4 adults, $3.50 seniors).

11141 S. Cottage Grove Ave. ✆ 773/785-8901. www.pullmanil.org. Mon–Fri 12–2pm;Sat 11am–2pm; Sunday 12–3pm. Train: Metra Electric line to Pullman (111th St.), turn right on Cottage Grove Ave. and walk 1 block to the Visitor Center.

International Museum of Surgical Science ✷ *Finds* This unintentionally macabre shrine to medicine is my pick for the weirdest tourist attraction in town. Not for the faint of stomach, it is run by the International College of Surgeons and is housed in a historic 1917 Gold Coast mansion designed by the noted architect Howard Van Doren Shaw, who modeled it after Le Petit Trianon at Versailles. Displayed throughout its four floors are surgical instruments, paintings, and sculptures depicting the history of surgery and healing practices in Eastern and Western civilizations. The exhibits are old-fashioned (no interactive computer displays here!), but that's part of the museum's odd appeal.

You'll look at your doctor in a whole new way after viewing the trepanned skulls excavated from an ancient tomb in Peru. The accompanying tools were used to bore holes in patients' skulls, a horrific practice thought to release the evil spirits causing their illness. There are also battlefield amputation kits, a working iron-lung machine in the polio exhibit, and oddities such as a stethoscope designed to be transported inside a top hat.

1524 N. Lake Shore Dr. (between Burton Place and North Ave.). ✆ 312/642-6502. www.imss.org. Admission $6 adults, $3 seniors and students. Free admission Tues. Tues–Sat 10am–4pm. Bus: No. 151.

Mexican Fine Arts Center Museum ✷ *Kids* Chicago's vibrant Pilsen neighborhood, just southwest of the Loop, is home to one of the nation's largest Mexican-American communities. This building, the largest Latino cultural institution in the country, may be the neighborhood's most prized possession.

This is truly a living museum. There are wonderful exhibits to be sure, showcasing Mexican and Mexican-American visual and performing artists, and often drawing on the museum's permanent collection of more than 2,400 works. But it's the visiting artists, festival programming, and community participation that make the museum really shine. Its Day of the Dead celebration, which runs for about 8 weeks beginning in September, is one of the most ambitious in the country.

The museum is very family oriented, offering a deluge of educational workshops for kids and parents. It also has a splendid gift shop, and it stages a holiday market, featuring items from Mexico, on the first weekend in December. Allow 1 hour.

1852 W. 19th St. (a few blocks west of Ashland Ave.). © 312/738-1503. www.mfacmchicago.org. Free admission. Tues–Sun 10am–5pm. Bus: No. 9. Subway/El: Blue Line to 18th St.

National Vietnam Veterans Art Museum 🟦🟦 (Finds)   This museum houses one of the most stirring art collections anywhere—and the only one of its kind in the world—telling the story of the men who fought in Vietnam. Works with titles such as *We Regret to Inform You, Blood Spots on a Rice Paddy,* and *The Wound* should give you an idea of the power of the images (over 700 in all) in this unique legacy to the war. Housed in a former warehouse in the Prairie Avenue district south of the Loop, the museum is modern and well organized. An installation suspended from the ceiling, *Above & Beyond* 🟦, comprises more than 58,000 dog tags with the names of the men and women who died in the war—the emotional effect is similar to that of the Wall in Washington, D.C. Allow 1 hour.

1801 S. Indiana Ave. (at 18th St.). © 312/326-0270. www.nvvam.org. Admission $5 adults, $4 seniors and students with ID. Tues–Fri 11am–6pm; Sat 10am–5pm; Sun noon–5pm. Closed major holidays. Bus: No. 3 or 4.

7 Exploring the 'Burbs

If you're in town for a while, or if you're staying with friends and relatives in the suburbs, it's worth venturing beyond the city limits to check out some of the sights in the surrounding areas. For a map of the greater Chicago area, see the "Chicago & Vicinity" map on p. 2.

OAK PARK

Architecture and literary buffs alike make pilgrimages to Oak Park, a near suburb on the western border of the city that is easily accessible by car or train. The reason fans of both disciplines flock to this same small town is that Ernest Hemingway was born and grew up here and Frank Lloyd Wright spent a great deal of his career designing the homes that line the well-maintained streets.

GETTING THERE

BY CAR   Oak Park is 10 miles due west of downtown Chicago. By car, take the Eisenhower Expressway west (I-290) to Harlem Avenue (Ill. 43) and exit north. Continue on Harlem north to Lake Street. Take a right on Lake Street and continue to Forest Avenue. Turn left here, and immediately on your right you'll see the **Oak Park Visitor Center** (see below).

BY PUBLIC TRANSPORTATION   Take the Green Line west to the Harlem stop, roughly a 25-minute ride from downtown. Exit the station onto Harlem Avenue, and proceed north to Lake Street. Take a right on Lake Street to Forest Avenue, and then turn left to the **Oak Park Visitor Center** (see below).

VISITOR INFORMATION

The **Oak Park Visitor Center,** 158 Forest Ave. (© **708/848-1500**), is open daily from 10am to 5pm April through October, and from 10am to 4pm November through March. Stop here for orientation,

The (Frank Lloyd) Wright Stuff

Oak Park has the highest concentration of houses or buildings anywhere designed and built by Frank Lloyd Wright, probably the most influential American architect. People come here to marvel at the work of a man who saw his life as a twofold mission: to wage a single-handed battle against the ornamental excesses of architecture, Victorian in particular, and to create in its place a new form that would be at the same time functional, appropriate to its natural setting, and stimulating to the imagination. Oak Park has, in all, 25 homes and buildings by Wright, constructed between the years 1892 and 1913, which constitute the core output of his Prairie School period.

maps, and guidebooks. There's a city-operated parking lot next door. From the center, the heart of the historic district and the Frank Lloyd Wright Home and Studio is only a few blocks away.

SITES

Frank Lloyd Wright Home and Studio ☆☆☆   For the first 20 years of Wright's career, this remarkable complex served first and foremost as the sanctuary from which Wright was to design and execute more than 130 of an extraordinary output of 430 completed buildings. The home began as a simple shingled cottage that Wright built for his bride in 1889 at the age of 22, but it became a work in progress, as Wright remodeled it constantly until 1911 (he left there in 1909). During this highly fertile period, the house was Wright's showcase and laboratory, but it also embraces many idiosyncratic features molded to his own needs rather than those of a client. With many add-ons—including a barrel-vaulted children's playroom and a studio with an octagonal balcony suspended by chains—the place has a certain whimsy that others might have found less livable. This, however, was not an architect's masterpiece, but the master's home, and every room in it can be savored for the view it reflects of the workings of a remarkable mind. The Home and Studio Foundation has restored the residence and studio to its 1909 vintage. Allow 2 hours.

951 Chicago Ave. ☎ **708/848-1976.** www.wrightplus.org. Admission $9 adults, $7 seniors and children 7–18, free for children under 7. Combined admission for Home and Studio tour and guided or self-guided historic district tour (see below) $15 adults, $11 seniors and children 7–18. Admission to home and studio is by guided tour only; tours depart from the Ginkgo Tree Bookshop Mon–Fri 11am, 1pm, and 3pm; Sat–Sun every 20 min. 11am–3:30pm. Facilities for people with disabilities are limited; please call in advance.

HISTORIC DISTRICT WALKING TOURS

An extensive tour of the neighborhood surrounding the Frank Lloyd Wright Home and Studio leaves from the **Ginkgo Tree Bookshop,** 951 Chicago Ave., on weekends from 10:30am to 4pm (tour times are somewhat more limited Nov–Feb). The tour lasts 1 hour and costs $9 for adults and $7 for seniors and children 7 to 18, and is free for children under 7. If you can't make it to Oak Park on the weekend, you can follow a self-guided map and audiocassette tour of the historic district (recorded in English, French, Spanish, German, Japanese, and Italian). Available at the Ginkgo Tree Bookshop from 10am to 3:30pm, the self-guided tour costs $9 for adults and $7 for seniors and children.

Unity Temple 🌟   After fire destroyed its church around 1900, a Unitarian/Universalist congregation asked one of its members, Frank Lloyd Wright, to design an affordable replacement. Using poured concrete with metal reinforcements—a necessity, owing to the small budget of $40,000 allocated for the project—Wright created a building that on the outside seems as forbidding as a mausoleum but that inside contains in its detailing the entire architectural alphabet of the Prairie School that has since made Wright's name immortal. Unity Temple is no simple meetinghouse in the tradition of Calvinist iconoclasm. Instead, its principal chapel looks like the chamber of the Roman Senate. Even so, the interior, with its unpredictable geometric arrangements and its decor reminiscent of Native American art, is no less beautiful.

Wright used color sparingly within Unity Temple, but the pale, natural effects that he achieved are owed in part to his decision to add pigment to the plaster rather than use paint. Wright's use of wood for trim and other decorative touches is still exciting to behold; his sensitivity to grain and tone and placement was akin to that of an exceptionally gifted woodworker. Other details to which the docent guide will call your attention, as you complete a circuit of the temple, are the great fireplace, the pulpit, the skylights, and the clerestory (gallery) windows. Suffice it to say, Unity Temple—only one of Wright's masterpieces—is counted among the 10 greatest American architectural achievements. Allow a half-hour.

875 Lake St. ⓒ **708/383-8873.** http://unitytemple.org. Self-guided tours $6 adults; $3 seniors, children, and students with ID. 45-min. guided tours Sat–Sun on the hr. 1–3pm at no extra charge. Mon–Fri 10:30am–4:30 pm; Sat–Sun 1–4pm. Church events can alter the schedule; call in advance.

ON THE TRAIL OF HEMINGWAY

Frank Lloyd Wright might be Oak Park's favorite son, but the town's most famous native son is Ernest Hemingway (who spent his first 18 years here). Maybe because Hemingway left when he had the chance and didn't write much about the town of his boyhood, Oak Park only recently has begun to rally around the memory of the Nobel and Pulitzer Prize–winning writer with the opening of a **Hemingway Museum,** 200 N. Oak Park Ave. (ⓒ **708/848-2222**). A portion of the ground floor of this former church, now the Oak Park Arts Center, is given over to a small but interesting display of Hemingway memorabilia. The museum is open Sunday through Friday from 1 to 5pm, and Saturday from 10am to 5pm.

. To see where Hemingway was born, on July 21, 1899, continue up the block to 339 N. Oak Park Ave., the home of his maternal grandparents. Hemingway's actual boyhood home, still privately owned, is located several blocks from here, not far from the Wright Home and Studio, at 600 N. Kenilworth Ave. The hours at the Hemingway Birthplace museum are the same as the Hemingway Museum above; an admission price of $7 for adults and $5 for seniors and children (free for children under 5) covers both museums.

THE NORTH SHORE
EXPLORING EVANSTON

Despite being a place much frequented by Chicagoans, Evanston, the city's oldest suburb, retains an identity all its own. A unique hybrid of sensibilities, it manages to combine the tranquility of suburban life with a highly cultured, urban charm. It's great fun to just wander amid the hip shops and cafes located in its downtown area or along funky Dempster Street at its southern end. **Northwestern University** (© **847/491-3741;** www.northwestern.edu) makes its home here on a beautiful lakefront campus, and many of its buildings—such as Alice Millar Chapel, with its sublime stained-glass facade, and the Mary and Leigh Block Gallery, a fine arts haven that offers a top-notch collection and always-intriguing temporary exhibitions—are well worth several hours of exploration in their own right.

For a bit of serenity, head to **Grosse Point Lighthouse and Maritime Museum,** 2601 Sheridan Rd. (© **847/328-6961**), a historic lighthouse built in 1873, when Lake Michigan still teemed with cargo-laden ships. Tours of the lighthouse, situated in a nature center, take place on weekends from June to September.

OTHER AREA ATTRACTIONS

Chicago Botanic Garden ⭐⭐ *Value*   Despite its name, the world-class Chicago Botanic Garden is located 25 miles north of the city in the suburb of Glencoe. This 385-acre living preserve includes eight large lagoons and a variety of distinct botanical environments—from the Illinois prairie to an English walled garden to a three-island Japanese garden. Also on the grounds are a large fruit and vegetable garden, an "enabling garden" (which shows how gardening can be adapted for people with disabilities), and a 100-acre old-growth oak woodland. If you're here in the summer, don't miss the extensive rose gardens (just follow the bridal parties who flock here to get their pictures taken). Allow 3 hours.

1000 Lake-Cook Rd. (just east of Edens Expressway/I-94), Glencoe. ℂ 847/835-5440. www.chicago-botanic.org. Free admission. Daily (except Christmas) 8am–sunset. Tram tours offered Apr–Oct. From Chicago, take Sheridan Rd. north along Lake Michigan or the Edens Expwy. (I-94) to Lake-Cook Rd. Parking $8.75 daily.

Ravinia Festival *★★ (Finds*   Want to know where the natives get away from it all? Come summertime, you'll find us chilling on the lawn at Ravinia, the summer home of the highly regarded Chicago Symphony Orchestra in suburban Highland Park. The season runs from mid-June to Labor Day and includes far more than classical concerts: You can also catch pop acts, dance performances, operatic arias, and blues concerts. Tickets are sold to both the covered pavilion, where you get a reserved seat and a view of the stage, and the lawn, which is the real joy of Ravinia: sitting under the stars and a canopy of leafy branches while listening to music and indulging in an elaborate picnic (it's a local tradition to try to outdo everyone else by bringing candelabras and fine china).

Don't let the distance from downtown discourage you from visiting, because Ravinia is served by an extremely convenient public-transportation system. Any evening a concert is scheduled, a special Ravinia Metra commuter train leaves at 5:50pm from the North Western train station at Madison and Canal streets (just west of the Loop). The train stops directly at the festival at 6:30pm, plenty of time to enjoy a picnic before an 8 o'clock showtime. After the concert, trains wait right outside the gates to take commuters back to the city. The round-trip train fare is $5, a real bargain considering that traffic around the park can be brutal.

Green Bay and Lake-Cook roads, Highland Park. ℂ 847/266-5100 or 312/RAVINIA. www.ravinia.org. Tickets: Pavilion $15–$50; lawn $10. Most concerts are held in the evening.

8 Kid Stuff

Chicago has plenty of places to take the kids—places, in fact, that make every effort to turn a bored child into a stimulated one.

Chicago Children's Museum *★★*   This museum has areas especially for preschoolers as well as for children up to age 10, and several permanent exhibits allow kids a maximum of hands-on fun. *Dinosaur Expedition* re-creates an expedition to the Sahara, allowing kids to experience camp life, conduct scientific research, and dig for bones. *Face to Face: Dealing with Prejudice and Discrimination* is a multimedia display that helps kids identify prejudice and find ways to deal with it. There's also a **three-level schooner** that children can board for a little climbing; *PlayMaze,* a toddler-scale cityscape; and an **arts-and-crafts area** where visitors can create original artwork to take home. Allow 2 to 3 hours.

Navy Pier, 700 E. Grand Ave. © **312/527-1000.** www.chichildrensmuseum.org. Admission $7 adults and children, $6 seniors. Free admission Thurs 5–8pm. Tues–Wed and Fri–Sun 10am–5pm; Thurs 10am–8pm. Bus: No. 29, 56, 65, or 66. Subway/El: Red Line to Grand/State; transfer to city bus or Navy Pier's free trolley bus.

Lincoln Park Pritzker Children's Zoo & Farm-in-the-Zoo *Value*
After hours of looking at animals from afar in the rest of the Lincoln Park Zoo, kids can come here for some hands-on experience. Children are encouraged to come touch a variety of small animals—hedgehogs, iguanas, rabbits—under the supervision of zookeepers. There's also a very popular glass-walled animal nursery, where zoo docents and keepers care for the babies of more exotic species—often, this means gorillas and chimpanzees—who are ill, born weak, or rejected by their mothers.

The newly renovated Farm-in-the-Zoo is a working reproduction of a Midwestern farm, complete with a white-picket-fenced barnyard, chicken coops, and demonstrations of butter churning and weaving. Of course, you'll also spot plenty of livestock, including cows, sheep, and pigs. Inside the Main Barn (filled with interactive exhibits), the main attraction is the huge John Deere tractor that kids can climb up into and pretend to drive. (Can you say photo opportunity?) Allow 1 hour.

2200 N. Cannon Dr. © **312/742-2000.** Free admission. Daily 9am–5pm. Bus: No. 151 or 156.

9 Sightseeing Tours

If you're in town for a limited amount of time, an organized tour may be the best way to get a quick overview of the city's highlights. Some tours—such as the boat cruises on Lake Michigan and the Chicago River—can give you a whole new perspective on the city's landscape.

ORIENTATION TOURS
Chicago Trolley Company   Chicago Trolley Company offers guided tours on a fleet of rubber-wheeled "San Francisco–style" trolleys that stop at a number of popular spots around the city, including Navy Pier, the Grant Park museums, the Museum of

Tips **Ticket to Ride**

One of the most distinctive ways to tour the city is by hopping aboard one of our iconic El trains. Although you can ride any-time yourself for $1.50, a guided train tour will give you new insights on the buildings outside the windows. The city's **Office of Tourism** runs a 40-minute train tour of the Loop on Saturdays at 11:35, 12:15, 12:55, and 1:35 from May through September; tickets are free, but must be picked up on the day of the tour at the Chicago Cultural Center, 77 E. Randolph St., a block east of the Randolph and Wabash station where the tour starts (© **312/744-2400**).

Science and Industry, Lincoln Park Zoo, and the cluster of theme restaurants in River North (Hard Rock Cafe, Planet Hollywood, and so on). You can stay on for the full 1½-hour ride or get on and off at each stop. The same company also operates the **Chicago Double Decker Company,** which has a fleet of London-style, red, two-story buses. The buses follow the same route as the trollies; if you buy an all-day pass, you can hop from bus to trolley at any point.

© **773/648-5000.** www.chicagotrolley.com. All-day hop-on, hop-off pass $20 adults, $17 seniors, $10 children 3–11. Family package (2 adults, 2 children) $54. Daily 9am–5pm year-round (in the winter the vehicles are enclosed and heated).

Gray Line   Part of a company that offers bus tours worldwide, Gray Line Chicago offers professional tours in well-appointed buses. A basic guided tour of the city takes 1½ hours; more extensive trips run 4 to 5 hours and include lunch. Some tours also include a cruise on Lake Michigan or a visit to the Sears Tower Skydeck. Gray Line also operates a trolley that runs through downtown Wednesday through Sunday; an all-day pass costs $20 for adults and $10 for children.

27 E. Monroe St., Suite 515. © **800/621-4153** or 312/251-3107. www.grayline. com. Tours cost $16–$45.

LAKE & RIVER CRUISES

Getting out on the lake is a great way to take in Chicago's incredi-ble skyline from a whole new vantage point, and when the weather cooperates, the sight of sunlight or moonlight sparkling off the city's skyscrapers never fails to thrill.

Chicago from the Lake   This company runs two different cruises: a 90-minute tour of architecture along the Chicago River, and historical cruises that travel on the lake and river to explore the development of the city. Complimentary coffee (Starbucks, no less), lemonade, cookies, and muffins are served. For tickets, call or stop by the company's ticket office, located on the lower level on the east end of River East Plaza. Advance reservations are recommended.

Departing from Ogden Slip adjacent to River East Plaza (formerly North Pier) at the end of E. Illinois St. ☎ **312/527-1977**. www.chicagoline.com. Tickets $25 adults, $22 seniors, $14 children 7–18, free for children under 7. Daily May–Oct.

Mystic Blue Cruises   A more casual alternative to fancy dinner cruises, this is promoted as more of a "fun" ship. Daily lunch and dinner excursions are available, as well as midnight weekend voyages. The same company offers more formal (and expensive) cruises aboard the **Odyssey,** and motorboat rides on the 70-passenger **Seadog,** if you really want to feel the water in your face.

Departing from Navy Pier. ☎ **877/299-7783**. www.mysticbluecruises.com. Lunch cruises $28–$31, dinner $55–$60, midday cruise $22, moonlight cruise $28. Cruises run year-round.

Shoreline Sightseeing   Shoreline schedules 30-minute lake cruises every half-hour from its three dock locations: the Shedd Aquarium, Navy Pier, and Buckingham Fountain in Grant Park. Shoreline has also gotten in on the popularity of architecture tours by offering its own version, narrated by an architectural guide (with higher prices than their regular tours).

Departing from Navy Pier, Shedd Aquarium, and Buckingham Fountain in Grant Park. ☎ **312/222-9328**. www.shorelinesightseeing.com. Tickets $10 adults, $9 seniors, $5 children under 12; architectural tours $18–20 adults, $17 seniors, $7–$8 children under 12. Daily May 1–Sept 30.

The Spirit of Chicago   This luxury yacht offers a variety of wining-and-dining harbor cruises, from a lunch buffet to the "Moonlight Dance Party." This can be a fairly pricey night out if you go for the whole dinner package; the late-night moonlight cruises are a more affordable option for insomniacs.

Departing from Navy Pier. ☎ **312/836-7899**. www.spiritcruises.com. Lunch cruises $35–45, dinner (seated) $70–$100, sunset and midnight cruises $32. Ask about children's rates. Daily year-round.

Wendella Sightseeing Boats   Wendella operates a 1-hour tour along the Chicago River, and a 1½-tour along the river and out onto Lake Michigan. (One of the most dramatic events during the boat tours is passing through the locks that separate the river from the lake.) Boats run from late April to early October. Scheduling for cruises depends on the season and the weather, but cruises usually leave every hour during the summer.

Departing from Michigan Ave. and Wacker Dr. (on the north side of the river at the Wrigley Building). (℮ 312/337-1446. www.wendellaboats.com. Tickets $16 adults, $14 seniors, $8 children under 12. Daily Apr–Oct.

Windy   The 148-foot-long, four-masted schooner (and its new sister ship, the *Windy II*) sets sail for 90-minute cruises two to five times a day, both day and evening. Of course, the boats are at the whims of the wind, so every cruise charts a different course. Passengers are welcome to help raise and trim the sails and occasionally take turns at the ship's helm (with the captain standing close by). The boats are not accessible for people with disabilities.

Departing from Navy Pier. (℮ 312/595-5555. Tickets $25 adults, $15 seniors and children under 12. Tickets go on sale 1 hr. before the 1st sail of the day at the boat's ticket office, on the dock at Navy Pier. Reservations (except for groups) are not accepted. Call for sailing times.

SPECIAL-INTEREST TOURS
ARCHITECTURE TOURS

Chicago is the first city of architecture, and the **Chicago Architecture Foundation (CAF),** 224 S. Michigan Ave. (℮ **312/922-3432,** or 312/922-TOUR for recorded information; www.architecture. org), offers first-rate walking, bike, boat, and bus tours to more than 60 architectural sites and environments in and around Chicago. The foundation also has another tour center in the John Hancock Center, 875 N. Michigan Ave. Below is a sampling of their offerings.

BY BOAT   Perhaps the CAF's most popular tour is its 1½-hour **Architecture River Cruise,** which glides along both the north and the south branches of the Chicago River. Although you can see the same 50 or so buildings that the cruise covers on your own by foot, traveling by water lets you enjoy the buildings from a unique perspective. The cruise points out both landmark buildings, such as the Gothic 1925 Tribune Tower, and contemporary ones, including the late-1980s NBC Tower, constructed in wedding-cake style in homage to the city's old zoning codes mandating that sunlight reach down to the street.

Tickets are $23 per person weekdays, $25 on weekends and holidays, and are scheduled hourly every day May through October from 11am to 3pm. The trips are extremely popular, so purchase tickets in advance through **Ticketmaster** (℮ **312/902-1500;**

www.ticketmaster.com/Illinois), or avoid the service charge and buy your tickets at one of the foundation's tour centers, 224 S. Michigan Ave. or the John Hancock Center, or from the boat launch on the southeast corner of Michigan Avenue and Wacker Drive.

BY BUS   Reservations are required for all bus tours, although walk-ins are welcome if there's space.

Highlights by Bus is a 3½-hour tour offered Saturdays at 9:30am that covers the Loop, Hyde Park, and the Gold Coast, plus several other historic districts. The tour includes a visit to the interior of Frank Lloyd Wright's Robie House. Tickets are $30 per person; tours depart from the Chicago Architecture Center at 224 S. Michigan Ave. To keep up with popular demand, the foundation adds Sunday morning tours periodically throughout the year.

A 4-hour bus tour of Frank Lloyd Wright sights in **Oak Park** is offered once a month on Saturday from May to October ($30). The tour includes walks through three neighborhoods and commentary on more than 25 houses—but does not take visitors inside Wright's home and studio. A separate 4-hour bus tour takes Wright fans inside the master's home and Oak Park's Unity Temple ($40). Both tours leave from the Chicago Architecture Center.

ON FOOT   If you prefer exploring on your own two feet, the CAF offers a variety of guided walking tours. For first-time visitors, I highly recommend two tours that give an excellent introduction to the dramatic architecture of the Loop: **Historic Skyscrapers,** which covers buildings built between 1880 and 1940, including the Rookery and the Chicago Board of Trade, and **Modern Skyscrapers,** which includes modern masterpieces by Mies van der Rohe and postmodern works by contemporary architects. The 2-hour tours cost $12 each ($20 for both) for adults and $9 each ($15 for both) for seniors and students. The tours are offered daily and depart from the Chicago Architecture Center at 224 S. Michigan Ave. Call ℂ 312/922-TOUR for exact tour times.

10 Staying Active

Perhaps because Chicago's winters can be so brutal, Chicagoans take their summers very seriously. In the warmer months, with the wide blue lake and the ample green parks, it's easy to think that the city is one big grown-up playground. The park district can be reached at ℂ 312/742-PLAY; for questions about the 29 miles of beaches and parks along Lake Michigan, call the park district's lakefront region office at ℂ 312/747-2474.

Another handy resource is ***Windy City Sports*** (© 312/421-1551; www.windycitysportsmag.com), a free monthly publication that you'll find at many retail shops, grocery stores, and bars and cafes.

BEACHES

Public beaches line Lake Michigan all the way up north into the suburbs and Wisconsin, and southeast through Indiana and into Michigan. The most well known is **Oak Street Beach,** the location of which at the northern tip of the Magnificent Mile creates some interesting sights as sun worshippers sporting swimsuits and carting coolers make their way down Michigan Avenue. The most popular is **North Avenue Beach,** about 6 blocks farther north, which has developed into a volleyball hot spot and recently rebuilt its landmark steamship-shaped beach house and added a Venice Beach–style outdoor gym; this is where the Lincoln Park singles come to play, check each other out, and fly by on bikes and in-line skates. For more seclusion, try **Ohio Street Beach,** an intimate sliver of sand in tiny Olive Park, just north of Navy Pier, which, incredibly enough, remains largely ignored despite its central location.

Beaches are officially open with a full retinue of lifeguards on duty beginning about June 20, though swimmers can wade into the chilly water Memorial Day to Labor Day. Only the bravest souls venture into the water before July, when the temperature creeps up enough to make swimming an attractive proposition. Please take note that the entire lakefront is not beach, and don't go doing anything stupid such as diving off the rocks.

BIKING

Biking is a great way to see the city, particularly along the lakefront bike path that extends for more than 18 miles.

To rent bikes, try **Bike & Roll,** which has locations at Navy Pier (© 312/595-9600) and North Avenue Beach (© 773/327-2706). Both are open from 8am to 10pm May through October (weather permitting). Rates for bikes are $9.75 an hour, $34 a day, with helmets, pads, and locks included.

Both the park district (© 312/742-PLAY) and the **Chicagoland Bicycle Federation** (© 312/42-PEDAL; www.chibikefed.org) offer free maps that detail popular biking routes.

IN-LINE SKATING

Bike & Roll, with locations at Navy Pier (© 312/595-9600) and North Avenue Beach (© 773/327-2706), charges $9.75 an hour or

$34 a day (you can have the skates 8am–10pm). A second spot is **Londo Mondo,** 1100 N. Dearborn St. (© **312/751-2794**), on the Gold Coast, renting blades for $7 an hour or $20 a day.

The best route to skate is the lakefront trail that leads from Lincoln Park down to Oak Street Beach. Beware, though, that those same miles of trail are claimed by avid cyclists.

11 In the Grandstand: Watching Chicago's Athletic Events

Alas, Chicago's professional sports glory has faded since the days when Michael Jordan was the most recognized athlete in the world. But Chicago fans are nothing if not loyal, and, for that reason, attending a home game in any sport is an uplifting experience. And look on the bright side: Now that our teams aren't doing so well, it's a lot easier to get tickets to games.

BASEBALL

Baseball is imprinted in the national consciousness as part of Chicago, not because of victorious dynasties, but rather because of the opposite—the Black Sox scandal of 1919 and the perennially losing Cubs (despite the Cubs' trip to the National League Championship Series—only one step away from the World Series—in 2003).

Let's start with the **Chicago Cubs.** The Cubbies haven't made a World Series appearance since 1945 and haven't been World Champs since 1908, but when the team plays in so perfect a place as Wrigley Field, with its ivy-covered outfield walls, its hand-operated scoreboard, its view of the shimmering lake from the upper deck, and its "W" or "L" flag announcing the outcome of the game to the unfortunates who couldn't attend, how could anyone stay away? Because Wrigley is small, just about every seat is decent.

No matter how the Cubs are doing, tickets ($12–$36) go fast; most weekend and night games are sold out by Memorial Day. Your best bet is to hit a weekday game, or try your luck buying a ticket on game day outside the park (you'll often find some season-ticket holders looking to unload a few seats).

Wrigley Field, 1060 W. Addison St. (© **773/404-CUBS;** www. cubs.mlb.com), is easy to reach. Take the Red Line to the Addison stop, and you're there. You could also take the no. 22 bus, which runs up Clark Street. To order tickets in person, stop by the ticket windows at Wrigley Field, Monday through Friday from 9am to

6pm, Saturday from 9am to 4pm, and on game days. Call ℂ **800/ THE-CUBS** for tickets through **Ticketmaster,** and you can also order online through the Cubs website. About a dozen tours of the ballpark are led each season; tickets are $15 and are sold through the Wrigley Field ticket office or Ticketmaster.

Alas, the **Chicago White Sox** can't count on the same kind of loyalty as the Cubs. Longtime fans rue the day owner Jerry Reinsdorf (who is also majority owner of the Bulls) replaced the admittedly dilapidated Comisky Park with a concrete behemoth that lacks the yesteryear charm of its predecessor (it's now known as **U.S. Cellular Field**). That said, sightlines at the new stadium are spectacular from every seat (if you avoid the vertigo-inducing upper-deck seats), and every conceivable amenity—from above-average ballpark food concessions to shops to plentiful restrooms—has been provided for your ease and enjoyment. Games are rarely sellouts—a residual effect, presumably, of Reinsdorf's sterile stadium and the blighted neighborhood that surrounds it. All of this makes it a bargain deal for bona fide baseball fans. Tickets cost $12 to $26 and are half-price on Mondays (kids get in for $1 on certain Sun games).

U.S. Cellular Field is at 333 W. 35th St. (ℂ **312/674-1000;** www.whitesox.mlb.com), in the South Side neighborhood of Bridgeport. To get Sox tickets, call **Ticketmaster** at ℂ **866/SOX-GAME** or visit the ticket office, open Monday through Friday from 10am to 6pm, Saturday and Sunday from 10am to 4pm, except on game days, when it opens at 9am. To get to the ballpark by subway/El, take the Red Line to Sox/35th Street.

BASKETBALL

Do not mention the name Jerry Reinsdorf or Jerry Krause to a Chicago sports fan unless you want to be pummeled like a speed bag. The owner and general manager, respectively, of the **Chicago Bulls** were—fairly or not—castigated by the public and local press after dismantling the world-famous six-time NBA championship Chicago Bulls following the 1998 season.

So you can imagine what a jolt it has been to hear about the Bulls losing 5, 10, or 15 games in a row, year after year. The **United Center,** 1901 W. Madison St. (ℂ **312/455-4500;** www.chicagosports. com), where the Bulls play, feels like an airplane hangar–size funeral parlor these days. For the time being, tickets, once impossible to come by, are worth about as much as the paper they're printed on. So grab yourself a courtside seat—there are plenty to go around.

FOOTBALL

The **Chicago Bears** play at a newly renovated **Soldier Field,** Lake Shore Drive and 16th Street (© **847/615-2327;** www.chicagobears.com). The stadium's most distinctive feature—its classically-inspired colonnade—was retained, but a giant addition that looks somewhat like a spaceship was crammed awkwardly on top. Architecturally, it's a disaster. But from a comfort perspective, the place is much improved—although that doesn't impress long-time fans that prided themselves on surviving blistering cold game days and horrifying bathrooms. But there is still something quintessentially Chicago about grilling up ribs and brats in the parking lot before the Bears go to battle against our arch enemy, the Green Bay Packers. Just make sure you dump a pint of peppermint schnapps in that thermos of hot chocolate before you experience "Bear Weather" for the first time.

HOCKEY

The **Chicago Blackhawks** have a devoted, impassioned following of fans that work themselves into a frenzy with the first note of the "Star Spangled Banner." The Blackhawks play at the **United Center,** 1901 W. Madison St. (© **312/455-4500;** www.chicagoblackhawks.com).

For a more affordable and family-friendly experience, catch the semipro **Chicago Wolves** at Allstate Arena (© **847/724-GOAL,** www.chicagowolves.com). The team has been consistently excellent over the past few years, and the games are geared toward all ages, with fireworks before the show and plenty of on- and off-ice entertainment.

7

Shopping

The art of merchandising has a rich history in Chicago. The original Marshall Field operated his namesake department store under the motto "Give the lady what she wants," pioneering many customer-service policies that are now standard (such as hassle-free returns). Catalogs from Chicago-based Sears and Montgomery Ward made clothes, books, and housewares accessible to even the most remote frontier towns. East to west, or back the other way, just about everything passed through Chicago.

Today, Montgomery Ward is no more, but Sears recently opened a new flagship store in the heart of the Loop, signaling the continued vitality of downtown Chicago as a shopping destination.

This chapter concentrates on the Magnificent Mile, State Street, and several trendy neighborhoods, where you'll find one-of-a-kind shops and boutiques that make shopping such an adventure.

SHOPPING HOURS As a general rule, store hours are 10am to 6 or 7pm Monday through Saturday, and noon to 6pm Sunday. Neighborhood stores tend to keep later hours, as do some of the stores along Michigan Avenue, which cater to after-work shoppers as well as tourists. Almost all stores have extended hours during the holiday season. Nearly all the stores in the Loop are open for daytime shopping only, generally from 9 or 10am to no later than 6pm Monday through Saturday. (The few remaining big downtown department stores have some selected evening hours.) Many Loop stores not on State Street are closed Saturday; on Sunday, the Loop—except for a few restaurants, theaters, and cultural attractions—is shut down pretty tight.

SALES TAX You might do a double take after checking the total on your purchase: At 8.75%, the state and local sales tax on non-food items is one of the steepest in the country.

1 Shopping the Magnificent Mile

The nickname "Magnificent Mile"—hyperbole to some, an understatement to others—refers to the roughly mile-long stretch of North Michigan Avenue between Oak Street and the Chicago River.

The density of the area's first-rate shopping is, quite simply, unmatched anywhere. Even jaded shoppers from other worldly capitals are delighted at the ease and convenience of the stores concentrated here. Taking into account that tony Oak Street (see below) is just around a corner, the overall area is a little like New York's Fifth Avenue and Beverly Hills's Rodeo Drive rolled into one. Window-shoppers and people-watchers will find plenty to amuse themselves because this is the city's liveliest corridor.

A NORTH MICHIGAN AVENUE SHOPPER'S STROLL

This shopper's stroll begins at Oak Street at the northern end of the avenue and heads south toward the river. It just hits the highlights; you're sure to find much more to tickle your fancy and tempt your wallet as you meander from designer landmarks to well-known chain stores.

The parade of designer names begins at the intersection of Michigan Avenue and Oak Street, including a couple housed in The Drake hotel, such as the legendary Danish silversmith **Georg Jensen,** 959 N. Michigan Ave. (© 312/642-9160), known for outstanding craftsmanship in sterling silver and gold, including earrings, brooches, watches, tie clips, and flatware; and **Chanel,** 935 N. Michigan Ave. (© 312/787-5500).

The newest luxury emporium in town is the spacious **Louis Vuitton** store at 919 N. Michigan Ave. (© 312/944-2010), where you'll find trendy handbags and the company's distinctive brown-and-gold luggage. A few doors down is famed Italian jeweler **Bulgari,** 909 N. Michigan Ave. (© 312/255-1313), which sells timepieces, necklaces, bracelets, rings, and silver gift items.

Giorgio Armani's sleek boutique, at 800 N. Michigan Ave. in the Park Hyatt Hotel (© 312/751-2244), faces the park that overlooks the historic Water Tower. Across the street, a few doors west of Michigan Avenue, is one of Chicago's hottest family destinations: **American Girl Place,** at 111 E. Chicago Ave. (© 877/AG-PLACE). The three-story doll emporium attracts hordes of young girls (and parents) hooked on the popular mail-order company's line of historic character dolls. A stage show brings stories from the American Girl books to life, and the store's cafe is a nice spot for a special mother-daughter lunch or afternoon tea.

The next block of Michigan Avenue has a New York vibe, thanks to the world's largest **Polo Ralph Lauren** (© 312/280-1655), a four-floor, wood-paneled mini-mansion, and **Tiffany & Co.** (© 312/944-7500), with its signature clock, jewels, and tabletop accessories (if you want to get your hands on one of the distinctive robin's-egg blue shopping bags without spending a fortune, the $50 sterling-silver key chains are the least expensive items in the store).

A few doors south are **Neiman Marcus,** 737 N. Michigan Ave. (© 312/642-5900), and, at 669 N. Michigan Ave. (© 312/642-6363), the hugely popular **Niketown,** a multilevel complex that helped pioneer the concept of retail as entertainment. A little farther south is a haven for reluctant male shoppers: the **Sony Gallery of Consumer Electronics,** 663 N. Michigan Ave. (© 312/943-3334), where the latest high-tech gadgets are displayed in a museumlike setting (head up to the 2nd floor to try out the newest PlayStation games).

Across the street, you'll probably see a line of people trailing out from the **Garrett Popcorn Shop,** 670 N. Michigan Ave. (© 312/944-2630), a 50-year-old landmark. Join the locals in line and pick up some caramel corn for a quick sugar rush.

At the intersection of Michigan Avenue and Erie Street is the appropriately barrel-shaped **Crate & Barrel,** 646 N. Michigan Ave. (© 312/787-5900). Crate & Barrel was started in Chicago, so this is the company's flagship location. Countless varieties of glassware, dishes, cookware, and kitchen gadgets for everyday use line the shelves. The top two floors are devoted to furniture.

Sharing the same address, at 645 N. Michigan Ave., are two big names in Italian fashion: shoemaker **Salvatore Ferragamo** (© 312/397-0464), which also sells men's and women's clothing; and **Ermenegildo Zegna** (© 312/587-9660), designer of finely tailored menswear. Continuing south, you'll find **Burberry,** 633 N. Michigan Ave. (© 312/787-2500), where the classic beige plaid has moved beyond trench coats to show up on chic purses, shoes, and bathing suits (if you're looking for luxury souvenirs, check out the collection of baby clothes and dog accessories).

Two shops are pulling younger, hipper shoppers into the renovated ground-floor retail wing of the Chicago Marriott: the **Virgin**

Megastore (© 312/645-9300), which, true to its name, has stock-piled a megacollection of CDs, videos, DVDs, books, and interactive games; and **Kenneth Cole New York** (© 312/644-1163), offering a line of contemporary shoes for women and men, along with men's sportswear and suits. Across the street, at 535 N. Michigan Ave., is **La Perla** (© 312/494-0400), home of very trendy and very expensive Italian lingerie.

THE MAGNIFICENT MALLS

WATER TOWER PLACE Chicago's first—and still busiest—vertical mall is Water Tower Place, a block-size, marble-sheathed building at 835 N. Michigan Ave. (© 312/440-3165), between East Pearson and East Chestnut streets. The mall's seven floors contain about 100 stores that reportedly account for roughly half of all the retail trade transacted along the Magnificent Mile. The mall also houses a dozen different cafes and restaurants.

Water Tower is a magnet for suburban teenagers (just like your mall back home!), and can get quite crowded during prime summer tourist season. Most of its stores are part of national chains (Gap, Victoria's Secret, etc.). But there are a few shops that make it worth a stop, including hip young designs from the British store **French Connection** (5th floor; © 312/932-9460) and wearable women's clothing at **Eileen Fisher** (2nd floor; © 312/943-9190). The department stores anchoring the mall are the Mag Mile outpost of the Loop's famed **Marshall Field's** (floors one to eight; © 312/335-7700) and a **Lord & Taylor** (floors one to seven; © 312/787-7400). One of Water Tower's best features is its funky food court **foodlife.**

900 NORTH MICHIGAN The most upscale of the Magnificent Mile's three vertical malls, 900 North Michigan (often called the Bloomingdale's building, for its most prominent tenant) avoids the tumult of Water Tower Place by appealing to a more well-heeled shopper. In addition to about 70 stores are a few good restaurants and a nice movie multiplex on the lower level. For mall information, call © 312/915-3916.

The Chicago outpost of **Gucci** (ground floor; © 312/664-5504) has the same hip attitude as the label's sexy clothing and much-in-demand purses. Also on the ground floor is **MaxMara** (© 312/475-9500), the Italian women's fashion house known for elegantly constructed coats and separates (some of which will cost you about as much as a flight to Italy). Other goodies worth checking out

---

Tips Lunch on the Mag Mile

If shopping has made you hungry, try the Food Court on the eighth floor of Chicago Place. A bright, airy space with a fountain and palm trees, you'll find the usual mall favorites as well as healthier dishes at **Pattie's Quick and Lite** (salads, wraps, pasta) and **Pita Pavilion** (Mediterranean). Don't miss the crispy french fries at the **Great Steak and Potato Company.** Grab one of the tables behind Pita Pavilion for a great Michigan Avenue view.

---

include funky European footwear at **Charles David** (2nd floor; © 312/944-9013), amazingly intricate French glassware at **Lalique** (ground floor; © 312/867-1787), silver and crystal splurge items at **Christofle** (ground floor; © 312/664-9700), and lovely hats made by a local designer at **Linda Campisano Millinery** (6th floor; © 312/337-1004).

CHICAGO PLACE   Chicago Place, 700 N. Michigan Ave. (© 312/266-7710), has been looking for an identity ever since opening in 1991. Although it is home to **Saks Fifth Avenue** (© 312/944-6500), the rest of the stores are not as upscale. The best reason to stop here is the good selection of import stores, the best of which are **Joy of Ireland,** where you can also stop for a spot of tea in the afternoon (© 312/664-7290), **Design Toscano** (© 312/587-1199), and **Russian Creations** (© 312/573-0792).

THE SHOPS AT NORTH BRIDGE   The newest addition to the Mag Mile shopping scene is this mall at 520 N. Michigan Ave. The anchor of the development is a four-story **Nordstrom** (© 312/464-1515). The mall includes the first Chicago locations for **A/X Armani Exchange** (© 312/467-5702), Giorgio Armani's younger and more affordable line, and **Tommy Bahama** (© 312/644-8388), which sells upscale tropical gear (plenty of Hawaiian-style prints and bright colors). The third floor is devoted to children's shops, the best of which is **The Lego Store** (© 312/494-0760)—look for the replicas of Chicago landmarks built out of those distinctive colored-plastic blocks. Future Easy Riders can get decked out in minisized motorcycle gear at the **Harley-Davidson** children's store (© 312/755-9520).

CHIC SHOPPING ON NEARBY OAK STREET

Oak Street has long been a symbol of exclusive designer-label shopping; if a store has an Oak Street address, you can count on its being expensive. This posh, 1-block stretch of exclusive shops is located at the northern tip of the Magnificent Mile, where Michigan Avenue ends and Lake Shore Drive begins. Most of Oak Street is closed on Sunday, except during the holiday season.

Without a doubt, the top independent designer shop in Chicago is **Ultimo,** 114 E. Oak St. (© 312/787-1171), which carries both men's and women's clothing and accessories. This is the place to find hot, up-and-coming designers before they show up in department stores. Ultimo's distinctive lush, red interior also is a welcome change from the minimalist design of so many other designer boutiques.

Oak Street is home to several fancy footwear moguls: Italian shoemaker **Tod's,** 121 E. Oak St. (© 312/943-0070); **Donald J Pliner,** 106 E. Oak St. (© 312/202-9600), whose eponymous founder got his start in Chicago; and elegant French designs from **Robert Clergerie,** 56 E. Oak St. (© 312/867-8720), displayed in a sleek, modern setting. Shoes, stationery—and most importantly, handbags—are available at **kate spade,** 101 E. Oak St. (© 312/ 654-8853), along with the Jack Spade line of men's accessories. The priciest accessories on this very pricey block are probably to be found at French luxury house **Hermès of Paris,** 110 E. Oak St. (© 312/787-8175).

Thread-count fanatics swear by the sheets from **Pratesi,** 67 E. Oak St. (© 312/943-8422), and **Frette,** 41 E. Oak St. (© 312/ 649-3744), both of which supply linens to the top hotels in Europe (and where sheet sets cost more than what some people pay in rent). Other shops include **Loro Piana,** 45 E. Oak St. (© 312/ 664-6644), for Italian cashmere and wool clothing, and **Marina Rinaldi,** 113 E. Oak St. (© 312/867-8700), a division of Italian clothing company MaxMara that specializes in women's clothing sizes 12 and above (making this a welcome respite from the fashion-model-size clothes at surrounding boutiques). **Dunhill,** 55 E. Oak St. (© 312-467-4455), sells upscale British menswear; there's even an old-style barbershop inside.

Anchoring the western end of the block are two haute heavyweights: **Barneys New York,** 25 E. Oak St. (© 312/587-1700), for chic clothing, stellar shoe selection, and always-interesting home accessories (prepare for attitude from the sales staff if you're not dressed to impress); and stratospherically hip Italian designer **Prada,** 30 E. Oak St. (© **312/951-1113**), which offers three floors of sleek, postmodern fashions for men and women, and plenty of the designer's signature handbags.

2 More Shopping Neighborhoods

RIVER NORTH

Along with becoming Chicago's primary art-gallery district, River North—the area west of the Magnificent Mile and north of the Chicago River—has attracted many interesting home-design shops, concentrated on Wells Street from Kinzie Street to Chicago Avenue. The neighborhood even has a mall of its own—**The Shops at the Mart** (© 312/527-7990)—in the Merchandise Mart, at Wells and Kinzie streets, with a standard collection of chain stores.

The rest of the **Merchandise Mart,** the world's largest commercial building, houses mostly interior design showrooms—which are open only to professional designers.

But furniture shoppers will also find plenty of treasures in River North, including **Manifesto,** 755 N. Wells St., at Chicago Avenue (© **312/664-0733**), offering custom-designed furniture, as well as imports from Italy and Austria, and **Mig & Tig,** 549 N. Wells St., at Ohio Street (© **312/644-8277**), a charming furniture and decorative-accessories shop. **Sawbridge Studios,** 153 W. Ohio St. (© **312/828-0055**), between LaSalle and Wells streets, purveys exquisite handcrafted furniture, accessories, and gift items from artisans across America in a handsome, lofted, gallery-type space with exposed brick walls. **Michael FitzSimmons Decorative Arts,** 311 W. Superior St. (© **312/787-0496**), is one of the top dealers anywhere for furniture and furnishings dating to the Arts and Crafts period.

ART GALLERY HOPPING

Since the 1960s, when the Chicago Imagists (painters Ed Paschke, Jim Nutt, and Roger Brown among them) attracted international attention with their shows at the Hyde Park Art Center, the city has been a fertile breeding ground for emerging artists and innovative art dealers. The primary gallery district today is concentrated in the River North neighborhood. More recently, a new generation of gallery owners has set up shop in the rapidly gentrifying West Loop neighborhood, where you'll tend to find more cutting-edge work.

Carl Hammer Gallery   A former schoolteacher and one of the most venerated dealers in Chicago, Carl Hammer touts his wares as "contemporary art and selected historical masterworks by American and European self-taught artists"—but it's the "self-taught" part that warrants emphasis. Hammer helped pioneer the field known as "outsider art," which has since become a white-hot commodity in the international art world. 740 N. Wells St. ✆ **312/266-8512.** Subway/El: Brown or Red line to Chicago.

Donald Young Gallery   Internationally renowned on the contemporary art scene since the late 1970s, Young has made his dramatic West Loop gallery into a haven for critically important artists working in video, sculpture, photography, painting, and installation, including Anne Chu, Gary Hill, Martin Puryear, Bruce Nauman, Cristina Iglesias, Robert Mangold, and Charles Ray. 933 W. Washington St. ✆ **312/455-0100.** Bus: No. 20 (Madison).

Vedanta Gallery   Owner Kavi Gupta (a former investment banker) is widely credited with kicking off the West Loop art scene when he developed this property as a home for new galleries. Vedanta specializes in contemporary art by national and international emerging artists, so you never quite know what you're going to see here. Also worth checking out in the same building are **Thomas McCormick Gallery** (✆ **312/226-6800**) and **Kraft/Lieberman Gallery** (✆ **312/948-0555**). 835 W. Washington St. ✆ **312/432-0708.** Bus: No. 20 (Madison).

Maya Polsky Gallery   Gallery owner Maya Polsky deals in international contemporary art, and also represents some leading local artists—including Chicago's most famous living artist, Ed Paschke. But she's best known for the contemporary and postrevolutionary art of Russia, including the work of such masters as Natalya Nesterova and Sergei Sherstiuk. 215 W. Superior St. ✆ **312/440-0055.** Subway/El: Brown or Red line to Chicago.

Rhona Hoffman Gallery   Like her former partner and spouse, Donald Young, the New York–born Hoffman maintains a high profile on the international contemporary art scene. Today she is the purveyor of such blue-chip players as Cindy Sherman, Sol LeWitt, and Jenny Holzer; she has also added young up-and-comers such as Dawoud Bey. 118 N. Peoria St. ✆ **312/455-1990.** Bus: No. 20 (Madison).

Richard Gray Gallery   Richard Gray is the dean of art dealers in Chicago. Specializing in paintings, sculpture, and drawings by leading artists from the major movements in 20th-century American and European art, Gray and his son, Paul, who now runs the Chicago gallery, have shown the work of such luminaries as Pablo Picasso, Jean Dubuffet, Willem de Kooning, Alexander Calder, Claes Oldenburg, Joan Miró, and Henri Matisse. John Hancock Center, 875 N. Michigan Ave., Suite 2503. (C) 312/642-8877. Subway/El: Red Line to Chicago.

Zolla/Lieberman Gallery   Bob Zolla and Roberta Lieberman kicked off the River North revival when they opened their gallery here in 1976. Today, Zolla/Lieberman represents a wide range of artists—including sculptor Deborah Butterfield, installation artist Vernon Fisher, and painter Terence LaNoue—and this gallery is generally considered the *grande dame* of the area. 325 W. Huron St. (at Orleans St.). (C) 312/944-1990. Subway/El: Brown Line to Chicago.

LINCOLN PARK

The North Side neighborhood of Lincoln Park has a variety of unique specialty shops (mostly locally owned and offering unique and interesting wares) that make it easy to browse through this leafy, picturesque community. Shops are located on the primary commercial arteries running through the area, including Armitage Avenue, Webster Avenue, Halsted Street, Clark Street, and Lincoln Avenue.

ARMITAGE AVENUE   Armitage Avenue has emerged as a shopping destination in its own right. The shops and boutiques here sell everything from artisan-made apparel to offbeat gifts. Most of the shops are concentrated between Halsted Street and Clybourn Avenue.

A number of clothing and accessories stores cater to the hip young women who live in the area. **Celeste Turner,** 859 W. Armitage Ave. ((C) 773/549-3390), offers sophisticated suits, dresses, and eveningwear from up-and-coming designers. **Art Effect,** 934 W. Armitage Ave. ((C) 773/929-3600), which bills itself as a "modern-day general store," stocks everything from cute blouses and creative jewelry to handmade picture frames, which makes for fun browsing. Bargain hunters shouldn't miss **Fox's,** 2150 N. Halsted St. ((C) 773/281-0700), a perennially crowded shop that offers designer clothing at a steep discount. The downside: Most clothing labels are cut out, so you might not know exactly which A-list name you're buying. Another great stop for designer clothes at real-people prices is the consignment shop **McShane's Exchange,** 815 W. Armitage Ave. ((C) 773/525-0282, see listing on p. 151). And don't miss the boutique of local-gal-made-good **Cynthia Rowley,** 808 W. Armitage Ave. ((C) 773/528-6160).

LAKEVIEW

BELMONT AVENUE & CLARK STREET   Radiating from the intersection of Belmont Avenue and Clark Street is a string of shops catering to rebellious kids on tour from their homes in the 'burbs (the Dunkin' Donuts on the corner is often referred to as "Punkin' Donuts" in their honor).

One constant in the ever-changing youth culture has been the **Alley,** 858 W. Belmont Ave., at Clark Street (© **773/525-3180**), an "alternative shopping complex" selling everything from plaster gargoyles to racks of leather jackets. It has separate shops specializing in condoms, cigars, and bondage wear.

All the latest men's (and some women's) fashion styles—from names such as Fresh Jive, Fuct, and Diesel—can be found under the same roof at the multiroom building housing the **Aero** and **Untitled** shops, 2707 N. Clark St. (© **773/404-9225**). Whether you're into tight, fitted fashion or the layered, droopy-pants look, it's here. **Tragically Hip,** a storefront women's boutique at 931 W. Belmont Ave. (© **773/549-1500**), next to the Belmont El train stop, has outlasted many other similar purveyors of cutting-edge women's apparel.

WICKER PARK/BUCKTOWN

Note: For a map of this area, see p. 89.

The go-go gentrification of the Wicker Park/Bucktown area has brought retailers with an artsy bent that reflect the neighborhood's bohemian spirit.

The friendly modern-day Marco Polos at **Pagoda Red,** 1714 N. Damen Ave., second floor (© **773/235-1188**), have imported

---

Moments Taking a Break in Wicker Park

When you're ready to rest your weary self, settle down at a local coffeehouse and soak in Wicker Park's artsy vibe. **Earwax Café,** 1564 N. Milwaukee Ave. (© **773/772-4019**), attracts the jaded and pierced set with a no-frills, slightly gritty atmosphere. **Filter,** across the street at 1585 N. Milwaukee Ave. (© **773/227-4850**), is a little more welcoming; comfy couches fill the main dining room, which features paintings by local artists. Both cafes are near the bustling intersection of North, Milwaukee, and Damen avenues—the heart of Wicker Park—and draw a steady stream of locals.

Chic Boutiques

Chicago has come into its own fashion-wise as a new generation of boutiques has sprung up, offering a fresh array of unique accouterments. These are some of the best.

Just around the corner from chic Oak Street is the newest fashionista haven, **Ikram,** 873 Rush St. (© **312/587-1000**). Run by Ikram Goldman, the shop stocks all the big names, from Valentino to Yves St. Laurent—and whatever else *Vogue* has declared "hot" for the season.

Business is booming at **Jolie Joli,** 2131 N. Southport Ave. (© **773/327-4917**), thanks to its collection of men's and women's wear by hard-to-find labels.

Wicker Park's **p45,** 1643 N. Damen Ave. (© **773/862-4523**), is a gold mine of urbane and cutting-edge fashion for men and women.

Browsing **Robin Richman,** 2108 N. Damen Ave. (© **773/278-6150**), feels more like poking around a big, antiques-filled closet than shopping for threads in Bucktown. While Richman carries a small assortment of men's and women's separates (mostly loose, unstructured pieces), the big draw here is her exquisite sweaters.

Tribeca, 2480½ N. Lincoln Ave. (© **773/528-5958**), is bright, cutesy, and essentially feminine, catering more to the style sensibilities of corporate Lincoln Park 20-somethings than hipster Wicker Park club hoppers. Hiley recently opened a second location at 1013 W. Armitage Ave. (© **773/296-2997**).

beautiful (and expensive) antique furniture and art objects, including Chinese concubine beds, painted Tibetan cabinets, Burmese rolling water vessels, cast-iron lotus bowls, bronze Buddhas, and Chinese inspiration stones. The three women who opened the upscale bazaar **Embelezar** a few years ago at 1639 N. Damen Ave. (© **773/645-9705**) purvey exotic merchandise from around the world, both old and new, including the famous Fortuny silk lamps—hand-painted in Venice at the only studio allowed to reproduce the original Fortuny designs. You'll find a well-edited selection of home accessories and jewelry at **Lille,** 1923 W. North Ave. (© **773/342-0563**).

3 Shopping A to Z

Chicago has shops selling just about anything you could want or need, be it functional or ornamental, whimsical or exotic. Although the following list only scratches the surface, it will give you an idea of the range of merchandise available. You'll find more shops in many of these categories, such as apparel and gifts, covered in the earlier sections of this chapter.

ANTIQUES

Architectural Artifacts, Inc. *(Finds* Chicago has a handful of salvage specialists that cater to the design trades and retail customers seeking an unusual architectural piece for their homes. This one is the best. Its brightly lit, well-organized, cavernous showroom features everything from original mantels, garden ornaments, and vintage bathroom hardware to American and French Art Deco lighting fixtures. Shoppers may also come across portions of historically significant buildings. 4325 N. Ravenswood Ave. (east of Damen Ave. and south of Montrose Ave.). © 773/348-0622. Subway/El: Brown Line to Irving Park.

Broadway Antique Market Want to shop vintage like a pro? Visiting Hollywood prop stylists and local interior designers flock here to find 20th-century antiques in near-perfect condition. In this two-level, 20,000-square-foot vintage megamart, you'll spot both pricey pieces (for example, an Arne Jacobsen egg chair) and affordable collectibles for less than $100 (Roseville pottery, Art Deco barware, Peter Max scarves). 6130 N. Broadway (½ mile north of Hollywood Ave. and Lake Shore Dr.). © 773/743-5444. Subway/El: Red Line to Granville.

Jay Robert's Antique Warehouse This mammoth space boasts 60,000 square feet of fine furniture, as well as fireplaces, stained glass, and an impressive selection of antique clocks. 149 W. Kinzie St. (at LaSalle St.). © 312/222-0167. Subway/El: Brown Line to Merchandise Mart.

BOOKS

Abraham Lincoln Book Shop This bookstore is truly the land of Lincoln, with one of the country's most outstanding collections of Lincolniana, from rare and antique books about the 16th president to collectible signatures, letters, and other documents illuminating the lives of other U.S. presidents and historical figures. The shop carries new historical and academic works, too. 357 W. Chicago Ave. (between Orleans and Sedgwick sts.). © 312/944-3085. Subway/El: Brown Line to Chicago.

Barbara's Bookstore This haven for small, independent press titles also has extensive selections of everything current. In addition, it has a well-stocked children's section, with sitting areas for the tots to peruse the books. Two other branches are a small tourist-targeted shop at Navy Pier, 700 E. Grand Ave. (© **312/222-0890**), and a shop in Oak Park at 1100 Lake St. (© **708/848-9140**). 1350 N. Wells St. (between Division St. and North Ave.). © **312/642-5044.** Subway/El: Brown Line to Sedgwick.

Children in Paradise Bookstore *Kids* This is Chicago's largest children's bookstore, with storytelling hours Tuesday and Wednesday and special events on Saturday. 909 N. Rush St. (between Delaware Place and Walton St.). © **312/951-5437.** Subway/El: Red Line to Chicago.

Prairie Avenue Bookshop This South Loop store does Chicago's architectural tradition proud with the city's finest stock of architecture, design, and technical books. 418 S. Wabash Ave. (between Congress Pkwy. and Van Buren St.). © **312/922-8311.** Subway/El: Red Line to Jackson.

Women & Children First *Kids* This feminist and children's bookstore holds the best selection in the city of titles for, by, and about women. 5233 N. Clark St. (between Foster and Bryn Mawr aves.). © **773/769-9299.** wcfbooks@aol.com. Subway/El: Red Line to Berwyn.

DEPARTMENT STORES

Bloomingdale's The first Midwestern branch of the famed New York department store, Bloomingdale's is on par in terms of size and selection with Marshall Field's Water Tower store. Among its special sections is the one for its souveniresque Bloomingdale's logo merchandise. 900 N. Michigan Ave. (at Walton St.). © **312/440-4460.** Subway/El: Red Line to Chicago.

Carson Pirie Scott & Co. Carson's still appeals primarily to working- and middle-class shoppers. But this venerable Chicago institution that was almost wiped out by the Chicago Fire has made a recent bid to capture the corporate trade, adding a number of more upscale apparel lines, plus a trendy housewares department, to appeal to the moneyed crowd that works in the Loop. 1 S. State St. (at Madison St.). © **312/641-7000.** Subway/El: Red Line to Monroe.

Lord & Taylor Lord & Taylor, one of two large department stores in Water Tower Place (see Marshall Field's, below), carries about what you'd expect: women's, men's, and children's clothing; cosmetics; and accessories. The formerly crowded first floor has gotten an upscale makeover, although the offerings remain fairly affordable.

The store's star department is definitely shoes, for its good selection and sales. Water Tower Place, 835 N. Michigan Ave. ✆ 312/787-7400. Subway/El: Red Line to Chicago.

Marshall Field's   Although it's now owned by Minneapolis-based Target Corporation, Chicagoans still consider Marshall Field's their "hometown" department store. The flagship store, which covers an entire block on State Street, is second in size only to Macy's in New York City. Within this overwhelming space, shoppers will find areas unusual for today's homogeneous department stores, such as the Victorian antique-jewelry department and a gallery of antique-furniture reproductions.

The breadth is what makes this store impressive; shoppers can find a rainbow of shirts for under $20, a floor or so away from the 28 Shop, the Field's homage to designer fashion. For a sophisticated take on the latest trends at a more affordable price, look for clothes from Field's own label, 111 State.

The Water Tower store—the mall's primary anchor—is a scaled-down but respectable version of the State Street store. Its eight floors are actually much more manageable than the enormous flagship, and its merchandise selection is still vast (although this branch tends to focus on the more expensive brands). 111 N. State St. (at Randolph St.). ✆ 312/781-1000. Subway/El: Red Line to Washington. Water Tower Place, 835 N. Michigan Ave. (at Pearson St.). ✆ 312/335-7700. Subway/El: Red Line to Chicago.

Neiman Marcus   Yes, you'll pay top dollar for designer names here—the store does, after all, need to live up to its Needless Mark-up moniker—but Neiman's has a broader price range than many of its critics care to admit. It also has some mighty good sales. The four-story store, a beautiful environment in its own right, sells cosmetics, shoes, furs, fine and fashion jewelry, and men's and children's wear. 737 N. Michigan Ave. (between Superior St. and Chicago Ave.). ✆ 312/642-5900. Subway/El: Red Line to Chicago.

Nordstrom   The newest arrival on the Chicago department store scene, Nordstrom has upped the stakes with its spacious, airy design and trendy touches (wheatgrass growing by the escalators, funky music playing on the stereo system). The company's famed shoe department is large but not overwhelming; more impressive is the cosmetics department, where you'll find a wide array of smaller labels and an "open sell" environment (meaning you're encouraged to try on makeup without a salesperson hovering over you). The Shops at North Bridge, 55 E. Grand Ave. (at Rush St.). ✆ 312/464-1515. Subway/El: Red Line to Grand.

Saks Fifth Avenue   Saks Fifth Avenue might be best known for its designer collections—Valentino, Chloe, and Giorgio Armani, to name a few—but the store also does a swell job of buying more casual and less expensive merchandise. Check out, for example, Saks's own Real Clothes or The Works women's lines. A men's department recently opened in a separate building across Michigan Avenue. Chicago Place, 700 N. Michigan Ave. (at Superior St.). ✆ **312/944-6500.** Subway/El: Red Line to Chicago.

MUSIC

Dusty Groove America   Dusty Groove covers a lot of ground, selling soul, funk, jazz, Brazilian, lounge, Latin, and hip-hop music on new and used vinyl and all new CDs. For the most part, all selections are either rare or imported, or both. 1120 N. Ashland Ave. ✆ **773/342-5800.** Subway/El: Blue Line to Division.

Jazz Record Mart   This is possibly the best jazz record store in the country. Albums are filed alphabetically and by category (vocals, big band, and so on), and there are a couple of turntables to help you spend wisely. 444 N. Wabash Ave. (at Grand Ave.). ✆ **312/222-1467.** Subway/El: Red Line to Grand.

Reckless Records   The best all-round local record store for music that the cool kids listen to, Reckless Records wins Brownie points for its friendly and helpful staff. There's also a location in Wicker Park, at 1532 N. Milwaukee Ave. (✆ **773/235-3727**). 3157 N. Broadway (at Belmont Ave.). ✆ **773/404-5080.** Subway/El: Red or Brown Line to Belmont.

PAPER & STATIONERY

Paper Source   The acknowledged leader of stationery stores in Chicago, Paper Source is now expanding throughout the country (with locations from Boston to Beverly Hills). The store's claim to fame is its collection of handmade paper in a stunning variety of colors and textures. You'll also find one-of-a-kind greeting cards and a large collection of rubber stamps for personalizing your own paper at home. The River North shop is the store's headquarters, but there's also a location in the trendy Armitage shopping district, at 919 W. Armitage Ave. (✆ **773/525-7300**). 232 W. Chicago Ave. (at Franklin St.). ✆ **312/337-0798.** Subway/El: Red or Brown Line to Chicago.

The Watermark   Chicago socialites come here to order their engraved invitations, but this stationery store also carries an intriguing selection of handmade greeting cards for all occasions. 109 E. Oak

St. (1 block from Michigan Ave.). © **312/337-5353**. Subway/El: Red Line to Clark/ Division.

SALONS & SPAS

Charles Ifergan   One of Chicago's top hair salons, Charles Ifergan caters to the ladies-who-lunch, and his rates, which vary according to the seniority of the stylist, are relatively high. If you're a little daring, you can get a cut for the price of the tip. On Tuesday and Wednesday evenings, junior stylists do their thing gratis— under the watchful eye of Monsieur Ifergan (call © **312/640-7444** between 10am and 4pm to make an appointment for that night). 106 E. Oak St. (between Michigan Ave. and Rush St.). © **312/642-4484**. Subway/ El: Red Line to Chicago.

Kiva   Named for the round ceremonial space used by Native Americans for quietness, cleansing, and relaxation of the spirit, Kiva is the city's reigning "super spa." The two-floor, 6,000-square-foot space offers spa, salon, nutrition, and apothecary services, and a nutritional juice and snack bar in a setting that evokes its namesake inspiration. Water Tower Place, 196 E. Pearson St. © **312/840-8120**. Subway/ El: Red Line to Chicago.

Salon Buzz   This hip coiffure parlor, operated by wizardly stylist Andreas Zafiriadis (who has wielded his scissors in Paris, Greece, New York, and California), is the hair salon of the moment, especially for young women in less-than-conservative creative professions. 1 E. Delaware Place (at State St.). © **312/943-5454**. Subway/El: Red Line to Chicago.

Studio 110   Another hip salon catering to the city's bright young things, Studio 110 adds a dash of humor the hairstyling business (witness the shiny disco balls overhead). Yes, you'll see plenty of glamorous gals here, but the staff is friendly and attitude-free. The salon also offers facials, manicures, and pedicures. 110 E. Delaware Place. © **312/337-6411**. Subway/El: Red Line to Chicago.

Truefitt & Hill _(Finds_   Women have their pick of hair and beauty salons, but men don't often come across a place like Truefitt & Hill, the local outpost of a British barbershop. You'll pay a steep price for a haircut here ($40 and up), but the old-world atmosphere is dead-on, from the bow-tied barbers to the antique chairs. 900 N. Michigan Ave., 6th floor. © **312/337-2525**. Subway/El: Red Line to Chicago.

Urban Oasis _(Finds_   After a long day of sightseeing, try a soothing massage in a subdued, Zen-like atmosphere. The ritual begins with a steam or rain shower in a private changing room, followed by the spa treatment you elect—various forms of massage (including a couples' massage, in which you learn to do it yourself), an aromatherapy wrap, or an exfoliating treatment. 12 W. Maple St., 3rd floor (between Dearborn and State sts.). ✆ 312/587-3500. Subway/El: Red Line to Clark/Division.

SHOES

Donald J Pliner   Light and airy, with Tibetan rugs, giant mirrors, and a polished hardwood floor, hometown retail hero Donald Pliner's Oak Street boutique evokes a contemporary art gallery and his shoe selection goes above and beyond whimsical. Cowboy boots, in basic black and outrageously funky colors, fly off the shelves. He also offers mules—in leopard and cow prints, no less—as well as many styles in colored furs. 106 E. Oak St. ✆ 312/202-9600. Subway/El: Red Line to Chicago.

G'Bani   On the corner of Oak and State, this funky, European-style boutique caters to men and women unfulfilled by designs made for the masses. The owner, a former fashion buyer for several high-style stores abroad, sells upscale clothing and shoes (priced $120–$900) often skewed toward fit fashionistas in their 20s through their 40s. 949 N. State St. ✆ 312/440-1718. Subway/El: Red Line to Chicago.

Lori's Designer Shoes ⟨Value⟩   Lori's looks like a local version of Payless Shoes, with shoeboxes stacked on the floor and women surrounded by piles of heels and boots that they try on and trade in search of the perfect fit. But the designer names on most of those shoes prove that this is a step above your typical discount store. A mecca for shoe-obsessed fashion slaves, Lori's stocks all the latest styles, at prices that average 10% to 30% below department-store rates. 824 W. Armitage Ave. (between Sheffield Ave. and Halsted St.). ✆ 773/281-5655. Subway/El: Brown Line to Armitage.

SPORTING GOODS

Niketown ⟨Overrated⟩   In the days when Michael Jordan was the city's reigning deity, Niketown was the place to bask in his glory. These days, Niketown is no longer unique to Chicago (it's sprung up in cities from Atlanta to Honolulu), and the store's celebration of athletes can't cover up the fact that the ultimate goal is to sell expensive shoes. But the crowds keep streaming in. 669 N. Michigan Ave. ✆ 312/642-6363. Subway/El: Red Line to Grand.

Sportmart   The largest sporting-goods store in the city, the flagship store of this chain offers seven floors of merchandise, from running apparel to camping gear. Sports fans will be in heaven in the first- and fifth-floor team merchandise departments, where Cubs, Bulls, and Sox jerseys abound. Cement handprints of local sports celebs dot the outside of the building. 620 N. LaSalle St. (at Ontario St.). ✆ 312/337-6151. Subway/El: Red Line to Grand.

TOYS

Saturday's Child You'll know from the vintage decor (wood floors, a pressed-tin ceiling) that this is no cookie-cutter modern shop. Instead, this is a place that values classic designs over the latest electronic gadgets. The clever toys range from rubber snakes and frogs to sidewalk chalk and kids' large-face wristwatches. 2146 N. Halsted St. (south of Webster Ave.). ✆ 773/525-8697. Subway/El: Brown Line to Armitage.

Toyscape The proprietors bar the door to Barbie at this cluttered Lakeview toyshop. Their tastes run to good old-fashioned wooden toys, musical instruments, and puppets, most of which don't require batteries. 2911 N. Broadway (between Diversey Pkwy. and Belmont Ave.). ✆ 773/665-7400. Subway/El: Brown Line to Diversey.

VINTAGE FASHION/RESALE SHOPS

The Daisy Shop A significant step up from your standard vintage store, The Daisy Shop specializes only in couture fashions. Well-dressed women from throughout the world stop by here in search of the perfect one-of-a-kind item. 67 E. Oak St. (between Michigan Ave. and Rush St.). ✆ 312/943-8880. Subway/El: Brown Line to Sedgwick.

Flashy Trash *(Finds* One of the best vintage stores anywhere, Flashy Trash mixes used and new clothing, from Todd Oldham jeans to used tuxes to dress-up accessories such as feather boas, wigs, and jewelry. 3524 N. Halsted St. (between Belmont Ave. and Addison St.). ✆ 773/327-6900. Subway/El: Red Line to Addison.

McShane's Exchange *(Finds* This consignment shop has a selection that's a few steps above the standard thrift store, and for designer bargains it can't be beat. The longer a piece stays in stock, the lower the price drops—and I've done plenty of double-takes at the price tags here: Calvin Klein coats, Prada sweaters, and Armani jackets all going for well under $100. McShane's also has another location at 1141 W. Webster St. (✆ 773/525-0211), with a similar selection. 815 W. Armitage Ave. (at Halsted St.). ✆ 773/525-0282. Subway/El: Brown Line to Armitage.

8

Chicago After Dark

Chicago's bustling energy isn't confined to daylight hours. The city offers something for everyone—from discriminating culture vultures to hard-core club-hoppers. But nightlife here has a distinctly low-key, Midwestern flavor. Chicago's thriving theater scene was built by performers who valued gritty realism and a communal work ethic; from the big-league Steppenwolf and Goodman theaters down to the scrappy storefront companies that keep springing up throughout town, that down-to-earth energy is still very much a part of theater here. Chicago also has a thriving music scene, with clubs devoted to everything from jazz and blues to alternative rock, reggae, and Latin beats. Music and nightclub haunts are scattered throughout the city, but many are concentrated in River West, Lincoln Park, Lakeview, and Wicker Park.

For up-to-date entertainment listings, check the local newspapers and magazines, particularly the "Friday" and "Weekend Plus" sections of the two dailies, the *Chicago Tribune* and the *Chicago Sun-Times;* the *Chicago Reader* or *New City,* two free weekly tabloids with extensive listings; and the monthly *Chicago* magazine. The *Tribune's* entertainment-oriented website, **www.metromix.com**; the *Reader's* website, **www.chireader.com**; and the local Citysearch website, **www.chicago.citysearch.com**, are also excellent sources of information, with lots of opinionated reviews. The "Entertainment and Night Life" section of Out Chicago's website, **www.out chicago.org**, provides a directory of links to bars, clubs, and performing-arts venues that welcome gay and lesbian visitors.

1 The Performing Arts

Chicago is a regular stop on the big-name entertainment circuit, whether it's the national tour of Broadway shows or pop music acts. High-profile shows sometime have their first runs here before moving on to New York. Thanks to extensive renovation efforts, performers now have some impressive venues where they can strut their stuff.

CLASSICAL MUSIC

For current listings of classical music concerts and opera, call the **Chicago Dance and Music Alliance** (℃ 312/987-1123).

Chicago Symphony Orchestra ✦✦   The Chicago Symphony Orchestra (CSO) is being led into its second century by music director Daniel Barenboim, and it remains among the best in the world—a legacy of the late maestro Sir Georg Solti, who captured a record-breaking 31 Grammy awards for his CSO recordings and showcased the orchestra at other major musical capitals during frequent international tours. Barenboim has proven a worthy successor to the baton, a talented conductor and pianist prodigy whom the CSO recruited from the Orchestre de Paris after Solti's death in 1997. Staking out his own legacy in the renovated and expanded Symphony Center complex, he has steadily introduced more modern works by 20th-century composers into the orchestra's repertoire. But you will certainly not be disappointed by the CSO's treatment of crowd-pleasing Beethoven or Brahms.

Although in high demand, good seats for all concerts often become available on concert days. Call Symphony Center or stop by the box office to check availability.

The **Civic Orchestra of Chicago,** the training orchestra of the Chicago Symphony since 1919, is also highly regarded and presents free programs at Orchestra Hall. The **Chicago Symphony Chorus** also performs there. Orchestra Hall, in Symphony Center, 220 S. Michigan Ave. ℃ 312/294-3000. www.cso.org. Tickets $10–$90; box seats $165. Subway/El: Red Line to Jackson.

OPERA

Lyric Opera of Chicago ✦✦   One of the top American opera companies, the Lyric attracts the very best singers in the world for its lavish productions. The Lyric's talented musicians and performers satisfy the opera snobs, while newcomers are often swept away by all the grand opera dramatics (English supertitles make it easy to follow the action).

The Lyric Opera performs in the handsome 3,563-seat Art Deco Civic Opera House, the second-largest opera house in the country, built in 1929. If you're sitting in one of the upper balconies, you'll definitely want to bring binoculars (if you're nice, the regulars sitting nearby may lend you theirs). There's only one problem with catching a show at the Lyric: the season, which runs through early March, sells out way in advance. Single tickets are sometimes available a few months in advance. Your other option is to call the day of a performance, when you can sometimes buy tickets that subscribers have turned in because they won't be using them. Civic Opera House, at Madison St. and Wacker Dr. © 312/332-2244. Fax 312/332-8120. www.lyricopera.org. Tickets $26–$125. Subway/El: Brown Line to Washington.

DANCE

Chicago's dance scene is lively, but unfortunately it doesn't attract the same crowds as our theaters or music performances. So although some of our resident dance troupes have international reputations, they spend much of their time touring to support themselves. Depending on the timing of your visit, you may have a choice of dance performances—or there may be none at all.

For complete information on local dance performances, call the Chicago Dance and Music Alliance information line at © 312/987-1123.

Hubbard Street Dance Chicago   If you're going to see just one dance performance while you're in town, make it Hubbard Street. Chicago's best-known dance troupe mixes jazz, modern, ballet, and theater dance into an exhilarating experience. Sometimes whimsical, sometimes romantic, the crowd-pleasing 22-member ensemble incorporates a range of dance traditions, from Kevin O'Day to Twyla Tharp, who has choreographed pieces exclusively for Hubbard Street. Although the troupe spends most of the year touring, it has regular 2- to 3-week Chicago engagements in the fall and spring. Offices at 1147 W. Jackson Blvd. © 312/850-9744. www.hubbardstreetdance.com. Tickets $25–$70.

Joffrey Ballet of Chicago   While this major classical company concentrates on touring, the Joffrey schedules about 6 weeks of performances a year in its hometown. Led by co-founder and artistic director Gerald Arpino, the company is committed to the classic works of the 20th century. Its repertoire extends from the ballets of Arpino, Robert Joffrey, Balanchine, and Jerome Robbins to the cutting-edge works of Alonzo King and Chicago choreographer Randy Duncan. The Joffrey continues to draw crowds to its popular rock ballet, *Billboards,* which is set to the music of Prince, and continues to tour internationally. The company is usually in town in the spring (March or April), October, and December, when it stages a popular rendition of the holiday favorite *The Nutcracker.* Offices at 70 E. Lake St. © 312/739-0120. www.joffreyballet.org. Tickets $30–$75.

THEATER

Ever since the Steppenwolf Theatre Company burst onto the national radar in the 1970s and early 1980s with gritty, in-your-face productions of Sam Shepard's *True West* and Lanford Wilson's *Balm in Gilead,* Chicago has been known as a theater town. Local theater troupes have gained respect for their risk-taking and no-holds-barred emotional style. Some of Broadway's most acclaimed dramas in recent years (Goodman Theatre's revival of *Death of a Salesman* and Steppenwolf's *The Grapes of Wrath,* to name just two) have been hatched on Chicago stages. Steppenwolf and Goodman have led the way in forging Chicago's reputation as a regional theater power-house, but a host of other performers are creating their own special styles. With more than 200 theaters, Chicago might have dozens of productions playing on any given weekend—and seeing a show here is on my must-do list for all visitors.

The listings below represent only a fraction of the city's theater offerings. For a complete listing of current productions playing on a given evening, check the comprehensive listings in the two free weeklies, the *Reader* (which reviews just about every show in town) and *New City,* or the Friday sections of the two dailies. The **League of Chicago Theatres'** website (www.chicagoplays.org) also lists all theater productions playing in the area.

GETTING TICKETS

To order tickets for many plays and events, call **Ticketmaster Arts Line** (© **312/902-1500**), a centralized phone-reservation system that allows you to charge full-price tickets (with an additional service charge) for productions at more than 50 Chicago theaters. Individual box offices will also take credit-card orders by phone, and many of the smaller theaters will reserve seats for you with a simple request under your name left on their answering machines. For hard-to-get tickets, try the **Ticket Exchange** (© **800/666-0779** outside Chicago, or 312/902-1888).

HALF-PRICE TICKETS   For half-price tickets on the day of the show (on Fri. you can also purchase tickets for weekend perform-ances), drop by one of the **Hot Tix** ticket centers (© **312/977-1755**), located in the Loop at 78 W. Randolph St. (just east of Clark St.); at the Water Works Visitor Center, 163 E. Pearson St.; in Lincoln Park at Tower Records, 2301 N. Clark St.; and in several suburban locations. Hot Tix also offers advance-purchase tickets at full price. Tickets are not sold over the phone. The Hot Tix website (www.hottix.org) lists what's on sale for that day beginning at 10am.

In addition, a few theaters offer last-minute discounts on their leftover seats. Steppenwolf Theatre Company often has half-price tickets on the day of a performance; call or stop by the box office 1 hour before showtime. The "Tix at Six" program at the Goodman Theatre offers half-price, day-of-show tickets; many of them are excellent seats that have been returned by subscribers. Tickets go on sale at the box office at 6pm for evening performances, noon for matinees.

DOWNTOWN THEATERS

Chicago Shakespeare Theatre on Navy Pier   This group's relatively new home is a visually stunning, state-of-the-art jewel. The centerpiece of the glass-box complex, which rises seven stories, is a 525-seat courtyard-style theater patterned loosely after the Swan Theater in Stratford-upon-Avon. But what keeps subscribers coming back is the talented company of actors, including some of the finest Shakespeare performers in the country.

The main theater presents three plays a year—almost always by the Bard—with founder and artistic director Barbara Gaines usually directing one of the shows. We Shakespeare Theatre subscribers are a very loyal lot, so snagging tickets can be a challenge; reserve well in advance, if possible. If you have a choice of seats, avoid the upper balcony—the tall chairs are fairly uncomfortable and you have to lean way over the railing to see all the action on stage—definitely not recommended for anyone with a fear of heights. 800 E. Grand Ave. ℂ **312/595-5600**. www.chicagoshakes.com. Tickets $48–$58. Subway/El: Red Line to Grand, then bus no. 29 to Navy Pier. Guaranteed parking in attached garage at 40% discount.

Goodman Theatre ℛ   The Goodman is the dean of legitimate theaters in Chicago. Under artistic director Robert Falls, the Goodman produces both original productions—such as Horton Foote's *The Young Man from Atlanta* before it went directly to Broadway— and familiar standards, including everything from Shakespeare to musicals. Its acclaimed revival of Arthur Miller's *Death of a Salesman,* starring Brian Dennehy, not only made it to the Broadway stage in 1999, but won four Tonys—more than any other production. Productions at the Goodman are always solid; you may not see anything revolutionary, but you'll get some of the best actors in the city and top-notch production values. 170 N. Dearborn St. ℂ **312/**

443-3800. www.goodman-theatre.org. Tickets $30–$50 main stage, $10–$40 studio. Subway/El: Red Line to Washington/State or Lake/State; Brown or Orange line to Clark/Lake.

Noble Fool Theater   The newest addition to the downtown theater scene is this comedy-focused company. If you're looking for a fun show downtown, where you can relax and let loose, this is the place to go. The Main Stage features a full-length play, usually a comedy; the Studio hosts Noble Fool's signature show, *Flanagan's Wake,* an "interactive" Irish wake that encourages audience participation (call in advance for tickets because it does tend to sell out). 16 W. Randolph St. (at State St.) © **773/202-8843**. www.noblefool.com. Tickets $32–$36 main stage, $25–$29 studio stage. Subway/El: Brown Line to Randolph or Red Line to Washington.

OFF-LOOP THEATERS

The thespian soil here must be fertile. It's continually mined by Tinseltown and TV, which have lured away such talents as Macy, John Malkovich, Joan Allen, Dennis Franz, George Wendt, John and Joan Cusack, Aidan Quinn, Anne Heche, and Lili Taylor. But even as those actors get lured away by higher paychecks, there's always a whole new pool of talent waiting to take over. This constant renewal keeps the city's theatrical scene invigorated with new ideas and new energy.

Court Theatre *(Finds*   This 250-seat theater, affiliated with the University of Chicago, started out heavily steeped in Molière but has branched into other classics of French literature, Shakespeare, and equally highbrow stuff—with some Oscar Wilde and Noel Coward thrown in for fun. Court Theatre's actors are considered among the finest in the city, and with good reason; they turn classic texts into vibrant, energetic live theater. 5535 S. Ellis Ave. (at 55th St.). © **773/753-4472**. www.courttheatre.org. Tickets $30–$40. Bus: No. 6 (Jeffrey Express).

Lookingglass Theatre Company ⚔   A rising star on the Chicago theatrical scene, Lookingglass has a style all its own, producing original shows and unusual literary adaptations in a highly physical and visually imaginative style. The company, founded more than a decade ago by graduates of Northwestern University (including *Friend* David Schwimmer), stages several shows each year. Lookingglass shows emphasize visual effects as much as they do acting, whether it's having performers wade through a giant shallow pool or take to the sky on trapezes. 821 N. Michigan Ave. © **312/337-0665**. www.lookingglasstheatre.org. Tickets $30–$50. Subway/El: Red Line to Chicago.

Steppenwolf Theatre Company *(Overrated* Once a pioneer of bare-bones guerilla theater, Steppenwolf has moved firmly into the mainstream, with a state-of-the-art theater and production budgets as big as any in town. The company has garnered many national awards and has also launched the careers of several highly respected and well-known actors, including John Malkovich, Gary Sinise, Joan Allen, John Mahoney (of *Frasier*), and Laurie Metcalf (of *Roseanne*). Famous for pioneering the edgy, so-called "rock 'n' roll," spleen-venting style of Chicago acting in the 1970s and 1980s, Steppenwolf lately has become a victim of its own success. No longer a scrappy storefront theater, it now stages world premieres by emerging playwrights, revivals of classics, and adaptations of well-known literary works. While the acting is always high caliber, shows at Steppenwolf can be hit or miss, and unlike the early days, you're certainly not guaranteed a thrilling theatrical experience. 1650 N. Halsted St. (at North Ave.). ℂ 312/335-1650. www.steppenwolf.org. Tickets $35–$50 main stage, $25–$28 studio. If they're available, rush tickets for the main stage are sold at half price (studio tickets for $10) an hour before a performance (call or stop by the box office). Subway/El: Red Line to North/Clybourn.

Victory Gardens Theater *(Finds* Victory Gardens is one of the few pioneers of off-Loop theater still standing since the 1970s. The company was rewarded with a Tony Award for regional theater in 2001—a real coup for a theater of this relatively small size. What the Tony committee recognized was Victory Gardens' unswerving commitment to developing playwrights. The five or six productions presented each season are all new works. The plays tend to be very accessible stories about real people and real situations—nothing too experimental. Even though most shows don't feature nationally known actors, the casts are always first-rate, and the plays usually leave you with something to think about. 2257 N. Lincoln Ave. (at Belden Ave.). ℂ 773/871-3000. www.victorygardens.org. Tickets $30–$35. Subway/El: Red or Brown line to Fullerton.

2 Comedy & Improv

In the mid-1970s, *Saturday Night Live* brought Chicago's unique brand of comedy to national attention. But even back then, John Belushi and Bill Murray were just the latest brood to hatch from the number-one incubator of Chicago-style humor, Second City. From Mike Nichols and Robert Klein to Mike Meyers and Tina Fey, two generations of American comics have honed their skills in Chicago before making their fortunes as film and TV stars.

ImprovOlympic *(Finds* ImprovOlympic was founded 20 years ago as a training ground for improv actors by the late, great, and inexplicably unsung Del Close, an improv pioneer who branched off from his more mainstream counterparts at Second City to pursue an unorthodox methodology.

The ImprovOlympic offers a nightclub setting for a variety of unscripted nightly performances, from free-form shows to shows loosely based on concepts such as *Star Trek* or dating. Like all improv, you're gambling here: It could be a big laugh, or the amateur performers could go down in flames. 3541 N. Clark St. (at Addison St.). ☎ 773/880-0199. www.improvolymp.com. Tickets $5–$12. Subway/El: Red Line to Addison.

Second City For more than 40 years, Second City has been the top comedy club in Chicago and the most famous of its ilk in the country. Photos of its vast class of famous graduates line the lobby walls, from Elaine May to John Belushi to current *Saturday Night Live* cast members Tina Fey, Horatio Sanz, and Rachel Dratch.

Today's Second City is a veritable factory of improv, with shows on two stages (the storied main stage and the smaller Second City ETC) and a hugely popular training school. The main-stage ensembles do change frequently, and the shows can swing wildly back and forth on the hilarity meter. Your best bet is to check the theater reviews in the *Reader,* a local free weekly, for an opinion on the current offering. To sample the Second City experience, catch the free postshow improv session (it gets going around 10:30pm); no ticket is necessary if you skip the main show (except Fri). 1616 N. Wells St. (in the Pipers Alley complex at North Ave.). ☎ 312/337-3992 or 877/778-4707. www.secondcity.com. Tickets $8–$17. Subway/El: Brown Line to Sedgwick.

3 The Music Scene

JAZZ

In the first great wave of black migration from the South just after World War I, jazz was transported from the Storyville section of New Orleans to Chicago. Jelly Roll Morton and Louis Armstrong made Chicago a jazz hotspot in the 1920s, and their spirit lives on in a whole new generation of musicians. Chicago jazz is known for its collaborative spirit and a certain degree of risk-taking—which you can experience at a number of convivial clubs.

Andy's Jazz Club Casual and comfortable, Andy's, a full restaurant and bar, is popular with both the hard-core and the neophyte jazz enthusiast. It's the only place in town where you can hear jazz

Lincoln Park & Wrigleyville After Dark

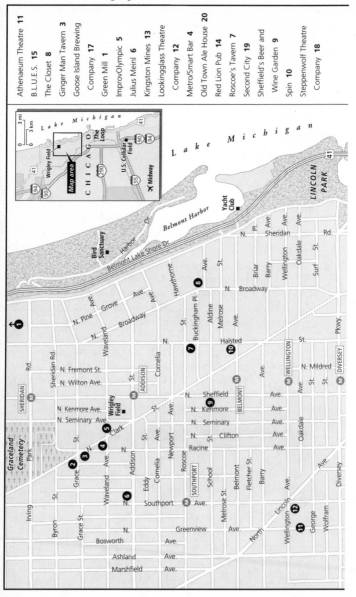

Athenaeum Theatre 11
B.L.U.E.S. 15
The Closet 8
Ginger Man Tavern 3
Goose Island Brewing
Company 17
Green Mill 1
ImprovOlympic 5
Julius Meinl 6
Kingston Mines 13
Lookingglass Theatre
Company 12
Metro/Smart Bar 4
Old Town Ale House 20
Red Lion Pub 14
Roscoe's Tavern 7
Second City 19
Sheffield's Beer and
Wine Garden 9
Spin 10
Steppenwolf Theatre
Company 18

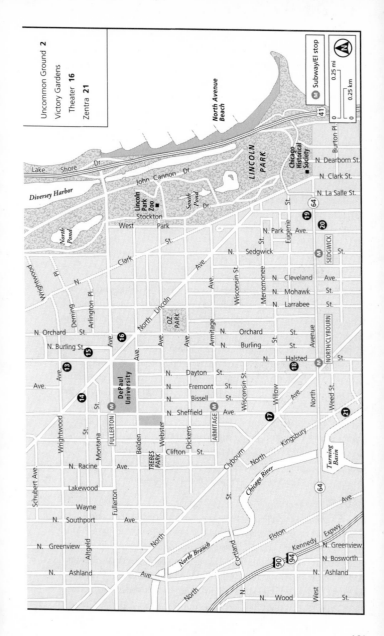

Uncommon Ground **2**
Victory Gardens
Theater **16**
Zentra **21**

Lake Shore Dr.

Diversey Harbor

North Pond

Windsinewood Pl.

Wrightwood Ave.

N. Racine Ave.

Lakewood

Wayne

N. Southport Ave.

N. Greenview

Altgeld

N. Ashland Ave.

Schubert Ave.

Fullerton

North

North Branch

Montana

Belden

Webster

Dickens

Clifton St.

TREBES PARK

Clybourn

Elston

North

Cortland

N. Wood

West St.

Kennedy Expwy.

N. Greenview

N. Bosworth

N. Ashland

Chicago River

Turning Basin

Kingsbury Ave.

Weed St.

North Ave.

Willow

N. Sheffield Ave.

N. Bissell St.

N. Fremont St.

N. Dayton St.

Wisconsin St.

N. Burling St.

N. Orchard St.

Armitage

N. Lincoln Ave.

OZ PARK

Clark St.

Arlington Pl.

Deming Pl.

N. Orchard St.

N. Burling St.

DePaul University

FULLERTON

ARMITAGE

SEDGWICK

NORTH/CLYBOURN

N. Larrabee St.

N. Mohawk St.

N. Cleveland Ave.

Menomonee

Wisconsin St.

N. Sedgwick

N. Park Ave.

Eugenie St.

North Ave.

West Park St.

Stockton

Lincoln Park Zoo

South Pond

John Cannon Dr.

LINCOLN PARK

Chicago Historical Society

N. Dearborn St.

N. Clark St.

N. La Salle St.

Burton Pl.

North Avenue Beach

41

90 94

64

64

16

15

13

14

2

17

18

19

20

21

Ⓜ Subway/El stop

0   0.25 mi
0   0.25 km

nearly all day long. 11 E. Hubbard St. (between State St. and Wabash Ave.). © 312/642-6805. Cover $4–$10. Subway/El: Red Line to Grand.

Green Mill ★ *(Finds)*   In the heart of Uptown, the Green Mill is "Old Chicago" to the rafters. A popular watering hole during the 1920s and 1930s, when Al Capone was a regular and the headliners included Sophie Tucker and Al Jolson, it still retains its speakeasy flavor. On Sunday night, the Green Mill hosts the Uptown Poetry Slam, when poets vie for the open mike to roast and ridicule each other's work. Most nights, however, jazz is on the menu, beginning around 9pm and winding down just before closing at 4am (5am Sat). Regular performers include vocalist Kurt Elling, who performs standards and some of his own songs with a quartet, and chanteuse Patricia Barber (they're both worth seeing if they're playing while you're in town). The Green Mill is a Chicago treasure and not to be missed. Get there early to claim one of the plush velvet booths. 4802 N. Broadway (at Lawrence Ave.). © 773/878-5552. Cover $6–$15. Subway/El: Red Line to Lawrence.

Jazz Showcase *(Kids)*   Spanning more than 50 years and several locations, founder Joe Segal has become synonymous with jazz in Chicago. His son, Wayne, recently took over the business, but this latest venue in the River North restaurant and entertainment district is the spiffiest yet, a spacious and handsome room with sharp black-and-white photographs of jazz greats, many of whom have passed through Segal's clubs. There are two shows a night, and reservations are recommended for big-name headliners. The club admits all ages (free for children under 12), has a nonsmoking policy, and offers a Sunday 4pm matinee show. The Segals's latest outpost is the new **Joe's Be-bop Cafe and Jazz Emporium** at Navy Pier, 600 E. Grand Ave. (© 312/595-5299), a Southern-style barbecue restaurant with live music nightly. 59 W. Grand St. (at Clark St.). © 312/670-2473. www.jazz showcase.com. Tickets $15–$20. Subway/El: Red Line to Grand.

BLUES

If Chicagoans were asked to pick one musical style to represent their city, most of us would start singing the blues. Thanks in part to the presence of the influential Chess Records, Chicago became a hub of blues activity after World War II, with musicians such as Muddy Waters, Howlin' Wolf, and Buddy Guy all recording and performing here. Today, the blues has become yet another tourist attraction (especially for international visitors), but the quality and variety of blues acts in town is still impressive.

Blue Chicago *(Kids)*   Blue Chicago pays homage to female blues belters with a strong lineup of the best women vocalists around. The 1940s-style brick-walled room, decorated with original artwork of Chicago blues vignettes, is open Monday through Saturday, with music beginning at 9pm. 736 N. Clark St. (between Chicago Ave. and Superior St.). ℂ 312/642-6261. www.bluechicago.com. Cover $6–$8. Subway/El: Red or Brown line to Chicago.

B.L.U.E.S.   On the Halsted strip, look for B.L.U.E.S.—the name says it all. This is a small joint for the serious blues aficionado—you won't miss a single move of the musicians standing on stage only yards away. Shows start at 9:30pm daily. 2519 N. Halsted St. (between Wrightwood and Fullerton aves.). ℂ 773/528-1012. www.chicagobluesbar.com. Cover $5–$10. Subway/El: Red or Brown line to Fullerton.

Buddy Guy's Legends *(Finds)*   A legend himself, the gifted guitarist runs one of the more popular and most comfortable clubs in town. You may catch Buddy on stage when he's in town. (Or, if you're lucky, one of his high-profile friends, such as Mick Jagger, will stop by for an impromptu jam session.) The kitchen serves good Louisiana-style soul food and barbecue. Buddy Guy's is planning a move 1 block north of the current location, so call first to check the address. 754 S. Wabash Ave. (between Balbo Dr. and 8th St.). ℂ 312/427-0333. www.buddyguys.com. Cover $10–$15. Subway/El: Red Line to Harrison.

Kingston Mines   Chicago's premier blues bar, Kingston Mines, is where musicians congregate after their own gigs to jam together and to socialize. Celebs have been known to drop by when they're in town shooting movies, but most nights the crowd includes a big contingent of conventioneers looking for a rockin' night on the town. But don't worry about the tourist factor—everyone's here to have a good time, and the energy is infectious. The show begins at 9:30pm daily, with two bands on two stages, and goes until 4am (5am Sat). 2548 N. Halsted St. (between Wrightwood and Fullerton aves.). ℂ 773/477-4646. www.kingstonmines.com. Cover $12–$15. Subway/El: Red or Brown line to Fullerton.

ROCK (BASICALLY)

Most Chicago bands concentrate on keeping it real, happy to per-form at small local clubs and not obsessing (at least openly) about getting a record contract. The city also is a regular stop for touring bands, from the big stadium acts to smaller up-and-coming bands. Scan the *Reader* or *New City* to see who's playing where.

Double Door *(Finds)*   This club has capitalized on the Wicker Park/ Bucktown neighborhood's ascendance as a breeding ground for rock and alternative music. Owned by the proprietors of Metro (see below), the club has some of the better acoustics and sight lines in the city and attracts buzz bands and unknowns to its stage. When you need to escape the noise, there's a lounge-type area, the Dirt Room, with pool tables in the basement. Concerts are staged Tuesday through Sunday. 1572 N. Milwaukee Ave. (at North Ave.). © 773/489-3160. www.doubledoor.com. Tickets $5–$15. Subway/El: Blue Line to Damen.

Metro   Metro, located in an old auditorium, is Chicago's premier venue for live alternative/rock acts on the verge of breaking into the big time. There's not much in the way of atmosphere—it's basically a big black room with a stage—but the place has an impressive history. Everybody who is anybody has played here when they were starting out, from REM to Pearl Jam to such local heroes as the Smashing Pumpkins. Newer "alternative" bands that are getting attention from MTV and radio stations show up at Metro eventually. Tickets are sold in person through the box office in the attached record shop, **Clubhouse** (sans service charges), or by phone through Ticketmaster. 3730 N. Clark St. (at Racine Ave.). © 773/549-0203, or 312/559-1212 for Ticketmaster orders. www.metrochicago.com. Tickets $12–$20. Subway/El: Red Line to Sheridan.

COUNTRY, FOLK & ETHNIC MUSIC

The mix of cultures and ethnicities in Chicago's neighborhoods translates into a wealth of music clubs catering to all kinds of musical tastes, from mellow folk and melancholy Irish to suave salsa and spicy reggae.

HotHouse *(Finds)*   This "Center for International Performance and Exhibition" schedules some of the most eclectic programming in the city, attracting well-known jazz and avant-garde musicians from around the world. When the heavy hitters aren't booked, you'll see anything from local musicians improvising on "invented instruments" to Afro-Cuban dance troupes to Japanese blues singers. 31 E. Balbo Dr. (at S. Wabash Ave.). © 312/362-9707. www.hothouse.net. Cover $10–$25. Subway/El: Red Line to Harrison.

Old Town School of Folk Music *(Finds)*   Country, folk, bluegrass, Latin, Celtic—the Old Town School of Folk Music covers a spectrum of indigenous musical forms. The school's home, in a former 1930s library, is the world's largest facility dedicated to the preservation and presentation of traditional and contemporary folk music. 4544 N. Lincoln Ave. (between Wilson and Montrose aves.). © 773/

728-6000. www.oldtownschool.org. Tickets $10–$30. Subway/El: Blue Line to Western.

CABARETS & PIANO BARS

Davenport's Piano Bar & Cabaret *Finds*   The youthful hipster environs of Wicker Park isn't the first place you'd expect to find a tried-and-true piano bar and cabaret venue. But Davenport's is doing its best to revive a fading art form. The piano bar in front is flashier than the subdued cabaret in back, featuring a singing wait-staff, blue-velvet banquettes, funky lighting fixtures, and a hand-painted mural-topped bar. 1383 N. Milwaukee Ave. (just south of North Ave.). © **773/278-1830.** www.davenportspianobar.com. Cover $10–$25. Subway/El: Blue Line to Damen.

Zebra Lounge *Finds*   The most wonderfully quirky piano bar in town, Zebra Lounge has a loyal following despite (or maybe because of) the campy decor. Just as you would expect, black-and-white stripes are the unifying decor theme at this dark, shoebox-size Gold Coast spot. For the past quarter century, it has been a raucous piano bar, attracting a multigenerational crowd of regulars. The scene is relatively mellow early in the evening, though it can get packed late into the night on weekends. 1220 N. State Pkwy. (between Division and Goethe sts.). © **312/642-5140.** No cover. Subway/El: Red Line to Clark/Division.

4 The Club Scene

Chicago is the hallowed ground where house music was hatched in the 1980s, so it's no surprise to find several dance clubs pounding away with a mostly under-30 crowd. Given the fickle nature of club goers, some places listed below might have disappeared by the time you read this.

Funky Buddha Lounge   Located a bit off the beaten path, west of the River North gallery district, this club blends in with its industrial surroundings. Inside is a different scene altogether: low red lighting, seductive dens with black-leather and faux leopard-skin sofas, lots of candles, and antique light fixtures salvaged from an old church. The DJs are among the best in the city, flooding the nice-size dance floor with hip-hop to bhangra, funk to African, and soul to underground house. Hugely popular Thursday nights pack in the young, mostly white club kids, but Fridays and Saturdays feature a cool, eclectic crowd decked out in funky gear. 728 W. Grand Ave. © **312/666-1695.** www.funkybuddha.com. Cover $15–$20. Bus: No. 65 (Grand Ave.), but take a cab at night.

Le Passage The Gold Coast's swankiest nightclub fits all the pre-requisites for chic exclusivity, starting with the semihidden entrance at the end of a narrow (but well-lit) alleyway just steps from Oak Street's Prada and Barneys New York stores. You descend down a long flight of stairs into an environment filled with expensive, gilded furnishings and exquisite decor imported from France; to gain access you must first pass muster with the gatekeepers manning the velvet rope. The beautiful, the rich, and the designer-suited come here for the loungy aesthetic. The soundtrack mixes R&B, soul, hip-hop, house, funk, and acid jazz. Another highlight is the stellar French fusion menu. 1 Oak Place (between Rush and State sts). ✆ 312/255-0022. Cover $15–$20. Subway/El: Red Line to Chicago.

Red Dog Another spot you have to reach by slipping down an alley, Red Dog is a loft space overlooking the action in Wicker Park. The throbbing beats of underground and industrial house attract serious clubgoers. As far as what to wear, anything goes. Dress up, down, casual, or extreme—you'll see pretty much everything here. The gay-themed Boom-Boom Room on Monday is hands-down the most exotic night on the social calendar, with club kids, drag queens, and platform dancers all bobbing to a house beat. Besides Monday, the club is open Wednesdays and weekends. 1958 W. North Ave. (at Milwaukee Ave.). ✆ 773/278-1009. Cover $6–$10. Subway/El: Blue Line to Damen.

Zentra Club hoppers often make the Middle Eastern/Moroc-can–flavored Zentra, which stays open into the wee hours, their last stop of the night. Plugged into a large four-room space, Zentra is riding the current trend wave of East meets West, with exotic Moroccan textiles, thick drapes, Indian silks, red lanterns and funky chrome fixtures, and even "Hookah Girls" proffering hits on hookah pipes packed with fruity tobacco blends. Upstairs caters to those who want to dance to progressive dance and techno sounds, while downstairs has DJs spinning mostly house and hip-hop. 923 W. Weed St. (just south of North Ave. at Clybourn Ave.). ✆ 312/787-0400. Cover $15–$20. Subway/El: Red Line to North/Clybourn.

5 The Bar & Cafe Scene

If you want to soak up the atmosphere of a neighborhood tavern or sports bar, it's best to venture beyond downtown into the surround-ing neighborhoods.

BARS
THE LOOP & VICINITY

The Berghoff   Women weren't admitted to the stand-up bar at The Berghoff—a Chicago institution with claim to the city's post-Prohibition liquor license no. 1—until they protested their way in the door in 1969. The only women's bathroom is in the dining room, but today Loop business types of both genders gather after work in the dark oak-paneled bar for one of The Berghoff's own drafts and a roast-beef sandwich. 17 W. Adams St. (between Dearborn and State sts.). ✆ 312/427-3170. Subway/El: Red Line to Jackson.

Miller's Pub   A true Loop landmark, Miller's has been serving up after-work cocktails to downtown office workers for more than 50 years; it's one of the few places in the area that offers bar service until the early morning hours. 134 S. Wabash Ave. (between Jackson Blvd. and Adams St.). ✆ 312/645-5377. Subway/El: Red Line to Jackson.

NEAR THE MAGNIFICENT MILE

Billy Goat Tavern *Value*   Tucked below the Wrigley Building is this storied Chicago hole-in-the-wall, a longtime hangout for newspaper reporters over the years, evidenced by the yellowed clippings and memorabilia papering the walls. But it's the "cheezeborger, cheezeborger" served at the grill that gave inspiration to the famous *Saturday Night Live* sketch. Despite all the press, the Goat has endured the hype without sacrificing a thing. 430 N. Michigan Ave. ✆ 312/222-1525. Subway/El: Red Line to Grand/State.

Signature Lounge   The drinks here are pricey, but you're not surprised, are you? Anyway, here you can get a drink and a fabulous view for the price of a trip to the John Hancock tower's observatory, two floors below. It's open until 1am Sunday through Thursday and until 2am on the weekends. 96th floor of the John Hancock Center, 875 N. Michigan Ave. ✆ 312/787-7230. Subway/El: Red Line to Chicago.

RIVER NORTH & VICINITY

Fado   The crowds have abated somewhat since Fado opened a couple years back, but this sprawling, multilevel theme-park facsimile of an Irish pub still lures the masses most nights. Bursting with woodwork, stone, and double-barreled Guinness taps (all of it imported from the Emerald Isle), Fado has several themed rooms, each designed to evoke a particular Irish pub style—country cottage and Victorian Dublin, for instance. Monday evenings feature Irish music sessions. 100 W. Grand Ave. ✆ 312/836-0066. Subway/El: Red Line to Grand.

Iggy's *(Finds)* The unofficial dress code is anything black at this dark, velvet-draped late-night haven for terminally hip insomniacs. Perfectly situated on a desolate strip on the edge of downtown that gives it an extra edge of mystery, Iggy's serves food and drink long after most of the city's other bars have called it a night (4am most nights). On Sunday nights in the summer, movies are screened on the backyard patio. 700 N. Milwaukee Ave. (at Huron St.). ② 312/829-4449. Subway/El: Blue Line to Chicago.

OLD TOWN

The center of nightlife in Old Town is Wells Street, home to Second City and other comedy clubs, as well as a string of reliable restaurants and bars. You're not going to find many trendy spots in Old Town; the nightlife here is geared toward neighborhood pubs and bustling restaurants, filled mostly with a late-20s and 30-something crowd.

Old Town Ale House This is one of Old Town's legendary saloons, a dingy neighborhood hangout since the late 1950s with a fading mural that captures the likenesses of a class of regulars from the early 1970s (John Belushi commandeered the pinball machines here during his days at the nearby Second City improv club). Put some quarters in the jukebox that's filled with an eclectic selection of crooner tunes, and just hang out. Open daily from noon to 4am (until 5am Sat). 219 W. North Ave. (at Wells St.). ② 312/944-7020. Subway/El: Brown Line to Sedgwick.

LINCOLN PARK

Lincoln Park, with its high concentration of apartment-dwelling singles, is one of the busiest nightlife destinations in Chicago. Since this is a residential neighborhood where prime real estate is at a premium, you won't find any warehouse-sized dance clubs here; most of the action is at pubs and bars. Concentrations of in-spots run along Armitage Avenue, Halsted Street, and Lincoln Avenue.

Goose Island Brewing Company *(Finds)* The first brewpub in the city features its own Honker's Ale on tap, as well as several other beers produced here and at an off-site distillery. Ask for a tasting menu to try them all (you can sample three glasses for $5). Goose Island has the added benefit of a casual full-service restaurant with more than just bar food. A brewery tour is conducted on Sunday at 3pm (including a free sample). Goose Island recently added an outpost in Wrigleyville, 3535 N. Clark St. (② 773/832-9040). 1800 N. Clybourn Ave. (at Sheffield Ave.). ② 312/915-0071. Subway/El: Red Line to North/Clybourn.

Red Lion Pub *(Finds)* An English pub in the heart of Lincoln Park, the Red Lion is a comfortable neighborhood place with a mix of old and young DePaul students, actors, and Anglophiles who feel right at home among the Union Jacks and photos of Winston Churchill. The British owner even claims the place is haunted. Old movies are screened on the TV during the day. 2446 N. Lincoln Ave. (between Fullerton and Wrightwood aves.). ℂ 773/348-2695. Subway/El: Red or Brown line to Fullerton.

WRIGLEYVILLE, LAKEVIEW & THE NORTH SIDE

Real estate in Wrigleyville and Lakeview is a tad less expensive than in Lincoln Park, so the nightlife scene here skews a little younger. You'll find a mostly postcollegiate crowd partying on Clark Street across from Wrigley Field (especially after games in the summer). But you'll also discover some more eclectic choices.

Ginger Man Tavern Ginger Man definitely plays against type on a row of predictable sports bars across the street from Wrigley Field. On game days, the earthy bar has been known to crank classical music in an attempt to calm drunken fans—or at least shoo them away. Pool tables (free on Sun) are always occupied by slightly bohemian neighborhood 20-somethings, who have more than 80 beers to choose from. 3740 N. Clark St. (at Racine Ave.). ℂ 773/549-2050. Subway/El: Red Line to Addison.

Sheffield's Beer and Wine Garden A popular neighborhood gathering spot is Sheffield's, 1 block north of Belmont, on the corner of School Street. Its large beer garden, furnished with what has got to be the only outdoor pool table in the city, is the main attraction during the summer. The bar boasts a selection of more than 80 beers, including one featured "bad beer" of the month. Sheffield's can get jammed with a young, loud crowd, but the attitude is welcoming—there always seems to be room to squeeze in one more person. 3258 N. Sheffield Ave. (between Belmont Ave. and Roscoe St.). ℂ 773/281-4989. Subway/El: Red or Brown line to Belmont.

WICKER PARK & BUCKTOWN

For an alternative scene, head over to Wicker Park and Bucktown, where slackers and some adventurous yuppies populate bars dotting the streets near the confluence of North, Damen, and Milwaukee avenues. Don't dress to impress if you want to blend in; a casually bohemian getup and low-key attitude are all you need to fit in.

Note: For a map of nightlife in the Wicker Park and Bucktown areas, please see the map "Dining & Nightlife in Wicker Park/Bucktown" on p. 89.

Tips Late-Night Bites

Chicago's not much of a late-night dining town, but if you know where to go, you can still get a decent meal past midnight. Here are a few spots that serve up real food until real late.

In the Loop, your best—and practically only—choice is **Miller's Pub** (p. 167), 134 S. Wabash Ave. (✆ **312/645-5377**), which offers hearty American comfort food until 2am daily. Many late-night visitors to this historic watering hole and restaurant are out-of-towners staying at neighboring hotels.

The acknowledged star of the late-night scene is the dark, moody **Iggy's** (p. 168), 700 N. Milwaukee Ave. (✆ **312/829-4449**). It's a bit off the beaten track (although an easy cab ride from nightspots in River North or Wicker Park), but the cool crowd descends here for pastas and breakfast items until 4am.

In River North, food is available until 4am at **Bar Louie,** 226 W. Chicago Ave. (✆ **312/337-3313**). The menu is a good step above mozzarella sticks and other standard bar food: Focaccia sandwiches, vegetarian wraps, and salads are among the highlights.

After a night out, Wicker Park and Bucktown residents stop by **Northside Café** (p. 92), 1635 N. Damen Ave. (✆ **773/384-3555**), for sandwiches and salads served until 2am (3am Sat). In nice weather, the front patio is the place to be for prime people-watching.

The bright, welcoming atmosphere at **Clarke's Pancake House,** 2441 N. Lincoln Ave. (✆ **773/472-3505**), is a dose of fresh air after an evening spent in dark Lincoln Park bars. Yes, there are pancakes on the menu, but plenty of other creative breakfast choices as well, including mixed skillets of veggies, meat, and potatoes. Clarke's is open 24 hours.

When the Lincoln Park bars shut down at 2am, the action moves to the **Wieners Circle,** 2622 N. Clark St. (✆ **773/477-7444**). This hot-dog stand is strictly no-frills: You shout your order across the drunken crowd and the only spots to sit are a few picnic tables out front. Open until 4am during the week and 6am on weekends.

Get Me High Lounge *(Finds)* If Wicker Park has a favorite late-night watering hole, it's likely this compact, atmospheric spot, owned by nightclub impresario and style-maker Dion Antic. Dimly lit with tealight candles hanging from the ceiling and humming with R&B music in the air, Get Me High has a devoted following, so get there early to claim one of the comfy couches in the back. 1758 N. Honore St. © 773/252-4090. Subway/El: Blue Line to Damen.

The Map Room *(Finds)* Hundreds of travel books and guides line the shelves of this globe-trotter's tavern. Peruse that tome on Fuji or Antarctica while sipping a pint of one of the 20-odd draft beers available. The Map Room's equally impressive selection of bottled brews makes this place popular with not only the tattered-passport crew, but beer geeks as well. Tuesday nights are theme nights featuring the food, music, and spirits of a certain country, accompanied by a slide show and travel tales from a recent visitor. There's live music on Friday and Saturday nights. 1949 N. Hoyne Ave. (at Armitage Ave.). © 773/252-7636. Subway/El: Blue Line to Damen.

CAFES

Julius Meinl Austria's premier coffee roaster chose Chicago—and even more mysteriously, a location near Wrigley Field—for its first U.S. outpost. The result is a mix of Austrian style (upholstered banquettes, white marble tables, newspapers hanging on wicker frames) and American cheeriness (lots of natural light, smiling waitstaff, smoke-free air). The coffee and hot chocolate are excellent, served European-style on small silver platters with a glass of water on the side. But it's the desserts that keep the regulars coming back. 3601 N. Southport Ave. (at Addison St.). © 773/868-1857. Subway/El: Brown Line to Southport.

Third Coast Just steps away from the raucous frat-boy atmosphere of Division Street is this laid-back, classic, independent coffeehouse. The below-ground space is a little shabby, but it attracts an eclectic mix of office workers, students, and neighborhood regulars. The full menu serves up food late, and the drinks run the gamut from lattes to cocktails. There's also often some kind of folk music on weekends. 1260 N. Dearborn St. (north of Division St.). © 312/649-0730. Subway/El: Red Line to Clark/Division.

Uncommon Ground When you're looking for refuge from the riotous exuberance of Cubs game days and party nights in Wrigleyville, Uncommon Ground offers an oasis of civility. Located just off busy Clark Street, the cafe has a soul-warming fireplace in winter (when the café's bowl—yes, bowl—of hot chocolate is a sight for cold eyes) and a spacious sidewalk operation in more temperate months. Breakfast is served all day, plus there's a full lunch and dinner menu. Open until 11pm Sunday through Thursday, midnight Friday and Saturday. 1214 W. Grace St. (at Clark St.). ☎ **773/929-3680**. Subway/El: Red Line to Addison.

An Escape from the Multiplex

Chicago has a fine selection of movie theaters—but even the so-called art houses show mostly the same films that you'd be able to catch back home (or eventually on cable). But three local movie houses cater to cinema buffs with truly original programming. The new **Gene Siskel Film Center**, 164 N. State St. (☎ **312/846-2600**; www.siskelfilmcenter.org; Subway/El: Red Line to Washington or Brown Line to Randolph), named after the well-known *Chicago Tribune* film critic who died in 1999, is part of the School of the Art Institute of Chicago. The center hosts an eclectic selection of film series in two theaters, including lectures and discussions with filmmakers. The Film Center often shows foreign films that are not released commercially in the United States.

The **Music Box Theatre**, 3733 N. Southport Ave. (☎ **773/871-6604**; www.musicboxtheatre.com; Subway/El: Brown Line to Southport), is a movie palace on a human scale. Opened in 1929, it was meant to re-create the feeling of an Italian courtyard; stars twinkle on the dark blue ceiling, and a faux-marble loggia and towers cover the walls. The Music Box books an eclectic selection of foreign and independent American films—everything from Polish filmmaker Krzysztof Kieslowski's epic *Decalogue* to a singalong version of *The Sound of Music*. (I saw the Vincent Price cult favorite *House of Wax*, complete with 3-D glasses, here.)

Facets Multi-Media, 1517 W. Fullerton Ave. (☎ **773/ 281-4114**; www.facets.org; Subway/El: Red or Brown line to Fullerton), a nonprofit group that screens independent film and video from around the world, is for the die-hard cinematic thrill-seeker. The group also hosts a Children's Film Festival (Oct–Nov) and the Chicago Latino Film Festival (Apr–May) and has an impressive collection of classic, hard-to-find films on video and DVD (which you can rent by mail).

6 The Gay & Lesbian Scene

Most of Chicago's gay bars are conveniently clustered on a stretch of North Halsted Street in Lakeview, making it easy to sample many of them in a breezy walk. A couple of helpful free resources published each week are the entertainment guide *Nightlines* and the club rag *Gab*. The bars and clubs recommended below don't charge a cover unless otherwise noted.

Berlin   Step into this frenetic Lakeview danceteria, and you're immediately swept into the mood. The disco tunes pulse, the clubby crowd chatters, and the lighting bathes everyone in a cool reddish glow. Don't bother showing up before midnight; the club stays open until 4am Friday and 5am Saturday. 954 W. Belmont Ave. (east of Sheffield Ave.). © 773/348-4975. www.berlinchicago.com. Cover after midnight Fri–Sat $5. Subway/El: Red or Brown line to Belmont.

The Closet   The Closet is an unpretentious neighborhood spot with a loud and constant loop of music videos (and sports games, when it matters) that draws mostly lesbian regulars, although gay men and straights show up, too. The space itself is not much bigger than a closet, which makes it easy to get up close and personal with other partiers. There's also a small dance floor that's usually packed on weekends. Open until 4am every night, until 5am on Saturdays. 3325 N. Broadway (at Buckingham St.). © 773/477-8533. Subway/El: Red or Brown line to Belmont.

Roscoe's Tavern *Finds*   The picture windows onto Halsted make Roscoe's, a gay neighborhood bar in business since 1987, an especially welcoming place, with its large antiques-filled front bar, an outdoor patio, a pool table, and a large dance floor. The 20- and 30-something crowd is friendly and laid-back—except on weekends when the dance floor is hopping. The adjoining cafe serves sandwiches and salads. 3356 N. Halsted St. (at Roscoe St.). © 773/281-3355. Cover after 10pm Sat $4. Subway/El: Red or Brown line to Belmont.

Spin   This dance club attracts one of Halsted Street's most eclectic crowds, a mix of pretty boys, nerds, tough guys, and the occasional drag queen. The video bar in front houses pool tables and plays a steady steam of dance-friendly music videos. The dance club, behind heavy drapes, thumps with house music. Spin keeps regulars coming back with daily theme parties, featuring everything from Friday-night shower contests to cheap drinks. 800 W. Belmont Ave. (at Halsted St.). © 773/327-7711. Subway/El: Red or Brown line to Belmont.

Index

See also Accommodations and Restaurant indexes below.

FROMMER'S® COMPLETE TRAVEL GUIDES

Alaska
Alaska Cruises & Ports of Call
Amsterdam
Argentina & Chile
Arizona
Atlanta
Australia
Austria
Bahamas
Barcelona, Madrid & Seville
Beijing
Belgium, Holland & Luxembourg
Bermuda
Boston
Brazil
British Columbia & the Canadian Rockies
Brussels & Bruges
Budapest & the Best of Hungary
California
Canada
Cancún, Cozumel & the Yucatán
Cape Cod, Nantucket & Martha's Vineyard
Caribbean
Caribbean Cruises & Ports of Call
Caribbean Ports of Call
Carolinas & Georgia
Chicago
China
Colorado
Costa Rica
Cuba
Denmark
Denver, Boulder & Colorado Springs
England
Europe
European Cruises & Ports of Call
Florida
France
Germany
Great Britain
Greece
Greek Islands
Hawaii
Hong Kong
Honolulu, Waikiki & Oahu
Ireland
Israel
Italy
Jamaica
Japan
Las Vegas
London
Los Angeles
Maryland & Delaware
Maui
Mexico
Montana & Wyoming
Montréal & Québec City
Munich & the Bavarian Alps
Nashville & Memphis
New England
New Mexico
New Orleans
New York City
New Zealand
Northern Italy
Norway
Nova Scotia, New Brunswick & Prince Edward Island
Oregon
Paris
Peru
Philadelphia & the Amish Country
Portugal
Prague & the Best of the Czech Republic
Provence & the Riviera
Puerto Rico
Rome
San Antonio & Austin
San Diego
San Francisco
Santa Fe, Taos & Albuquerque
Scandinavia
Scotland
Seattle & Portland
Shanghai
Sicily
Singapore & Malaysia
South Africa
South America
South Florida
South Pacific
Southeast Asia
Spain
Sweden
Switzerland
Texas
Thailand
Tokyo
Toronto
Tuscany & Umbria
USA
Utah
Vancouver & Victoria
Vermont, New Hampshire & Maine
Vienna & the Danube Valley
Virgin Islands
Virginia
Walt Disney World® & Orlando
Washington, D.C.
Washington State

FROMMER'S® DOLLAR-A-DAY GUIDES

Australia from $50 a Day
California from $70 a Day
England from $75 a Day
Europe from $70 a Day
Florida from $70 a Day
Hawaii from $80 a Day
Ireland from $60 a Day
Italy from $70 a Day
London from $85 a Day
New York from $90 a Day
Paris from $80 a Day
San Francisco from $70 a Day
Washington, D.C. from $80 a Day
Portable London from $85 a Day
Portable New York City from $90 a Day

FROMMER'S® PORTABLE GUIDES

Acapulco, Ixtapa & Zihuatanejo
Amsterdam
Aruba
Australia's Great Barrier Reef
Bahamas
Berlin
Big Island of Hawaii
Boston
California Wine Country
Cancún
Cayman Islands
Charleston
Chicago
Disneyland®
Dublin
Florence
Frankfurt
Hong Kong
Houston
Las Vegas
Las Vegas for Non-Gamblers
London
Los Angeles
Los Cabos & Baja
Maine Coast
Maui
Miami
Nantucket & Martha's Vineyard
New Orleans
New York City
Paris
Phoenix & Scottsdale
Portland
Puerto Rico
Puerto Vallarta, Manzanillo & Guadalajara
Rio de Janeiro
San Diego
San Francisco
Savannah
Seattle
Sydney
Tampa & St. Petersburg
Vancouver
Venice
Virgin Islands
Washington, D.C.

FROMMER'S® NATIONAL PARK GUIDES

Banff & Jasper
Family Vacations in the National Parks
Grand Canyon
National Parks of the American West
Rocky Mountain
Yellowstone & Grand Teton
Yosemite & Sequoia/Kings Canyon
Zion & Bryce Canyon

FROMMER'S® MEMORABLE WALKS

Chicago	New York	San Francisco
London	Paris	

FROMMER'S® WITH KIDS GUIDES

Chicago	Ottawa	Vancouver
Las Vegas	San Francisco	Washington, D.C.
New York City	Toronto	

SUZY GERSHMAN'S BORN TO SHOP GUIDES

Born to Shop: France	Born to Shop: Italy	Born to Shop: New York
Born to Shop: Hong Kong, Shanghai & Beijing	Born to Shop: London	Born to Shop: Paris

FROMMER'S® IRREVERENT GUIDES

Amsterdam	Los Angeles	San Francisco
Boston	Manhattan	Seattle & Portland
Chicago	New Orleans	Vancouver
Las Vegas	Paris	Walt Disney World®
London	Rome	Washington, D.C.

FROMMER'S® BEST-LOVED DRIVING TOURS

Britain	Germany	Northern Italy
California	Ireland	Scotland
Florida	Italy	Spain
France	New England	Tuscany & Umbria

HANGING OUT™ GUIDES

Hanging Out in England	Hanging Out in France	Hanging Out in Italy
Hanging Out in Europe	Hanging Out in Ireland	Hanging Out in Spain

THE UNOFFICIAL GUIDES®

Bed & Breakfasts and Country Inns in:	Southwest & South Central Plains U.S.A.	Mexio's Best Beach Resorts
California	Beyond Disney	Mid-Atlantic with Kids
Great Lakes States	Branson, Missouri	Mini Las Vegas
Mid-Atlantic	California with Kids	Mini-Mickey
New England	Central Italy	New England & New York with Kids
Northwest	Chicago	New Orleans
Rockies	Cruises	New York City
Southeast	Disneyland®	Paris
Southwest	Florida with Kids	San Francisco
Best RV & Tent Campgrounds in:	Golf Vacations in the Eastern U.S.	Skiing & Snowboarding in the West
California & the West	Great Smoky & Blue Ridge Region	Southeast with Kids
Florida & the Southeast	Inside Disney	Walt Disney World®
Great Lakes States	Hawaii	Walt Disney World® for Grown-ups
Mid-Atlantic	Las Vegas	Walt Disney World® with Kids
Northeast	London	Washington, D.C.
Northwest & Central Plains	Maui	World's Best Diving Vacations

SPECIAL-INTEREST TITLES

Frommer's Adventure Guide to Australia & New Zealand	Frommer's France's Best Bed & Breakfasts and Country Inns
Frommer's Adventure Guide to Central America	Frommer's Gay & Lesbian Europe
Frommer's Adventure Guide to India & Pakistan	Frommer's Italy's Best Bed & Breakfasts and Country Inns
Frommer's Adventure Guide to South America	Frommer's Road Atlas Britain
Frommer's Adventure Guide to Southeast Asia	Frommer's Road Atlas Europe
Frommer's Adventure Guide to Southern Africa	Frommer's Road Atlas France
Frommer's Britain's Best Bed & Breakfasts and Country Inns	The New York Times' Guide to Unforgettable Weekends
Frommer's Caribbean Hideaways	Places Rated Almanac
Frommer's Exploring America by RV	Retirement Places Rated
Frommer's Fly Safe, Fly Smart	Rome Past & Present

Booked aisle seat.

Reserved room with a view.

With a queen – no, make that a king-size bed.